A TRIBUTE TO HELMUTH NYBORG

Edited by Richard Lynn

A Tribute to

HELMUTH NYBORG

Contributors

RICHARD LYNN (ED.), ADRIAN FURNHAM, ANTHONY HOSKIN, EDWARD DUTTON, EMIL KIRKEGAARD, GRÉGOIRE CANLORBE, GREGORY CONNOR, GUY MADDISON, HEINER RINDERMANN, HENRIK ALBECK, JOHN FUERST, LARS LARSEN

ARKTOS
LONDON 2024

ΛRKTOS

⊕ Arktos.com   ⓕ fb.com/Arktos   ◗ @arktosmedia   ⓘ arktosmedia

ISBN

978-1-915755-19-3 (Paperback)
978-1-915755-20-9 (Hardback)
978-1-915755-21-6 (Ebook)

Front cover photo

Erik Refner/Ritzau Scanpix

Editing

Richard Lynn
Constantin von Hoffmeister

Cover & Layout

Tor Westman

CONTENTS

CHAPTER 1

HELMUTH NYBORG: LIFE AND WORK OF A CONTROVERSIAL PSYCHOLOGIST

RICHARD LYNN

HELMUTH NYBORG is the most controversial Danish psychologist and the sixth most controversial intelligence researcher
internationally, according to Carl & Woodley of Menie (2019),
surpassed only by Arthur Jensen, William Shockley, Hans Eysenck,
Charles Murray and Philippe Rushton, in that order. He has published
research arguing that men have on average a five point higher IQ than
women [1], that white people tend to be more intelligent than blacks
[4], that migration from third world countries to Denmark would
cause a dysgenic [2] effect on the country's average IQ [3], that immigration from non-Western countries leads to a decline in the average intelligence of the receiving Western country [5] and that atheists
tend to be more intelligent than religious people. [6][7][8][9] A former
professor of child and developmental psychology at Aarhus University
and Olympic canoeist, his main research topics include the connection
between hormones and intelligence, the inheritance of intelligence,

1

the evolution of intelligence, and the relationship between sex, race and intelligence. Nyborg's controversial work has made him both enemies and friends, fifteen of whom have contributed to this Festschrift to honour him and his achievements.

Helmuth Sørensen Nyborg was born on the 5th of January 1937, in Løsning, a small country village in the mideastern part of continental Jutland, during a snowstorm that was so fierce that the doctor's horse got trapped in a snowdrift and he never got through to assist with the problematic birth. His mother weighed only 45 kg. and he weighed short of a tenth of that, so he was stuck for a long time in the birth canal and born cyanotic, that is, with bluish skin discolouration caused by insufficient blood oxygen, and with a cranium squeezed like a cone.

His father, Kaj Bertel Sørensen, trained as a blacksmith but when he finished his apprenticeship was unable to get a job as such and worked as a low-paid stoker at the local slaughterhouse during the severe economic depression in the 1930s. His mother, Gerda Astrid Sørensen, née Jeppesen, trained as a seamstress but she was also unable to find a permanent job as such and was unemployed, so the family, including his 5-year older brother, Bjarne, had to move to the larger city of Vejle. There his father got work, again as a stoker at a slaughterhouse, while his mother worked occasionally as a tailor for more well-to-do people, or washed urinals at a nearby diabetes hospital.

On April 9th, 1940, when Nyborg was four years old, the German army invaded Denmark. Nyborg still recalls the horrifying sight and vibrating sound of heavy German bomber airplanes cruising just 200-300 meters above their working-class city block, close to the harbour. Most of his family members soon went underground as para-military freedom fighters, notwithstanding the fact that the Danish government in this early phase of the war still cooperated with the Germans and later requested citizens to report the names of freedom fighters to the Gestapo (the secret Nazi police). Armed German soldiers soon patrolled the streets in pairs, and Nyborg recalls that he was sometimes stopped on the way to school, and they cuddled his blond head. A soldier once said: "Ach, schönes Kind, du bist doch ein guter Arier" — at a time when Nyborg was acutely aware that these same soldiers might the next day shoot his father, if they caught him in an act of sabotage. He was expressly forbidden to talk to German soldiers about family matters.

Nyborg remembers his primary school as a vexatious experience. He disliked standing with military precision in a straight line every morning outside the school before class; he disliked the endless memorising and the collective singing of Christian and nationalistic songs every morning. He was bored by mindless repetitions in class and hated the various kinds of physical punishments he was regularly exposed to, including being hit repeatedly with a bamboo cane, a pedagogical instrument frequently used at this time. In class, he wondered how on earth flies could mate, and outside, how delicate were the flight strategies of birds, and why dogs differed so much in play and by size and breed.

Nyborg recalls his life began after school when he went to the local library to read just about everything within reach, without telling his parents. A later favourite activity after the end of the war in 1945 was that he and his older brother filled water pipes with gunpowder, obtained from German machine gun belts left in a nearby wasteground, to make effective bombs. One day disaster struck. His father, a war-time expert in explosives, surprised him experimenting in the basement with a variety of explosive chemicals, bought with his little spare money. Nyborg recollects that his father confiscated them all with the words: "You stupid child! You could have flattened the whole city block. What's to become of you?" Friends were more optimistic. They called him "Fessor".

At age fourteen, Nyborg decided it was time to leave school. The principal called his parents and suggested that he join a small private school. Considering the poor financial family situation, he would support an application for a free scholarship, but to no avail. All the principal could do was to write a letter, describing Nyborg as a bright kid, who, despite disappointingly little interest and effort. had attained good knowledge. His behaviour had "most of the time" been acceptable. Nyborg was later told that, at the day of departure, the principal had told his parents that he in fact expected Nyborg to return to school someday, which sounded exceedingly unlikely to everybody.

In the following years, Nyborg took up kayaking, did various unskilled jobs and worked in a mercantile company. In 1956, at the age of 19, he became both Danish junior and senior champion in sprint kayak, won a prestigious international 1000-meter international competition in East Berlin in front of most of the European elite canoeists, and joined the Royal Danish Marines. He was selected to participate in the 1956 Summer Olympiad in Melbourne, Australia and the Danish Olympic Committee wrote a letter recommending that he be given ample time to train in his kayak during his military service. He fell ill shortly before the Olympiad, however, suffering from pleurisy, an inflammation of the thin layers that separate the lungs from the chest wall, so he had to spend several months in a military hospital in Copenhagen during the Melbourne Olympiad. He was afterwards dismissed permanently from military service, and doctors told him that he would never be able to compete in sports again. Nyborg characteristically disagreed.

From 1957, he served on various Swedish and Norwegian tank ships, as greaser, motorman and donkeyman, but also found time and materials for welding together a variety of gymnastic devices for physical rehabilitation on board. He brought his kayak with him whenever possible and sometimes paddled in dangerous waters.

In 1959, at the age of 22, Nyborg returned to Denmark to obtain a license as a wireless radio operator at the Copenhagen Navigation School. He continued to train with his kayak and was elected for the Danish Olympic team for the 1960 Rome Olympiad. Here he won a bronze medal together with three others in 4x500 meter sprint kayak. On that victorious day, Nyborg declared that his sports career had ended the moment they crossed the finish line on the sunny surface of *Lago de Albani*. Enough time for that, he said.

Nyborg then married Merete Østrup, musical librarian assistant and later social worker, and immediately after took to the sea as ship radio officer on various cargo ships sailing Middle- and Far-Eastern waters for a couple of years. Together they had two children. Their son, Casper, born in 1966, was run down on his bicycle by a careless car driver at the age of 15, shortly before he was to attend gymnasium. He suffered a severe brain damage but managed nevertheless to pass a two-years gymnasium entrance test. He tragically died in a fire accident many years later, while staying in a protected home. Their daughter, Catrine, was born in 1968 and is currently working as a financial accountant in a large public corporation. She has two children, Thor and Stinna. Nyborg and Merete divorced in 1990.

In 1962, Nyborg enrolled in a one-year course at a private school to catch up with what he had missed. He financed the costs by establishing an atelier for photographing children, students, and circus artists — including the world-famous clown Charlie Rivel and his three acrobatic sons — as well as technical and commercial installations and reproductions. There he sat, a 25-year-old sailor, among 51 much younger, but also previously failed, adolescents, and discovered to his surprise that school could be fun. Encouraged, he continued by studying classical languages from 1963 to 1965 and this way qualified for university entrance. He now needed a pause from studying, however, and took to the sea again, serving as radio officer on a couple of polar expedition/supply ships, specially built for navigating in Arctic waters. This ended his maritime career.

In February 1966, Nyborg, now 29, entered the University of Copenhagen and began studying psychology. He started with great expectations, but his hopes were soon dashed by the uninspiring teaching there. Some professors essentially recapitulated their own books, others enthusiastically referred to speculative outdated psychodynamic theories, still others promoted subjective, highly abstract, ideological, phenomenological, or holistic surface approaches, or recounted endless clinical cases devoid of data and replication.

It was a temporary relief to Nyborg that he got permission to follow the "Magister's line", where students could do their own research along with self-studies of the ordinary cand. psych. pensum. However, meetings with the professors about study reforms got nowhere, and they typically "forgot" previous student suggestions for changes. As tensions grew at Copenhagen University in 1968, psychology students finally decided to plaster a huge poster high up outside the university building, saying: "Ned med Professorvældet" (Down with professorial dominance). Access to the psychology laboratory, an impressive university stairway, was physically blocked with several dozen long, compact oak benches, stacked on top of each other. Phone calls were answered with: "This is the Psychology Students' Laboratory", and rector Mogens Fog, former communist and freedom fighter during the Second World War, was denied access. It all ended with a revision of the obligatory book lists; students and staff became represented on most important committees, and the general line of teaching became more "progressive", which at the time meant more left-oriented social constructivist. For this 1968-typic mindless blunder, Nyborg feels remorseful and has since then made many attempts to correct it.

One day in 1968, Nyborg heard a lecture by Gerhard Nielsen, who had just been appointed to a full professorship at the University of Aarhus, where he was to establish a new department of psychology. Nielsen remarked that he needed to hire a few professors and a small select group of students at Copenhagen University for a start. Nyborg went into his office after the lecture and greeted him: "Dear professor, I am your new assistant", inspired by the famous American psychologist James McKeen Cattell, who is believed to have hired himself with these words to the famous Wilhelm Wundt, who had established the world's first psychology laboratory at the University of Leipzig. These two scholars eventually formalised the study of intelligence and Cattell wrote his dissertation there with the title *Psychometrische*

Untersuchungen (Psychometric Investigations). Nielsen apparently knew the story, smiled, and asked Nyborg to sit down and give his view on the future of psychology in Aarhus. After this, he asked Nyborg when he expected to pass his third and final exam in psychology in Copenhagen. Nyborg replied that he expected to pass the first part of this summer. Nielsen's smile immediately faded away and the audience was clearly over. However, a few days later he called Nyborg back and told him that he had conferred with student instructors and others, and that Nyborg was welcome in the select group of students. Later that year, they all moved to Jutland to set up psychology at the University of Aarhus.

During the next years, from 1968 to 1971, Nyborg studied and lectured, published a couple of papers on experimental psychology in a professional journal, which later became part of his doctoral thesis, and was then awarded a one-year scholarship, providing sufficient time for him to finalise the Magister's degree (mag. Art) in psychology at Aarhus University. One of the requirements for obtaining a Danish Magister's degree is to write a six-week thesis on a topic given by a committee. Nyborg's subject matter was to account for the relationship between psychology and genetics — not an attractive assignment for a left-leaning student activist. However, six weeks later Nyborg delivered a sizeable manuscript, which in 1972 was published as the first book in Danish on behavioural genetics: *Psychology and Genetics — An introduction to Psychogenetics* (p. 135) by Munksgaard Press in Copenhagen.

The preparation of this thesis fundamentally changed Nyborg's scientific outlook, political orientation, and personal life, and eventually led him into three court cases. From being a left-oriented social constructivist activist, largely believing that man was made by society, he completely changed his academic stance. He first established an obligatory series of lectures on behavioural genetics for sophomore psychology students. This immediately annoyed not only many left-oriented students, but also similarly politically tilted colleagues.

The result was that the Marxist-dominated administration cancelled Nyborg's genetics course each time he worked abroad so he had to re-establish it repeatedly on return. The atmosphere at the institute grew increasingly toxic over the following three decades with politically charged confrontations at board meetings and in the coffee room. One colleague secretly circulated a pugnacious paper for years among students, explicitly warning them in detail about Nyborg's position, before he started his obligatory series of lectures on developmental and child psychology. The Study Board "counterbalanced" Nyborg's recommend papers on IQ, biological, or behavioural genetics for the obligatory student reading list, with a "moderating" paper. Nyborg once gave a large group of psychology students a lower grade for col-lectively excluding discussion of a paper on the obligatory reading list — How much can we boost IQ and Scholastic Achievement — writ-ten in 1969 by the prominent educational researcher Arthur Jensen from the University of California, Berkeley. The students resolutely filed a collective complaint, and a committee raised their grade, effec-tively undermining student knowledge of intelligence research as well as Nyborg's authority. Nyborg repeatedly suggested more courses in statistics, introductory courses in neuropsychology and experimental psychology, increased emphasis on international research papers for psychology students, and raised the publication rate in international journals, but these suggestions were typically either left unanswered or rejected.

Before attaining his Mag., Art degree, Nyborg lectured from 1968 to 1971 on social and personality psychology. Afterwards, he taught perceptual psychology for a couple of years, then experimental, and then clinical neuropsychology. He also ran a series of experi-ments on field dependency, tactile stimulation, and optic-vestibular conflict in relation to the perception of directions in space. They culminated in a doctoral thesis on the ways in which humans typi-cally solve experimentally created perceptual conflicts, as a function of optic-vestibular-somaesthetic interaction, interpreted in terms of psychological differentiation theory. Nyborg collated these works in 1974 in a book: *The rod-and-frame test and the field dependence dimension: Some methodological, conceptual, and developmental considerations.* In 1972, Nyborg was awarded a two-year medical research fellowship at the Psychiatric Hospital in Aarhus, Denmark, at the recommendation of Professors Eric Strömgreen, internationally acknowledged for his many times reprinted international textbook in psychiatry and Bleuler medal recipient, and Mogens Schou, a founding father of lithium therapy. Schou and Professor Raben Rosenberg, then director of the Central Psychiatric Laboratory, provided space for Nyborg's studies in psychopharmaco-therapy and work on individual perceptual, intellectual and personality development in children and adults with sex chromosome abnormalities. Nyborg co-authored a book with two medical colleagues, as well as a series of papers, on women with Turner's syndrome. They lack X chromosome material, have abnormal hormone levels, and suffer, among other things, from a specific cognitive visuo-spatial deficit. He also studied males with Klinefelter syndrome and karyotype XXY, as well as males with XYY.

In 1976–1977, Nyborg obtained an Alexander von Humboldt award to work as senior research fellow at the Max-Planck-Institute of Behavioural Physiology in Seewiesen in Germany. There he took over Nobelist Konrad Lorentz's apartment after he left. He did experiments on the development of behavioural responses to optic-vestibular (somesthetic) conflict solutions in humans, lobsters, and fish, together with Professor Hermann Schöne, and studied cybernetic models for evolution and developmental ethology. Some of the most prominent zoologists, ethologists and biologists of the time either stayed there or briefly visited the Institute. One example is the well-known Austrian ethnologist, Irenäus Eibl-Eibesfeldt, who took over an office next to Nyborg's. Among many other matters, they discussed the nurture-oriented works of Margaret Mead, the then famous cultural anthropologist from Columbia University. Mead was a student of Professor

Franz Boas, whose position Nyborg later questioned in his paper *Race as Social Construct*. Mead's two books: *Coming of Age in Samoa* (1928) and *Sex and Temperament in Three Primitive Societies* (1939) contended that in some cultures men were not dominant. Eibl-Eibesfeldt was highly critical of Mead's methods and subjective and politicised account of the malleability of human nature. When Nyborg questioned him for data, Eibl-Eibesfeldt recommended Nyborg to go down to the cellar and take a good look at the kilometres of 8 mm film Eibl-Eibesfeldt had taken of the actual behaviour of people in the different cultures that Mead previously had visited and described. He had mounted a specially designed 45-degree camera mirror, disguising the line of sight, and then filmed people in the same cultures in terms of variations in sexual equality and cultural harmony. Eibl-Eibesfeldt said that these showed that Mead misrepresented the facts about sex roles, equality, flexibility, and cultural impact.

The Humboldt Stiftung generously sponsored a three-week bus tour around Germany for the hundreds of foreign scientists holding a stipend that year. Nyborg early got word that Elisabeth, the wife of Nobel Prize winner in physics Werner Heisenberg would serve as tourist guide in one of the buses, so he sprinted up to it and asked if he could be allowed to sit in the front seat, beside her, on the whole tour around Germany. This she, discretely amused, granted him. Werner Heisenberg had died shortly before, on February 1st. 1976 at the age of 74, after a long and celebrated career in physics, and Nyborg wanted, rather than sightseeing, to learn in detail about her husband and his work as the creator of quantum mechanics, as Heisenberg was characterised in 1932 by the Nobel Committee. Elisabeth told him about how she met Werner at a classical music concert, and they had fallen in love. She told about what profound dilemma it were for Werner to choose between a promising career in music and an unknown path in physics. She said that Heisenberg sometimes talked like a mystic as when he claimed that elementary particles could be created and destroyed, and that the smallest units in the universe were not physical objects but rather forms and ideas, somewhat as Plato had said about form and content, remembered Nyborg from his earlier Greek studies. Elisabeth said that Heisenberg found that Einstein and de Broglie were wrong when they assumed that the momentum and position of particles could be measured simultaneously, partly because method and object could not be separated. Nyborg admits that he found some of these ideas almost bordered on social constructivism, as when Elisabeth mentioned that Heisenberg claimed that elementary particles do not exist objectively but only mathematically tabulated in numbers with our knowledge of them — this reminded him of when even the otherwise critical rationalist philosopher Karl Popper and Nobelist John Eccles divided the world into three spheres: physical things, consciousness, and a pure world of logical relations, with the latter third world capable of informing our mathematics. Also, Ulric Neisser's speculative cognitive psychology came to mind, as when he had said that "[c]ognitive processes surely exist, so it can hardly be unscientific to study them" (*Cognitive Psychology*, 1967, p. 5; see later). Elisabeth also provided frank, if brief, personalised highlights of some of the many important scientists and politicians that she and Werner knew, had met, or interacted with before, during, and after the Second World War. Scientists included Niels Bohr, seen as a good friend, Albert Einstein as a more remote genius, and widely differing co-workers like Wolfgang Pauli, Arnold Sommerfeld, Max Born, Edward Teller (the father of the hydrogen bomb and somewhat autistic) and Paul Dirac at Cambridge. She talked with sadness about the intense and sometimes hostile atmosphere among scientists and organisations, based not only on personal and professional differences but also in relation to the many unsolved burning moral questions with respect to the Second World War. She talked about Werner's risky attempts to rescue Jewish colleagues from the Nazis, giving him the nickname *Der Weisse Jude*.

Unfortunately, Elisabeth refused to provide details of Werner's meetings with top Nazi officials and German politicians and of his mysterious wartime visit to Niels Bohr at his Copenhagen institute. Did they exchange views on German and American nuclear war programmes, or did Werner want primarily to warn Jewish Niels about the likelihood of future persecution of Jews in Denmark? Elisabeth rather preferred to talk about how sorry she felt about Werner's many unsuccessful attempts to become full professor at a German university, where he was repeatedly met with academic and political resistance. On a lighter note, Elisabeth readily reported on their many travels together, how Werner joked about whether they could find sufficient time for taking a short cut, and when Werner and Niels Bohr mused, during a holiday in Heisenberg's alpine Austrian Berghaus, about how they had to clean lots of trashy dishes in a bit of dirty water with one dirty handkerchief: "It's like physics", Werner said, "where we have dirty science and method, but nevertheless come out with clean concepts."

After the bus arrival in Berlin, Nyborg and four others had had some wine and merrily grabbed Elisabeth by the shoulders and forced her to walk between them in the middle of the famous Kurfürstendamm boulevard in the highly stylised goose step or *Stechschritt* march fashion, like Nazi soldiers used to do. She protested vigorously: "Aber Sie sind doch ganz verrückt. So was macht man nicht mehr hier" (*You are completely mad. Nobody does this anymore here*). As it happened, the German minister for education also walked the Kurfürstendamm, heading for the same restaurant, and couldn't but watch the incident. Afterwards, he jokingly commented on the incident, to Elisabeth's great embarrassment. Nyborg was asked on the occasion to give a speech on behalf of the foreign scientists, so he conveyed their gratitude to the Humboldt Stiftung and the minister for their generous support of international scientific cooperation, but Nyborg also jokingly made a couple of deliberate linguistic errors, to which the minister responded: "Nie wieder habe ich so viele Wörter gehört — mit so wenig Grammatik" (*I have never previously heard so many words with so little grammar*).

In 1979–1980, Nyborg worked as a Senior Research Fellow in the Department of Experimental Psychology at the University of Oxford. He became a member of University College, disputedly the oldest Oxford college, founded in 1249. At his first college lunch, he was (intentionally?) seated in between two faculty members, obviously world class historians, who questioned him in great detail about the political, economic, and strategical role of the Danish military and merchant fleets throughout the centuries in relation to England. They inquired about particulars of Lord Nelson's decision and strategy of the bombardment of Copenhagen and the military and economic consequences of the capture of the Danish Navy in 1807. At another lunch, Nyborg came to sit next to a female scholar and congratulated her on her sole female appearance as a sign that the college now hired women. She said this was not so and that she was only there for a brief visit, but the college actually began hiring women around that time. In the evenings, Nyborg would meet with colleagues from many different disciplines for a drink before dinner and have a learned conversation in a marvellously decorated room with solid dark wooden panels. At the appropriate time, the oldest faculty member dining that evening rose to his feet and led the guests of the day, followed by faculty in descending order of age into the spectacular dining hall. The students then rose to their feet as the possession arrived and took place at the elevated high table, with the eldest seated at the head. When all were seated, the senior scholar rose, took a wooden hammer, slammed it down on the table, and then took up what looked like a table tennis bat. From it, he began to read aloud the first line of the Latin text of the so-called Grace, which translates *Blessed be God in his gifts*. Then the appointed student of the day rose to his feet and responded: *And holy in all his works*. Then followed a series of line exchanges between the scholar and the student, all read aloud in Latin. Nyborg was told that students carefully monitored the reading speed of each day to find a long-time winner. After this, faculty members were served an exquisite three-course dinner with a select wine for each, whereas the students were offered two ordinary courses and free tap water.

Nyborg enjoyed the intellectually stimulating atmosphere in the psychology department provided by luminaries like Professors Peter Bryant, Donald Broadbent, and Michael Argyle. He enjoyed the ordinary Wednesday departmental lectures, where, for example, his friend Professor Jeffrey Grey would begin his talk by saying he really did not have anything new to say, only the same old boring stuff, and then always came up with some new perspectives. He was entertained by the cultural clashes, as when a bragging prominent American physiology professor, clad in a radiant Hawaii shirt, was elegantly torn to pieces. One day during the traditional afternoon tea, Nyborg conversed with a young American guest teacher, and a distinguished Oxford professor came over and kindly asked what she was doing in the department. She said: "I teach statistics and I am very good at that". "Ooouh! Gooood for youuu!" he said, turned around and briskly walked away. "What went wrong?" she asked Nyborg. "A cultural clash", he answered. "Certainly, in the US you can openly be proud of yourself, but here in Oxford you better proceed in a humbler way." Nyborg found it also amusing to receive a welcome note from the college steward, regretting that they unfortunately had run out of pre-war port wine. The note further said that it is not customary to invite one's wife for daily faculty dinners, but female guests are welcome to join on Sundays. Nyborg's wife was reportedly not that amused.

The prominent American psychologist Jerome Bruner had an office right opposite Nyborg's but kept his archive in Nyborg's office. He often dropped in to collect papers and then lectured on his much-favoured social constructivist position, which, alas, fell on utterly barren ground. Nyborg found it much more informative to talk with the Dutch biologist and ornithologist Nico Tinbergen, who had received the Nobel Prize in physiology or medicine in 1973, together with Karl von Frisch and Konrad Lorentz, the latter being the director of the Max Planck Institute for Behavioural Physiology where Nyborg worked for one-and-a-half years, three years earlier. It came as no surprise to Nyborg that the seriously minded Tinbergen took the trouble to learn Danish as he wanted to go to Greenland to study birds there and so thought it useful to be able to talk in the same language as the Danish authorities there. As an ethologist, Tinbergen person-ally expressed a deep concern for the future of mankind — much like Darwin did shortly before he died — but then Tinbergen excused himself with a characteristically humble remark that he perhaps just behaved like a frail and pessimistic old man. A couple of months ear-lier, Tinbergen had suffered a mental breakdown and was hospitalised after he gave an invited public lecture, where the left-oriented un-dergraduate organisers, apparently unknown to him, transmitted his speech via loudspeakers to a hostile crowd of left-oriented students demonstrating outside in the street, activists who afterwards viciously attacked him verbally.

However, Oxford debates were often polite, elegant, incisive, even if in a snobbish way, and most often illustrative, according to Nyborg. The legendary Professor Hans Eysenck from London was thus once asked, at the end of a lengthy and at times convoluted discussion in Oxford by internationally leading personality researchers, if he could briefly summarise his "Giant Three" factor theory. "Well", said Eysenck, "when you meet people, you may get anxious and run away — that's Neuroticism; or you can attack them, that's Psychoticism; or you can stay and socialise with them, that's Extraversion — what else can you do?"

Looking back at his time in Oxford at the Department of Experimental Psychology, Nyborg says that he found it at the same time intellectually stimulating and worrying. In addition to the Tinbergen incident, left-oriented "progressive" bullies also attacked the animal research laboratory on the fifth floor, so all faculty had afterwards to pass an annoying security gate before they could get through to their research and teaching. This confirmed Nyborg's previous suspicion of an ongoing left-oriented, social constructivist attack, occupation, and deconstruction of critical disciplines at European and American universities, a worry that has concerned him ever since (Nyborg, 2003, 2011).

In 1979, Nyborg attended the NATO Conference on Intelligence and Learning at York University in England. There was a strike at the British Railway, so Nyborg rented a car. He put up a note, asking whether other conference participants might be interested in joining him on the way back to Oxford. Ulric Neisser from Cornell University, USA, known as one of the fathers of cognitive psychology, wrote yes, as he had to reach Heathrow Airport for a flight back to the United States. One of Neisser's most widely shared ideas at the time was that mental processes could be measured *per se* and analysed afterwards. Nyborg reports that he — to the great amusement of Peter Bryant, the famous Oxford professor of developmental psychology, who sat in the back of the car — had a five-hour heated discussion about the decisive proof for the reality of mental or cognitive processes in an entirely physical brain. Contrary to Arthur Jensen, who was always willing to let data change his own theories when new data appeared, Nyborg got the impression that Neisser's great intellect and academic success all too easily let him go even faster and further out of a scientifically problematic line, where his strong belief trumped the absence of data, and where the obligatory need for Popperian falsification seemed not to disturb him unduly. Neisser's stand reminded Nyborg that the behaviourist B. F. Skinner who, only eight days before he died, famously delivered a speech at the APA Annual Convention meeting in 1990, where he said that: "So far as I am concerned, psychology is the creationism of psychology" and "the efforts to reinstate or recreate creative self or mind that do not exist in science ... Introspection is not a scientifically respectable method and, regrettably, biology cannot be taught in the US."

Between 1977 and 1991, Nyborg published a series of papers on sex differences in spatial ability in relation to plasma hormone level, treatment, and karyotype. This, plus a literature review, inspired him to suggest a new theory for developing differences in spatial ability as a function of different ratios of cerebral levels of oestradiol and testosterone — the "Optimal Oestrogen Range" theory — which can be considered a forerunner of his later "General Trait Covariance model" (see Chapter 9).

In 1984, Nyborg received a combined NATO Senior Research Fellowship and Fulbright stipend that allowed him to visit the Institute for Behavioral Genetics at Boulder University in Colorado, USA, for a year as guest professor. It was a follow-up on his interests in behavioural genetics and developmental neurobiological work, and Nyborg enjoyed the company of luminaries like the then young and budding Robert Plomin, now highly esteemed professor at King's College in London, as well as that of the director John DeFries, Steven Vandenberg, James Wilson, and others.

In 1985, Nyborg spent four months as a visiting professor at the Kinsey Institute for Sex, Gender and Reproduction at Indiana University, where he studied prenatal sex hormone effects on the developing brain and pubertal hormone effects on subsequent body, brain, behaviour and sexual orientation. He found the academic style there more relaxed than Oxford's. When on the first day he met with director June Reinisch, she greeted him: "Hi Helmuth. Welcome!" She then gave him a big hug, a smack kiss right on the mouth, and said: "Take a sweet" (from a huge one-meter-high fountain standing in the middle of the office) — and off she hurried, much too late for a meeting. On a later occasion she appeared as lead singer in a rock band, celebrating a major renovation of the Kinsey Institute, to the obvious bewilderment of some of the professors invited from other departments at Bloomington University. Nyborg also learned that next to the Vatican's collection of forbidden books and sex gadgets, the Kinsey Institute holds the greatest pornographic collection in the world.

To inquire deeper into models for child development, the diagnosis and treatment of childhood disorders, and sex hormonal correlates of prenatal and later development, Nyborg worked next for half a year at the Department of Child Health and Development at the University of London, thanks to a Senior Research Fellowship and with further support from the Research Foundation at the University of Aarhus. At the Hospital for Sick Children, he gained practical skills in measuring and quantifying child development from world-class experts like James Tanner and Michael Preece, to be applied in a Danish cohort-sequential study of the body, brain, and behavioural development of children and young adults aged 8 to 18+. As professor Tanner was away at the beginning of Nyborg's visit, working at a Texan institute in the US, Nyborg was allowed to take over his large office. However, one day Nyborg heard a loud angry voice coming from the outside corridor, saying: "What! Do you tell me that somebody has taken over my office?" Then the door opened, Tanner came in and said: "Who the hell are you?" and Nyborg turned his chair and responded: "Well, who the hell are you?" The great professor couldn't but smile after a second or five, and then suggested that they cut his large office in half with a book shelf, and there the two worked in perfect harmony for the rest of the time Nyborg spent there. Hearing about Nyborg's bronze medal in kayak at the Rome 1960 Olympiad, Tanner lit up and gave a detailed recap of his book series on biophysical and other differences among successful Olympians in different disciplines. He argued that genetic differences in bodily mechanics greatly trump training efforts, so that a weightlifter would risk dying from exhaustion in a marathon run, whereas a slim long-distance runner would be laughed out in the heavy-weight lifting room. Tanner could not explain why Nyborg had never met a black champion sprint canoer during his international sports career, even though many blacks have fast twitching muscles.

In 1987, Nyborg attended the Behavior Genetics Association conference in Minneapolis. During a lecture by David Fulker, he came to sit next to an unknown old man, who suddenly rose to his feet, interrupted the lecturer, and pointed, in a very loud voice, to an error in a formula the lecturer had written on the blackboard. He next turned to

Nyborg and said in a voice that could easily be heard by others in the lecture hall that he wouldn't spend more time on idiots who couldn't write proper population genetics formulas. He then said to Nyborg, "Let's both go and have a cup of coffee, and you can tell me about your interests." However, out of the auditorium, the old man said he had a serious prostate problem, so if Nyborg would escort him to the men's room, he could on the way tell him about his research. Gradually, Nyborg came to realise that the old, half-deaf, angry man was William Shockley, who was awarded the Nobel Prize in 1956, together with John Bardeen and Walter Brattain, for discovering the transistor effect. During the next 20 minutes or so, in the men's room, Nyborg would summarise his work, but Shockley cut him off and said: "You don't have to repeat, man. I got the Nobel Prize, you know! What you told me was that you find that IQ means a lot and is about 60–80 % genetic, which are both correct, and that the brain, thinking, intelligence and behaviour are entirely physical things that can be studied as such, which is also correct. Please send me your works — but only the summaries!". Shockley had, in his later years, begun to defend eugenics, support the idea of genetic improvement of people, defend Arthur Jensen's intelligence research, and discuss the likelihood of genetic race differences in IQ. For all this he was rated the second-most controversial intelligence researcher in the world, behind Arthur Jensen, according to the previously mentioned study in the journal *Intelligence* by Carl and Woodley of Menie (2019). Shockley died in 1989 of prostate cancer.

In 1989–1990, Nyborg worked as guest professor at the Rockefeller University, Laboratory of Neuroendocrinology in New York City. Most of the 80+ Rockefeller faculty members are associated with the most prestigious scientific organisations in the US, including the National Academy of Sciences, and no less than 38 Nobel Prize winners have had an affiliation there. Nyborg focussed on biological and medical sciences and experimented with the neuroendocrine development and learning in the rat. He wanted to test a prediction of his human

"General Trait Covariance Model", that precocious human children (and by implication, rats) reach an earlier asymptote in intelligence and learning curves than do more slowly developing normal children (and rats). He found that medically enforced precocious development of laboratory rat behaviour stunted their post-pubertal cognitive development, relative to untreated kin controls. The study was published in 1991, with colleagues from Rockefeller under the title: *Neonatal hyperthyroidism disrupts hippocampal LTP and spatial learning*. A follow-up note elaborated on the *Steroid and thyroid hormones and neural plasticity* aspects.

One day, a staff member came into Nyborg's laboratory and asked what academic colours his Danish University had. Admitting that he had no idea, she led him into an impressive wardrobe at the university, full of spectacular gowns. After inquiring about Nyborg's professorial rank — part-time, assistant, associate, tenured, full, and to the kind of dissertation — Ph.D., or Doctor of Philosophy, she handed over to Nyborg a gown in spectacular colours, making him look like a cardinal or pope. Only then was he allowed to join the annual parade across campus, together with the PhDs of the year and the then 90+-year-old David Rockefeller, to the graduation ceremony.

By sheer luck, Nyborg met Henrik Albeck at Rockefellers. Henrik is a Danish biochemical engineer, working for eight years at the Kreek Laboratory, where methadone treatment for heroin addiction was developed. Together, Albeck and Nyborg began to cooperate on a series of studies on drug abuse and bodily, behavioural, brain and cognitive status. The results of the studies were presented at various international conferences, and are now summarised in chapter 3 in this Festschrift.

In 1992, Nyborg worked at the Primate Research Centre at the University of Washington in Seattle, where he discovered that monkeys cannot solve an adapted version of the three-dimensional Shepard-Metzler mental rotation test. That same year, he analysed data on racial/ethnic variation in male testosterone levels, together with Professor Lee Ellis from Minot State University. They found that middle-aged American blacks have slightly higher serum testosterone than Hispanics and non-Hispanic whites and took this to mean that it could explain, at least in part, some racial differences in the incidence of cardiovascular diseases, hypertension, and prostate cancer.

In 1994, Nyborg got married a second time, to Charlotte Bondesen. They were divorced five years later without having children. He then worked as a visiting professor at the Institute for Psychiatric Research at the Psychiatric Hospital in Aarhus. Here he studied relations between sex hormones and psychosis. He also completed and published a book he had begun at Rockefeller University with the title *Hormones, sex, and society: The science of physicology*. Here Nyborg further elaborates on the idea that abstract explanatory concepts, like mind, psyche, cognitive schemata, desires and will, are better substituted by measurable, coupled, intra- and inter-systemic mass-molecular interactions with chemical and physical addresses before we can talk realistically about causal relations. In a review of the book, Eysenck (1996) wrote: "Nyborg is an internationally recognized expert on sex hormones, and the psychological effects they have on a variety of functions. This book ... presents to the reader the outcome of a life-time's work in this extremely important field. As such, it is well written, reads easily, and is very convincing".

In 1997, Nyborg elaborated on this view in a contribution to a Festschrift he produced for Professor Hans Eysenck, published as *The Scientific Study of Human Nature: Tribute to Hans J. Eysenck at Eighty*. He handed over this Festschrift to Eysenck at the 7th Meeting of the International Society for the Study of Individual Differences he arranged in July.1997 at the University of Aarhus, shortly before Eysenck's untimely death a couple of months later. At a commemorative occasion for Eysenck in November of that year in London, Nyborg gave an invited talk, where he, in passing, referred to the strange phenomenon that there is something rotten in the state of England, because, if you visit scientific libraries in England, you find the collected works of Freud and countless other meta-physicists, but not the collected works of Eysenck the scientist.

In a chapter on "Molecular Creativity, Genius and Madness" in the Festschrift (1997b), Nyborg called attention to the dilemma that creativity research seems to degenerate at a time when modern societies call for more of it. He suggested that creativity could perhaps be analysed in terms of his General Trait Covariance (GTC) model, an idea elaborated in a more complex Nonlinear, Dynamic, Multifactor, Multiplicative, Multidimensional Molecular (ND4M) model for the study of body, brain, and behavioural development.

Nyborg mentioned in the Epilogue to the Eysenck Festschrift, "Psychology as Science", that the philosopher William James wanted to redefine psychology in terms of natural science. In his *Principles of Psychology* (1890), James characterised psychology as not a science, but only as the hope for a science. As he said: "The waters of metaphysics leak at every point ... A string of raw facts; a little gossip and wrangle about opinion; a little classification and generalization on the mere descriptive level; a strong prejudice that we have states of mind ... but not a single law in the sense in which physics shows us laws ...".

In 1998, Nyborg wrote the paper *Molecular Mind in a Molecular World: Applied Physiology*, followed by one on *Personality, psychology, and the molecular wave: Covariation of genes with hormones, experience, and traits*, in an attempt to address this fundamental problem at a molecular level. Both papers refer to Nyborg's 1994 book on *Physiology* in recommending a natural science interpretation, where psychological phenomena are assigned causal status only if given physio-chemical addresses in the body and/or brain, before they can be assumed to enjoy equal causal standing and a scientific quantitative interpretation.

Nyborg spent four months in 1998, working with Benny Lautrup, professor in theoretical physics, on mathematical dimensioning of molecular models, while a visiting professor at the Niels Bohr Institute at Copenhagen University. Arthur Jensen joined Nyborg there and was invited to give a lecture on his intelligence research in the famous lecture theatre where Einstein, Bohr, Fermi, Teller, and many other luminaries regularly discussed future physics in the heydays of the Copenhagen School of Physics and quantum mechanics. Jensen confessed that he felt honoured and said afterwards that he preferred to speak to physicists and other natural scientists rather than to psychologists, because the latter too often lost sight of the essentials.

In 1999, Nyborg met Mette Lund Jensen, who was 28 years his junior and studied psychology. They got married in 2016 and first had twins, Tim and Tom, who were born prematurely and did not survive long. Then came Martin, born in 2006 when Nyborg turned 70. Mette is presently working at Skejby University Hospital as the departmental clinical psychologist for a large cancer section, servicing about 700 medical doctors and other health workers, teaching medical and psychology students, and has a private practice.

Later in 1999, Nyborg was invited to the Santa Fe Institute in Santa Fe, New Mexico, where he continued to work with physical models for human body, brain, and behavioural development. The raison d'être was a project, however, envisioned by George Cowan, a legendary physical nuclear chemist and co-developer of the first two nuclear bombs, for studying the physical aspects of brain development in children. Cowan told Nyborg that he had access to a substantial amount of dollars for a large-scale project on child development, which he wanted Nyborg to help run and where neuroscience principles were applied in the understanding of how the physiological development of children's brains relates to behavioural development. However, after lengthy negotiations, they both agreed that although international brain imaging and other techniques had made some progress in this direction, neither the Santa Fe Institute nor Nyborg were adequately equipped for such an endeavour.

In 2000, Nyborg organised and chaired a symposium on "Secular changes in intelligence", co-sponsored by the International Society for the Study of Individual Differences and the Behaviour Genetics

Society, at the University of Vancouver, Canada. The symposium discussed the secular increases in intelligence that have occurred during the twentieth century, known as the Lynn-Flynn effect because Lynn and Flynn had shown them independently. Nyborg told me that James Flynn said that he was quite poor, so Nyborg offered to share a hotel room with him, but Flynn said the next morning that during the night he had to retreat to a small couch in the front-room because of snoring sounds of unknown origin. Flynn expressed the view that the Lynn-Flynn effect was probably not on g. Flynn repeatedly asserted that the racial differences in intelligence have no genetic basis. This Nyborg disputed and Russell Warne later (2021) has shown it is highly improbable. Flynn later admitted, according to an interview in *The Guardian* in 2016, that his much hoped-for advantageous effects for blacks' IQ, of being reared in a white middle class family, disappeared when they reached the age of 17, as shown by Weinberg, Scarr & Waldman (1992) and by me (Lynn, 1994). Flynn died on December 11th, 2020, of intestinal cancer.

Nyborg next worked at the University of California at Berkeley with Arthur Jensen on g factor-related analyses. Their first paper came out in 2000, providing strong support for Charles Spearman's hypothesis that variation in the size of mean black-white differences on various psychometric tests is directly related to variation in the size of the tests' loading on the g factor. Their second paper regressed black and white occupational status and income differences on psychometric g, and disproved the widespread notion of unfavourable discrimination on job status and income against blacks, after matching for g. In fact, when g was considered, whites turned out to be relatively more disadvantaged. Their third paper showed that very low and very high serum testosterone levels affect g scores adversely. Jensen's Danish grandparents came from Copenhagen and Nyborg remembers him as a committed scientist, who spent most of his time fully occupied with one project after another and writing books and papers. However, he was extremely generous, both personally and professionally. He would cook sophisticated Indian dinners for others and prepare their next day's morning meal the evening before by filling oatmeal and special ingredients in a machine designed for slow cooking through the night. Jensen had an extensive knowledge of classical music and only reluctantly gave up a musical career as a clarinettist and director of the San Jose Symphony Orchestra. The sitting room in his sea-side house in Kelseyville, California, was dominated by two enormous loudspeakers, playing classical music at a level that perhaps contributed to his advancing deafness in his later years. Nyborg's wife, Mette, woke up one night and sensed smoke, so they roused Jensen, who was sleeping in the room next door. They all went down half a floor — in undies — to the dim daily room, where Jensen sniffed briefly in the air, shook his head, and then said that he couldn't smell a thing. Mette insisted, but Jensen characteristically replied: "This is not something I would worry about", and off he went to bed again, reflecting his stable introversion and low neuroticism scores. Next day it appeared that there had been a fire in the basement, and everything had burned out. Jensen's wife, Barbara, later told Nyborg that Jensen had long not been able to "smell a thing". This perhaps also explains his tolerance for hot Indian dishes. Once Nyborg lived for a short while in the Jensen's' rented apartment in London, Jensen was about to leave to give a speech in the House of Lords, so he asked Barbara to cook an Indian dish. "What ingredients?" asked Barbara. Jensen hurried back, wrote down 31 ingredients from the top of his head, gave a hasty instruction on how to cook, and off he went in his best suit. On another occasion, Mette, who is an instructor in Latino rhythms, taught Jensen to dance the tango, which took a little time. Professionally Nyborg remembers Jensen as invariably willing to change his theories if data wasn't supportive, contrary to what most of his many detractors asserted. For instance, Jensen concluded (1998) in his *The g Factor* book that a sex difference in g is either completely absent, inconsistent, or of varying directions. At an international conference, Nyborg gave a speech that confirmed my own theory that there are no sex differences before age

15, but after we see an increasing male advantage reaching 4 to 5 IQ points in adults. Jensen subsequently went up to the podium, faced Nyborg directly and said: "Well, it seems I have to revise my position in the sex difference matter." Once a reviewer pointed out an error in the dispersion of black IQ in their submitted paper on a race difference study. Jensen, seated next to Nyborg in his marvellous study in the Kelseyville seaside house, said: "Please, do the statistics again, Helmuth, even for the third time." Nyborg could still find nothing wrong with the analysis, so Jensen called Doug Dettermann, the legendary founder and editor of the journal *Intelligence*, on the phone. He immediately realised that it was the printer who had made an error in the pre-print edition, which only the reviewers had seen. After the correction was made, Jensen expressed unexpectedly great relief because, he said, critics had been after him for forty years and if they found even a miniscule and honest error, they had used this to dismiss his entire monumental work. In 2003, Nyborg edited a Festschrift for Arthur Jensen — *The Scientific Study of General Intelligence: Tribute to Arthur R. Jensen.* Jensen died in the Kelseyville house in 2012, from Parkinson's disease, at the age of 89.

In 2002, Nyborg realised that he was still under attack, now for his work on sex differences in intelligence. This interest grew out of the observation of a sex difference in his doctoral work on individual differences in visuo-vestibular interaction. He there found that females' perception of directions in space depended, on average, significantly more on information from the visual-spatial surroundings than that of males, who relied more on vestibular-proprioceptive signals. Nyborg first saw this as an experimental nuisance to be eliminated in an elegant experimental design, but soon realised that it was statistically robust. He did a systematic search in the literature and found multiple studies reporting sex differences in orientation and in two- and three-dimensional visuo-spatial test batteries. He then decided to take a closer look at some other data he had collected in a cohort-sequential study of 8–18+ year olds, where principal component analysis of a large battery of very inhomogeneous intelligence tests for a very small sample of 62 adolescent males and females confirmed a higher male IQ of between 3–8 IQ points, depending on the method applied. This confirmed previous results by me (Lynn, 1999, 2002) and by Lynn & Irwing (2004).

Nyborg's results were published in 2005 in a paper — "Sex-related differences in general intelligence g, brain size, and social status" by the journal *Personality and Individual Differences*. It immediately created a furore at his institute, in other departments of the university, and in left-leaning media. The university's switchboard was almost blocked for days by angry people, demanding Nyborg to be fired. Colleagues from other departments also complained, and Nyborg was asked to respond to criticisms at TV and radio stations from early morning to late night for several days.

The director of his Psychology Department, a former member of the Communist Party in Denmark, Professor Dr. Phil. Jens Mammen, told the media that he considered this a "serious case", so he began a witch-hunt against Nyborg at the Institute, in the media, and in the magazine *Forskerforum*, published by Nyborg's own Union and distributed regularly to several thousand of his academic colleagues, supported from time to time by the dean, Professor Svend Hylleberg, for many years to come. Mammen repeatedly ordered Nyborg to attend excruciating meetings at the university, where the dean and legal representatives from the university were also present. Nyborg was neither informed about the specific purpose of these meetings, nor was he given the obligatory advice that he might better be accompanied by a defendant, as they might have disciplinary consequences. The director pressed Nyborg under protest to present preliminary calculations and conclusions, which were meticulously noted and used later. He also officially confiscated Nyborg's huge raw database under protest and then set down a committee, manned by two Danish mathematical statisticians without formal qualifications in intelligence research and a Swedish psychologist. Without himself having any formal qualifications in intelligence research, Mammen even presented the committee with a personal, detailed, multi-page instruction, where he specified the large number of critical aspects he explicitly wanted the committee to focus on.

At another of many meetings, again with no purpose specified a priori, the director brought with him a 2–3-meter-long machine print-out of raw data — scribbled all over with his personal handwritten comments and questions, work that must have taken months to do. The dean then tragi-comically wrapped the long data roll over an image frame hanging on the wall, so it could be inspected in its flow down the wall, first with heads tilted backward, and out along the floor, with heads bent over. Then followed a long cross-examination of 69-year old Nyborg, demanding of him to recall tiny details from memory about the project, such as whether one or more identifiable subjects, out of many hundreds, were called in for testing on a particular day, exposed to a particular instrument or method, ten or more years previously. At another faculty meeting, Nyborg was first informed verbally that the university had decided to initiate a disciplinary hearing for doing flawed research, unworthy of a professor at the University of Aarhus. At a later meeting, Nyborg was told at the beginning that the university had spied on him on the internet with the help of a colleague, lector Lars Hem. He had "discovered" that Nyborg had informed and discussed his case with international colleagues, and this put the university in a bad light, said Dean Hylleberg. Nyborg had been disloyal and violated academic decorum, and for this the university would open yet another disciplinary hearing. Alas, with Nyborg near 70, the legal advisers at the university suddenly realised that two such long-lasting disciplinary hearings could not be completed before his forthcoming retirement. In this situation, the university suggested that if Nyborg would voluntarily and immediately step down from his professorship, the university would close the cases. It even offered to pay back Nyborg the amount of 23.000 Danish kroner (about $3,000), which he had already spent out of his private money on tickets, conference booking, and hotel, in accordance with a previous university grant — but only if Nyborg refrained from participation in the long-planned international intelligence conference. Nyborg saw no reason to back down from his position and joined the conference, nevertheless. The punishment was swift. "You are immediately relieved of all your professorial duties and have to clear your office desk." An implication of this was that he also had to close his research centre and dismiss his research assistant who had been working for him for many years. His name as adviser on the final print-out of a PhD thesis he had long counselled was immediately substituted with a name of a colleague with no formal training in the subject. The internationally acknowledged PhD student then left the university and science altogether in protest. All academic information about Nyborg was immediately removed from the university system (which was illegal).

Nyborg then submitted his case to the Danish Committees on Scientific Dishonesty, chaired by a judge. The committee cleared him of accusations of fraudulent research, but Rector Lauritz Holm-Nielsen still found him guilty of official misconduct, so he gave Nyborg a serious warning with no possibility of revocation, but nevertheless had to reinstate him — in an empty office room, but only for six months until he turned 70. The university kept its promise and never reimbursed Nyborg the private money he had used in accordance with the university grant. Nyborg's psychology institute refused to publicly announce the time and place for his farewell lecture.

About fifty internationally eminent scientists with expertise in the areas of intelligence and behaviour genetics and several editors of the relevant international journals came to Nyborg's rescue and wrote protest-letters to Aarhus University (see www.helmuthnyborg. dk), but this massive academic protest did not make the university change any of its decisions. A final blow came after almost 40 years of service, when his psychology institute refused to award the emeritus status that his critics were granted. As a director said, Nyborg holds values which he did not himself share, and certainly did not want to be presented to the public as representative of his institute. The sex difference in IQ that Nyborg reported in his 2005 study was later fully substantiated in a large, representative study by Nyborg in 2015, published in the journal *Intelligence* under the title "Sex differences across different racial ability levels: Theories of origin and societal consequences". Later attempts to make Aarhus University apologise, rehabilitate, and pay back the money he was granted have failed.

Nyborg came under fire again, this time for his paper "The decay of Western Civilization: Double relaxed Darwinian Selection", which was published in 2012 in *Personality and Individual Differences* by Elsevier Science. Nyborg here argued that low-IQ, high-fertility immigration from southern non-Western countries lowers the average IQ in receiving high-IQ, low-fertility countries, as do the extent to which native women with higher education have fewer children than women with little or no education. Both trends have had dysgenic effects for Denmark.

Two colleagues, lector Morten Kjeldgaard from Aarhus University and adjunct Jens Kvorning from Aalborg University, filed, together with Professor Mammen, a case against Nyborg's paper at the Danish Committee on Research Misconduct (DCRM), where they launched more than 20 different types of academic critique, including scientific misconduct, plagiarism, misleading statistics, construction of data, and the use of a ghostwriter. They also requested the committee to demand withdrawal of Nyborg's paper. They even wrote directly to the publisher, Elsevier Science, to also demand retraction. The DCRM consented to advise Nyborg to withdraw his paper, which he categorically refused. Elsevier Science set down a committee, manned by four of the most eminent international researchers in the relevant fields — Professors Ian Deary from Scotland, John Loehlin from the US, Jelte Wicherts from Holland, and William Revelle from the US. Following their assessment, the *Personality and Individual Differences* journal published an editorial in 2015, acquitting Nyborg of all charges of fraud. Nyborg then sued DCRM at a higher Danish court to have its verdict reversed. The DCRM was forced to do so in 2016 and Nyborg was awarded DKR 200,000 (approximately US$ 25,000) to cover the costs of the case.

Nyborg continues his research today. In 2017, he published *Common paradoxes in the study of sex differences in intelligence*. In 2019, he published *Race as Social Construct*, where he refuted the National Geographic Magazine's deliberate misrepresentation of race research(ers). In 2020, he published a paper with Emil Kirkegaard, falsifying previously found pupil size–IQ relations, another paper on the missing relationship between *Gout and Achievement*, and still another paper illustrating that if series of general psychopathology questions (in casu: MMPI items) become subjected to machine learning, we might obtain a highly reliable intelligence test, utilising all information. In 2021, Nyborg co-authored a paper on the bleak *Future of Secularism* (2021), with Lee Ellis, Anthony Hoskin and Edward Dutton. A further paper, written with Jordan Lasker and Emil Kirkegaard, supported *Spearman's Hypothesis in the Vietnam Experience Study and National Longitudinal Survey of Youth '79*. Still another paper, now in submission, reported that *Europeans Have Larger Testes than Sub-Saharan Africans but Lower Testosterone Levels*; it is co-authored by Edward Dutton and Emil Kirkegaard.

Nyborg will be remembered for five achievements. The first is his *General Trait Covariance* model for androgen-oestrogen balance related to prenatal and pubertal sexual differentiation of bodily, neural, and behavioural traits (see chapter 9). The second is Nyborg's *Physiology Program*, set out in his book as a scientific approach to the effects of ultimate evolutionary forces and the proximate examination of the development of human differences in body, brain and behaviour (see chapter 1 and 9).

The third is the illustration that his physiology research programme can be of use as a framework for the quantification and testing of a natural science hypothesis, set forth long ago by the physicists and mathematicians Ludwig Boltzmann (1859) and Alfred Lotka (1921; see chapter 1). They theorised that Darwin's predominantly descriptive theory of natural selection can be subjected to natural science scrutiny. Boltzmann thus wrote in 1886, in *Der zweite Hauptsatz der mechanischen Wärmetheorie*, that the Darwinian selection principle works when organisms compete for available energy and those most efficient in capturing and using energy survive and prosper. Lotka added in 1921 that Darwin's natural selection principle can be quantified as a physical law and that the selective principle of evolution is the one that favours the maximum useful energy flow transformation. To test these hypotheses, Nyborg first searched for a natural experimental setting, where the availability of energy varies systematically, and the variation can be estimated in precise available energy terms and provide a metric scale. The average earth surface solar energy flux, Wm^{-2} declines as a function of the latitude of the curved surface of the Earth, and this provided a perfect venue for this. Nyborg then used the various distances, in degree latitude, that prehistoric anatomically modern humans had migrated up north over a 275.000-year period, before they settled down, as measures of the multi-generational residential distance away from the equator (central or centroid position). He finally reduced likely disturbances to the latitudinal migration model from multiple major latitudinal re-migrations in north and central East Asia by restricting the geographic selection to African countries and only those European countries situated between -15-to +30-degree longitude. With declining Wm^{-2} serving as an independent variable, it now became possible for him to quantify and test the following hypothesis: the further north prehistoric migrants went before they settled down, the scarcer became available Wm^{-2}, the harder becamethe competition for capturing available energy, to more increased directive monotonous selection pressure for evolving a still more efficient adaptive response repertoire, to materialise in the form of still larger and more efficient brains. He quantified the former in measured cranial capacity [cm^3] and the latter by estimated

IQ+ [points], respectively. Preliminary analyses confirm, according to Nyborg, that Wm^{-2} correlates inversely -0.733 (r^2 = 0.597) with cranial capacity; -0.952 (r^2 = 0.907) with IQ+ (a proxy for g); and -0.996 (r^2 = 0.913) with skin colour. Wm^{-2} further correlates -0.930 (r^2 = 0.865) with genetic distance from Kenya, as estimated by DNA y-haplotype frequency. This provides early support for the hypothesis that natural Darwinian selection can be quantified, tested retrospectively, and confirmed in a pseudo-experimental natural science design. Nyborg added further support to the hypothesis by showing that prehistoric longitudinal migration neither implies noticeable variation in energy flux, nor elicits adaptive responses in cranial capacity, IQ, and other covariant traits. His results provide, by the way, also quantitative support for my own Cold Winter theory. A full report on these results is in progress.

The fourth is his replacement of the controversial and much disputed (self) descriptive race categorisation by neutral, quantitative, ecologically relevant categories that causally link polygene-based ecotypes to natural respective multi-generational geo-bio-climatic ecozones of origin (conf. chapter 4). Nyborg succeeded with this endeavour by first splitting the multitude of latitudinally distributed earthly geo-bio-climatic belts into five ecozones, each defined by its differentially declining selective average Wm^{-2} flux. The African equatorial ecozone number 5 thus receives a daily average of 5,422.87 Wm^{-2} and the northern ecozone 1 only 1,727.91. Further DNA y-haplotype frequency analysis allowed Nyborg to reconstruct the prehistoric origin, in years, generations, and geographic residence, of the five anatomically modern human ecotypes, by matching their migrated genetic distance from Kenya to their prehistoric long-lasting latitudinal geo-bio-climatic settlements, using data from Becker & Rindermann (2016), and to Nyborg's own prehistoric family DNA y-haplotype frequency data by the private company 23andMe. The matched reconstruction indicated that the black ecotype 5 either existed or originated about 275,000 years ago near Kenya, that some brown descendants reached the Middle East about 76,000 years ago, that some of Nyborg's now olive-skinned predecessors entered southern Europe 46,000 years ago, and that some white-skinned extended family members reached northern Europe between 28,000 to 18,000 years ago.

The fifth achievement is that Nyborg has provided the missing explanation for the observed timing of the evolution of high white, largely male, European civilisation. This analysis took point of departure in the historical data from Charles Murray's (2003) bibliometric study, indicating that this historically exceptional civilisation began flourishing in the 14th century in Italy, spread fast up north during the next five centuries, to reach its fullest extent when covering the globally small north-western polygon of Europe. From there it eventually spread to European offshoot countries like the USA, Canada, and Australia. Nyborg's geo-temporal ecotype/ecozone analyses now allows us not only to map the long evolutionary history of European civilisation in time and ecozone space, but also to predict the specific successive polygene-based ecotype trait adaptations needed to gradually evolve the full covariant trait pattern required for high civilisation.

Nyborg is currently writing up papers documenting these observations and predictions, but some of them have already been presented at various international meetings, including the Fifteenth American Renaissance Conference in Nashville in Tennessee, USA, July 2017, The Scandza Forum Meeting in Oslo, Norway, 2nd. November 2019, and at various meetings of the London School of Intelligence, before they were cancelled by a left-oriented mob. The last study was presented at the international meeting in Germany in August 13–15, 2021, under the title: "Thermodynamic Evolution of Intelligence".

It is, Nyborg believes, a sign of the widespread feebleness of current academic and political life that conference participants at the Nashville meeting had to be defended against a large aggressive left-oriented mob by armed park rangers. One scientist who nevertheless went outside the conference building was beaten up, thrown in a lake, and had to visit a hospital. Left-oriented Antifa activists tried to sabotage both the Scandza Forum meeting in 2019 in Copenhagen (with considerable success despite substantial police protection) and in 2021 in Oslo, where heavily armed Norwegian police had to physically remove about 50 loud activists. It neither bodes well for future free academic speech and research that the series of meetings by the London School of Intelligence group were attacked by left-oriented hooligans and eventually cancelled by the University College administration in London. Several participants in the London School meetings have since been attacked and some even sacked. The position of the German conference hotel, where Nyborg presented his thermodynamic lecture in 2021, had to be kept secret for all but an invited group of international researchers and the organisers for a realistic fear of disruption. Nyborg reports that several other presentations had to be cancelled or were blocked, and some even had to be defended by police armed with machine guns, dogs, and marine patrol boats, while left- oriented media, instead of reporting this academic scandal, remained silent. YouTube and Facebook have removed several of his video presentations.

Nyborg asserts that he nevertheless plans to continue and extend his previous critique of left-oriented activism, social constructivism, and weak university administration, continuing his previous publications (1997 and 2003). He further aims to extend his biophysical Physicology project by attempting to quantify the flux and many dynamic manifestations of free energy in a continual causal analysis of human evolution and current existence in terms of graphic network thermodynamics. A paper on this is in progress. However, he readily admits that to get there we have a long way yet to go. He reminds us of what Lotka said back in 1925 about his projects on the *Biophysics* or *General Mechanics of Evolution*: "The individual data appear, as yet, as more or less disconnected facts, or as regularities for which no proper place is found in the existing scheme of present-day science ... something of a scientific hobby by amateurs ... often totally lacking in any fundamental guiding principles or connecting theory ... but as results ... accumulate, the need of their unification ... into a distinct discipline of science, becomes more and more acutely felt in physical biology" (read Physicology, according to Nyborg).

Nyborg realises too that if the strong and facile social constructivist headwinds, currently sweeping through contemporary universities, continue to combine with dishonest, closed-minded, incompetent political academic leaders' de-platforming scientists they do not like and cancelling correct research, and with predominantly left-oriented media in charge, then continuing to work for the biophysical quantification of human evolution and development looks like a Sisyphean punishment for him.

I nevertheless have no doubt that Nyborg will continue to his death to try and prove his most basic hypothesis that "[m]an(kind) is a nanoscopic, local, irreversible, polygene-informed, negentropic reflection of an unforgiving, thermodynamic, energy flux, materialised on its evolutionarily optimised biophysical way through a gargantuan, meaningless universe".

References

Becker, D. & Rindermann, H. (2016). The relationship between cross-national genetic distances and IQ-differences. *Personality and Individual Differences*, 98, 300-310.

Boltzmann, L. (1886). Über die mechanische Bedeutung des zweiten Hauptsatzes der Wärmetheorie. Wien: k.k. Hof- und Staatsdr. https://www.deutsche-digitale-bibliothek.de/item/LAQBFEUXDOCKGMGCKA7RBFEJSSHLDNF7

Carl, N. & Woodley, M. of Menie (2019). A scientometric Analysis of Controversies in the Field of Intelligence Research. *Intelligence, 77.* https://doi.org/10.1016/j.intell.2019.101397

Guardian, The (Sept. 17th, 2016). Beyond the Flynn effect: new myths about race, family and IQ? By Peter Wilby: https://www.theguardian.com/education/2016/sep/27/james-Flynn-race-iq-myths-does-your-family-make-you-smarter.

Eysenck, H. J. (1996). Special Review: Helmuth Nyborg: Hormones, Sex, and Society: The Science of Physicology. *Personality & Individual Differences*, 21, 631-632.

James, W. (1880). The *Principles of Psychology* (Chapter V). New York: Henry Holt and Company.

Jensen, A.R. (1998). *The g factor: The science of mental ability.* Westport. Connecticut: Praeger.

Lotka, A. (1925). *Elements of Physical Biology.* Baltimore: Williams & Wilkins Company.

Lynn, R. (1994). Some reinterpretations of the Minnesota trans-racial adoption study. *Intelligence*, 19, 21-28.

Lynn, R. (1999). Sex differences in intelligence and brain size: a developmental theory. *Intelligence*, 27,1-12.

Lynn, R.(2002). Sex differences on the Progressive Matrices among 15-16 year olds: some data from South Africa. *Personality and Individual Differences*, 33, 669-677.

Lynn, R. & Irwing, P. (2004) Sex differences on the Progressive Matrices: a meta-analysis. *Intelligence*, 32, 481-498.

McEwen, B. S., Coirini, H., Frankfurt, M., Gould, E., Nyborg, H., Pavlides, C., Schumacher, M., Westind-Danielsson, A. & Woolley, C. (1990). Steroid and thyroid hormones and neural plasticity. *European Journal of Pharmacology*, 183, 1. https://doi.org/10.1016/0014-2999(90)91390-W.

Murray, C. (2003). *Human Accomplishment: The Pursuit of Excellence in the Arts and Sciences, 800 B.C to 1950.* New York: Harper Collins Publishers.

Neisser, U. 1967). *Cognitive Psychology.* New York: Psychology Press.

Nyborg, H. (1972). *Psychology and Genetics — An introduction to Psychogenetics* (in Danish). Copenhagen: Munksgaard.

Nyborg, H. (1974). *The rod-and-frame test and the field dependence dimension: Some methodological, conceptual, and developmental considerations.* Copenhagen: Dansk Psykologisk Forlag.

Nyborg, H. (1994). *Hormones, Sex, and Society: The Science of Physicology.* Westport, CT: Praeger.

Nyborg, H. (1997a). Psychology as science. In H. Nyborg (Ed) *The Scientific Study of Human Nature: Tribute to Hans J. Eysenck at Eighty.* Oxford: Pergamon.

Nyborg, H. (1997b). Molecular Creativity, Genius and Madness. In: *The Scientific Study of Human Nature: Tribute to Hans Eysenck at Eighty*, In H. Nyborg (Ed) Oxford: Pergamon, pp. 422-461.

Nyborg, H. (1998). Molecular man in a molecular world: Applied physiology. *Psyche & Logos*, 18, 457-474.

Nyborg, H, (2003). The sociology of psychometric and bio-behavioral sciences: A case study of destructive social reductionism and collective fraud in 20th century academia. In: H.Nyborg (Ed.) *The Scientific Study of General Intelligence: Tribute to Arthur R. Jensen.* Oxford: Elsevier/Pergamon.

Nyborg, H. (Ed.) (2003a). *The Scientific Study of General Intelligence: Tribute to Arthur R. Jensen.* Oxford: Elsevier/Pergamon.

Nyborg, H. (2005). Sex-related differences in general intelligence *g*, brain size, and social status. *Personality and Individual Differences, 39,* 497-509.

Nyborg, H. (2011). The greatest collective scientific fraud of the 20th century: The demolition of differential psychology and eugenics. *Mankind Quarterly,* 51, 241-268.

Nyborg, H. (2012). The decay of western civilization: Double relaxed Darwinian selection. *Personality and Individual Differences,* 53, 118-125.

Nyborg, H. (2015). Sex differences across different racial ability levels: Theories of origin and societal consequences. *Intelligence,* 52, 44-62.

Nyborg, H. (2019). Race as social construct. *Psych,* 1, 139-165.

Pavlides, C., Westlind-Danielsson, A. I., Nyborg, H. & McEwen, B. S. (1991). Neonatal hyperthyroidism disrupts hippocampal LTP and spatial learning. *Experimental Brain Research.* 85. 559-564.

Warne, R. T. (2021). Between-group mean differences in intelligence in the United States are >0% genetically caused: Five converging lines of evidence *American Journal of Psychology,* 134, 480-501.

Weinberg, R. A., Scarr, S., & Waldman, I. R. (1992). The Minnesota transracial adoption study: A follow-up of IQ test performance at adolescence. *Intelligence,* 16, 117-135.

CHAPTER 2

A CONVERSATION WITH HELMUTH NYBORG

GRÉGOIRE CANLORBE

G RÉGOIRE CANLORBE: How did you move from Olympic canoeing to an academic career? Which of those two activities was the most physically and mentally demanding?

Helmuth Nyborg: The change was easy. Preparation for the 1960-Olympiad in Rome took five years in advance with three hours training from 6–9 am and again from 6–9 pm — before dinner was an option — year-round. Such a program taxes social, family, metabolic, and intellectual life considerably. So, as I shared a room in the Olympic village with gold medalist Erik Hansen, with whom and two others I won the bronze medal, I simply told him that my career in kayaking ended at 3:08 pm when we passed the goal line. He found it hard to believe, but I kept my promise and entered the academic halls instead.

Grégoire Canlorbe: You are currently working on a thermodynamic approach to the biocultural evolution of intelligence. How do you sum up your theory as it stands?

Helmuth Nyborg: Actually, already back in 1994, I wrote a book on *Hormones, Sex, and Society: The Science of Physiology*, where I argued that science would advance by skipping much abstract philosophical thinking about Man's nature and instead turn to the study of *Molecular Man in a Molecular World*. The jump from there to thermodynamics is short. Currently I am trying to quantify 275,000 years of prehistoric competition between individuals in the struggle for capturing and transducing available energy (Wm-2), survival, and procreation, in a retrospective, pseudo experimental design, that is, to redefine classic Darwinian thinking along the lines suggested back in the 18th century by the two famous physicists Ludwig Boltzmann and Alfred Lotka.

Grégoire Canlorbe: When it comes to intelligence, what does the second law of thermodynamics imply? (Namely, that the entropy of an isolated system like the universe allegedly is necessarily increasing) Do you believe the universe's average intelligence is necessarily decreasing?

Helmuth Nyborg: The second law of thermodynamic is about isolated systems and is therefore not of great use for understanding the way humans work, because they are open systems. We therefore need to call upon a fourth thermodynamic model for open far-from-equilibrium systems. It is easy to understand why global intelligence has been declining steadily since 1850: low IQ people become more numerous and have more surviving children than high IQ people, and IQ is about 80% inherited. It then has to declime.

Grégoire Canlorbe: A line of criticism occasionally heard against the coevolution idea (i.e., the idea that gene and culture are influencing each other in their mutual evolution) is that cultural patterns in a population are indeed influencing genes in said population — but that genes do not have the slightest influence on cultural patterns in turn. Thus any population subject to the influence of a certain culture is allegedly led to becoming biologically adapted to said culture at the end of a few generations: that is how, for instance, the Berber, Afghan ethnicities, and various populations who were conquered by the Islamic Arabs allegedly ended up becoming culturally Arabized –and biologically adapted to the Arabic culture. What is your take on such claims?

Helmuth Nyborg: The whole idea of biocultural co-evolution assumes that cultural aspects can be measured and quantified as accurate as the biological aspects. This is not the case, and this makes, in my opinion, the whole idea of biocultural co-evolution untenable, as previously argued in Nyborg (1994).

As said above, we better entirely circumvent stubborn problems based on how more or less abstract culture works, for example by trying to retrospectively define and quantify the prehistoric circumstance under which different peoples around the world have evolved, which polygene adaptation they were forced to make in order to stay alive and prosper and which left surprisingly lasting polygene traces reflected in existing global differences in traditional behavior, which even the naked eye can see so readily today. The recent failing attempts to make Afghanistan democratic illustrate the point well in blood, violence, stubborn anachronistic tradition, wasted money and human despair.

Grégoire Canlorbe: An early investigator of the evolution of intelligence, Hippolyte Taine, expressed himself as follows in 1867: "The man-plant, says Alfieri, is in no country born more vigorous than in Italy; and never, in Italy, was it so vigorous as from 1300 to 1500, from the contemporaries of Dante down to those of Michael Angelo, Cæsar Borgia, Julius II., and Macchiavelli. The first distinguishing mark of a man of those times is the integrity of his mental instrument. Nowadays, after three hundred years of service, ours has lost somewhat of its temper, sharpness, and suppleness (…) It is just the opposite with those impulsive spirits of new blood and of a new race [that were the Italians of the Late Middle Ages and of the Renaissance]." Do you sense that analysis is grounded at a thermodynamical level?

Helmuth Nyborg: The mathematician and physicist Lord Kelvin (1824–1907) said in 1883 something to the effect that if you cannot measure a phenomenon and express it in numbers, you don't know what you are talking about. You may be at the beginning of knowledge but have certainly not advanced to the state of science, whatever the matter may be.

This problem is not only Taine's but has been with us since dawn. People think of a phenomenon, say "impulsive spirit" or "motivation", then they reify it and ascribe it causal value. Suddenly they have an explanation. Why did I do it? Well, I was motivated. They don't see that this is a circular explanation: how do you know you were motivated? Well, I did it. Much current sociology and psychology works in an abstract "conceptus-sphere".

This kind of muddled thinking was common in the past and is still prevalent today. One current widespread form is Social Constructivism, exemplified by, say, unsubstantiable theories of "systemic racism" or, "glass ceiling" in "gender research" (where gender is loosely what you feel; a lived cultural proxy for real, measurable, biological sex differences).

Grégoire Canlorbe: Thank you for your time. Please feel free to add anything else.

Helmuth Nyborg: It worries me to think that the political scientist Charles Murray (2003) has a valid point, when he concluded that Western thinking has been decaying since 1850. This most likely has to do with declining global and local average IQ.

In that connection, it hurts to watch the left-oriented political activist overtake of many modern universities and media, with their associated unprofessional "Cancel Culture", "Critical Race Studies" and politically motivated data-poor gender and LGBTQ+++ activist reports.

It is terrifying to realize that so many weak academic administrators today carelessly allow left-oriented student hooligans to attack, and have sacked serious researchers they have a political distaste for — instead of furiously defending free speech and independent research in the Academy.

It is saddening to see that so many modern universities seem to have completely forgotten the Humboldtian ideals of a free university, and instead have allowed their organization to degrade into mindless mass-producing institutions, where political correctness all too easily overturns rational science, where sober IQ research is tabooed, where dissident researchers are isolated, beleaguered, sacked, or must lecture behind armed police lines.

All this bodes well neither for free and usable science and the future of European democracy, nor for the sustainability of enlightened societies.

CHAPTER 3

HELMUTH NYBORG'S CONTRIBUTIONS TO DRUG ADDICTION RESEARCH

HENRIK ALBECK

D URING THE YEARS 1995–2006, Nyborg took an interest in the field of drug addiction research as a natural part of his interest in psycho-neuro-endocrinology. This interest led Nyborg to attend the annual meetings of the College on Problems of Drug Dependence (CPDD) where he contributed eight papers. His work in the field centred on the psychometric structure of the personality of people prone to drug addiction, including alcohol, opioids and nicotine addiction particularly seen in relation to plasma testosterone levels. The empirical bases for Nyborg's studies was the so called Agent Orange database from the Center for Disease Control (CDC) in Atlanta, USA, a database collecting health and biographical data with respect to some 2,000 variables from 4,462 American Vietnam War veterans. The original purpose of this database was to investigate the deleterious effect of the herbicide Agent Orange (used during the Vietnam War as part of the war effort) on the human body. Nyborg developed the use of the database into a rich source for drug addiction research. These studies eventually turned Nyborg into one of the leading experts in the use of the Agent Orange database as acknowledge by people at CDC.

Below eight cases are given of Nyborg's contributions to the field of drug addiction research.

1. COVARIANT DEVELOPMENT OF DRUG ABUSE, BODY, INTELLIGENCE, PERSONALITY, AND PSYCHOPATHOLOGY AS A FUNCTION OF TESTOSTERONE

In a study in 1994, Nyborg examined the development of drug abuse/ dependency in terms of his General Trait Covariance (GTC) model (Nyborg, 1994). The full GTC model predicts body, brain, intellectual and personality development from genes, sex hormones and experience. The shorter version of the model, used in in this study, relates plasma testosterone to drug abuse/dependency and general development. For use in his endocrinological models, Nyborg also defined a grouping variable named "Androtype" by dividing the veterans into five groups (A1 — A5, A5 corresponding to the highest level) based on the rank of the veteran's plasma testosterone levels. The full GTC model predicts body, brain, intellectual and personality development from genes, sex hormones and experience. Nyborg classified the total Agent Orange database with 4,429 middle-aged US male veterans into four groups: (1) No drug abuse (Never), (2) Abuse in the military only (OnlyMil), (3) Abuse only after active service (NowOnly), (4) Abuse during and after service (Sustained). Discriminant function analysis suggested that plasma testosterone is a powerful discriminator among the groups, so the average testosterone levels for the four drug use groups were determined. Using Nyborg's GTC model to predict the most likely development based on the veterans androtype (definition above), Nyborg compared the actual data with respect to the bodily, intellectual, personality, and psycho-pathologic characteristics of the different groups. The results of this investigation were as follows: the Never group has a testosterone level similar to the population average, which classifies them as androtype A3 according to Nyborg's

GTC-model. Both OnlyMil and NowOnly groups had above average level, classifying these groups as androtype A4. The Sustained
group had the highest mean testosterone levels, approaching that
of androtype A5 in the GTC model. Nyborg had previously discovered that high testosterone (androtype A5) males tend towards low
IQ, brief education, high Extroversion, Neuroticism, Psychoticism,
Depression, Hypomania and high frequency of delinquent behavior.
In general, the higher the testosterone levels, the lower the body mass
index and intelligence, the lesser education, the more personality and
psychopathology problems, seen most clearly within the Sustained
group. Nyborg interpreted the findings in terms of his physicology
theory: Physicology sees humans as complex carbon-based molecular
organizations whose development and behavior depends on DNA
instructions and on how these instructions modulate hormones in the
nonlinear dynamic interaction within a physico-chemical environment (Nyborg, 1996). Drug abuse/dependence reflects, in Nyborg's
view, a combined intra-systemic gene — endocrine disturbance with
an effect on body and brain development promoting maladaptive
responses to intra–extra-systemic mismatches.

2. A MULTIDIMENSIONAL STUDY OF ENDOCRINE AND PSYCHOLOGICAL FACTORS IN ALCOHOL ABUSE

Nyborg analyzed here the structure of 17 psychological and 9 endocrine variables with respect to their effects on alcohol intake in 2,836
middle-aged white American males from the Agent Orange database.
Psychological variables included: Spcarman general intelligence g, level of education, Eysenck's personality dimensions (Psychoticism — P,
Extraversion — E, Neuroticism — N, and Social Desirability — L)
and 11 MMPI psychopathology scores (Hypomania, Psychopathy,
Ego-strength, Introversion, Depression, Obsession Compulsion,
Schizophrenia, Paranoia, Hypochondria, Hysteria, and Femininity).
Endocrine variables included Plasma Testosterone (t), T4, Dihydro-
epi-androsterone sulfate (DHEAS), Cortisol (9 AM), Luteinizing

(LH) and Follicle stimulating hormone (FSH), Thyroid stimulating hormone (TSH), T3 uptake and Body Mass Index (BMI). Nyborg defined four groups with respect to alcohol intake with one group defined as drinking no alcohol ever. Among the alcohol-drinking veterans Nyborg formed three groups by K-mean clustering of their log-transformed alcohol consumption. A design was formulated with the 17 psychological and 9 endocrine variables as a function of the alcohol consumption grouping. This design was then analyzed by MANOVA to determine the discriminatory power of the 17 psychological and 9 endocrine variables with respect to the 4 alcohol consumption groups described above. The MANOVA design proved highly significant (p < 0.000001) with a moderate discriminatory power (Wilks' index = 0.77). The following variables — listed in order of discriminative power — demonstrated significant discriminatory power: Psychoticism, Hypomania, T3 uptake, Spearman g, L, P, Education, Ego-strength, Introversion, N, t, BMI, E, Depression, Obsession-Compulsion, Schizophrenia, T4, Paranoia, Hypochondria, and DHEAS. Nyborg compared the results from this study to his previous study of non-alcoholic drug abuse (Nyborg, Albeck, & Larsen, 1996) and found a number of similarities between non-alcoholic abusers and alcohol abusers with respect to physiology, intelligence and personality.

3. PLASMA TESTOSTERONE—A RISK FACTOR IN NICOTINE DEPENDENCE?

Two of Nyborg's previous studies had suggested that plasma testosterone (t) relates to physiological and psychological traits that dispose for drug and alcohol abuse (Nyborg, Albeck, & Larsen, 1996), (Nyborg & Albeck, 1998). In this study, Nyborg used as previously the Agent Orange database (CDC, 1988) to see whether t and t-related traits can be used to discriminate non-smokers and ex-smokers from current smokers in 4,462 representative middle-aged American males. An ANOVA analysis showed significant group differences: current smokers have 21% (or 128.6 ng/dl) higher plasma testosterone level than non-smokers, and 18% higher testosterone than ex-smokers. Ex-smokers do not differ from non-smokers (+2.4% or 14.75 ng/dl, non-significant). An Exploratory Classification Tree analysis then ranked 27 biological, psychological and psycho-pathological variables according to how well they predict nicotine dependence. Testosterone came out with the best discriminatory power, closely followed by Intelligence and Education; followed by Eysenck's Psychoticism, MMPI-2 Hypomania, Lie score, MMPI-2 Psychopathy and T4 (thyroxine). All other parameters had lower discriminatory power. Discriminant Function Analysis indicated, however, that effect sizes were small. Nyborg concluded that even though plasma t is the best of the predictors in the study and t differences among current, ex-smokers and non-smokers are significant, the small effect size makes this variable significant as a predictor only in very large samples.

4. RASCH INTERVAL SCALING OF ANXIETY RELATED MMPI SCALES AS PREDICTORS IN DRUG ADDICTION

Nyborg regularly used the Rasch-analysis for constructing statistically valid psychometric scales in the models to be investigated. Nyborg (2000) combined Rasch-scale constructs of MMPI-defined scales with scales as defined in the MMPI-manual. MMPI (Minnesota Multiphasic Personality Inventory) scales traditionally used in psychiatric diagnosing. Though the validity of these scales has been demonstrated, it has been suggested in the statistical literature that the additive raw score method of calculation is not optimal for scale construction, as it can lead to scales with uncertain interval properties. The Rasch scales of measurement are designed to obtain interval properties of the scales extracted from the underlying items. In the study, Nyborg specifically looked at the MMPI scale definitions concerned with anxiety, namely "Acute Anxiety State" (AAS) and "Anxiety and Tension" (AT), and their involvement in drug use. Nyborg had at his disposal the above-mentioned CDC database (CDC, 1988) with the full MMPI battery of items for 4,462 American men (mean age=38.4

years, SD=2.5 years). The Rasch scale showed a high Spearman rank correlation with the MMPI raw score based scales r(AAS)=0.999; t(4460)=1321.8; p<0.0001 and r(AT)=0.990; t(4460)=466.8; p<0.0001, as expected. Alcohol and general drug abusers (according to DSM-III, Diagnostic and Statistical Manual of Mental Disorders) both showed a significantly elevated level of AAS and AT over non-abusers. Nyborg had previously demonstrated that testosterone is a factor in drug addiction; when factored out, the drug addiction behavior still showed an independent effect with respect to "Acute Anxiety State" and "Anxiety and Tension".

5. CHILDHOOD DEVIANT BEHAVIOR AS A PREDICTOR FOR ADULT DRUG ABUSE

Nyborg examined the effect of childhood deviant behavior as a predictor for drug abuse later in life using the Agent Orange database (CDC 1988). Nyborg had at his disposal records of the following antisocial behaviors occurring before the age of 15: 1) Truancy, 2) Expulsion, 3) Arrest, 4) Run away from home, 5) Lying, 6) Drunk, 7) Stealing, 8) Vandalism, 9) Poor Grades, 10) Trouble at School, 11) Starts fights and 12) Total number of positives for disorderly conduct. A tendency of disorderly behavior early in life was reflected in a tendency to disorderly behavior in adult life both with respect to the total numbers of problems in job, family and in public (Spearman r=0.38; p<0.00001) as well as on the DMS-III scale for Antisocial Personality (r=0.63; p<0.00001). Nyborg next looked at the relationship between a variable with four levels of drug abuse: 1) No use, 2) Abuse + no dependence, 3) No abuse + dependence and 4) Abuse + dependence. He found a significant, positive correlation both between a range of early life deviant behaviors and drug abuse; the factors showed significant ranged from "Start fights" with R=0.08 to R=0.19 for "Drunken driving". Nyborg further used Structural Equation Modeling to study whether the personality structures differed among the various behavioral groups with deviant and drug use patterns. It turned out that the correlation matrices for the Eysenckian PENL (Psychoticism, Extroversion, Neuroticism, Lie) personality dimensions did not differ significantly either among the four drug abuse groups or between levels of deviant behavior. However, the following Generalized Linear Model: "Drug Abuse Behavior"=f ("Number of Antisocial Incidences", P, E, N, L) showed highly significant effects for "Antisocial Incidences", Psychoticism and the Lie scale. The significant correlations of adult testosterone levels with drug abuse and adult deviant behavior (r=0.11; p<0.00001 and r=0.12; p<0.00001, respectively) pointed to a common endo-crinological component. Moreover, testosterone correlated significantly with personality dimensions Psychoticism (r=0.07) and the Lie scale (r=-0.09), which suggests a common physiological component for drug abuse and antisocial behavior.

6. GENERAL INTELLIGENCE g AS A PROTECTIVE FACTOR AGAINST DRUG USE

Spearman's century-old measure of general intelligence, g, is acknowledged as a major determinant for a successful life. Nyborg accordingly hypothesized that high g protects against drug abuse and tested this by comparing the g level of non-drug users to those taking a variety of drugs. The point of departure for the analysis was a sample of 4,462 middle-aged military male veterans (CDC, 1988). These persons were questioned about their drug use patterns supplemented with 19 highly varied cognitive tests. The cognitive data were factor analyzed in order to derive a high-quality g. Nyborg found that users of heroin or marijuana have significantly lower g than non-users. Cocaine use did not relate to the user's mean g-level, but there was a significant lower variance among users, pointing to a higher degree of homogeneity in g among users of cocaine than non-users. Only in the group with a high-dose intake of more than 90 drinks per month alcohol intake was g significantly negatively correlated to alcohol intake. Even though a high-dose alcohol intake was related to g, a family history of alcohol abuse had no effect on g. Nyborg finally found that the debut age for drug use is positively (and statistically highly significantly) correlated with g (N=2820; r=0.09); t=5.02; p<0.000001). Nyborg concluded that low g is associated with an increased risk of being a drug user. As g is highly heritable (about 70%), and has many physiological correlates in the brain, Nyborg speculated that the protective role of g reflects individual differences in inborn capability to deal with everyday life complexity and thus to foresee the harmful consequences of drug intake.

7. DRUG ABUSE IN MENTAL ILLNESS ASSESSED THROUGH THE ASSOCIATION BETWEEN DRUG ABUSE PATTERNS AND PSYCHIATRIC INVENTORIES

It is has been suggested that drug abuse can be considered as a kind of self-medication. Nyborg therefore examined the association of drug (alcohol, marijuana, heroin, cocaine) abuse in relation to psychiatric status. Nyborg had at his disposal an archival database of 4,462 male veterans, who had been evaluated with respect to several psychiatric scales: DSM-III (Diagnostic and Statistical Manual of Mental Disorders), Somatization past year and DIS (Diagnostic Interview Schedule): depression past year, general anxiety past year and frequency of problems within past 6 months of insomnia, concentration, memory, short temper, aggression/anger, "loss of interest", "feeling distant" and "feeling life meaningless", MMPI (Minnesota Multiphasic Personality Inventory): hypochondria, depression, hysteria, psychopathy, paranoia, obsession-compulsion, schizophrenia and hypomania. With respect to current alcohol abuse/dependence (according to DIS) the strongest (and significant) Spearman correlations were observed with respect to psychopathy (r=0.21), hypomania (r=0.18) and aggression/anger (R=0.17). With respect to drug abuse (according to DIS), the strongest (and significant) correlations were observed to psychopathy (r=0.16), hypomania (r=0.14) and schizophrenia (r=0.13). Also in relation to current smoking of marijuana, current cocaine use and current use of heroin, both the psychopathy and hypomania scales demonstrated the strongest correlations. The drug use pattern of the veterans was recorded at both entry into the military and approximately 20 years later. These data were used for an examination of the relationship between sustained drug use and psychiatric status. This showed that sustained marijuana use had the strongest (and significant) correlations to hypomania (r=0.08), "feeling distant" (r=0.07) and schizophrenia (r=0.07). Sustained heroin use showed the strongest (and significant) relations to "feeling life meaningless" (r=0.13) and psychopathy (r=0.12). Nyborg concluded that the psychopathy and hypomania scales are the psychiatric scales with the strongest relation to drug abuse.

8. ALCOHOL/SMOKE/DRUG USE DECREASES WITH INCREASING AGE

Nyborg noted that in 1665 the French moral philosopher Francois Duc de La Rochefoucauld wrote: "When we age it is not we who leave our vices it is the vices that leave us." To test the hypothesis that drug use declines with age, Nyborg again used the Agent Orange database (CDC, 1988). He analyzed the relationship between frequency of current drug use [None; Marijuana; Hard] to age, using a generalized linear model with a logit link i.e. log (Odds of drug use [None; Marijuana; Hard]) = $a_0 + a_1 \times Age$. Age and testosterone (t) was standardized by z-transform. He found that marijuana as well as hard drug use showed similar, negative and significant slopes of $a_1 = -0.681$ and $a_1 = -0.605$, respectively. This supports the hypothesis that drug use frequency drops with age. Nyborg further found that alcohol use (as well as smoking) showed a significant and similar decline ($a_1 = -0.182$ and $a_1 = -0.207$, respectively), These rates of decline were substantially smaller than those found for marijuana and hard drug use. As he had previously demonstrated the frequency of drug use increase with increased plasma levels of testosterone (t), Nyborg analyzed the interaction between age and t by adding t to the logit model. Both age and t showed similar sized and significant effects on the frequency of drug use, but the effects worked in opposite directions: t increased the use of hard drug (a_1t=0.362) and marijuana (a_1t=0.492), and age lowered the use of hard drugs (a_1a=-0.456) and marijuana (a_1a=-0.544). Nyborg found a significant interaction between age and t for hard drugs ($a_1a t$=-0.216) and for marijuana ($a_1a t$=-0.121). A similar pattern was seen for alcohol use ($a_1a t$=-0.103), but the effect was less powerful. In contrast, smoking did not show a significant interaction between age and t, but was still significantly affected by age (a_1a=-0.132) and t (a_1t=0.475).

In summary, during his years of researching drug addiction, Nyborg was able to make solidly substantiated findings in the field because of the size of the Agent Orange database and the usefulness of his model. Nyborg interpreted his results within the framework of his "General Trait Covariance (GTC)" model and "Physicology" philosophy (Nyborg, 1994). Thus, Nyborg's research became more than a mere reporting of descriptive statistics concerning drug abuse; rather, he was able to put the numbers into a broader philosophical context.

References

CDC. (1988). *Agent Orange database*. Atlanta, GA: Center for Disease Control.

Nyborg, H. (1994). *Hormones, sex and society: The science of physicology*. Westport, CT: Praeger.

Nyborg, H. (1996). Nonlinear gonadal hormone modulation of the brain and behavior. In U. Halbreich (Ed) *Gonadal hormones, sex and behavior* (Chapter 9). New York: American Psychiatric Press.

Nyborg, H., Albeck, H. & Larsen, L. (1996). Covariant development of drug abuse, body, intelligence, personality and psychopathology as a function of testosterone. *Problems of Drug Dependence 1996*: Proceedings of the 58th Annual Scientific Meeting. San Juan, PR: National Institute on Drug Abuse.

Nyborg, H. & Albeck, H. (1998). A multidimensinal study of endocrine and physiological factors in alcohol abuse. *Problems of Drug Dependence*, 1998: Proceedings of the 66th Annual Scientific Meeting. Scottsdale, AZ: National Institute on Drug Abuse.

CHAPTER 4

LINEAR AND PARTIALLY LINEAR MODELS OF BEHAVIORAL TRAIT VARIATION USING ADMIXTURE REGRESSION

GREGORY CONNOR & J. G. R. FUERST

Abstract

THE ADMIXTURE REGRESSION methodology exploits the natural experiment of random mating between individuals with different ancestral backgrounds to infer the environmental and genetic components to trait variation across racial and ethnic groups. This paper provides a statistical framework for admixture regression based on the linear polygenic index model and applies it to neuro-psychological performance data from the Adolescent Brain Cognitive Development (ABCD) database. We develop and apply a new test of the differential impact of multi-racial identities on trait variation, an orthogonalization procedure for added explanatory variables, and a partially linear semiparametric functional form. We find a statistically significant genetic component to neuropsychological performance differences across racial identities, and find some possible evidence of nonlinearity in the link between admixture and neuropsychological performance scores in the ABCD data.

1. Introduction

Helmuth Nyborg has published extensively on the intersection between self-identified race, ethnicity and intelligence (Hartmann, Kruuse, & Nyborg, 2007; Nyborg & Jensen, 2001; Nyborg & Jensen, 2000). While defending the traditional concept of race, Nyborg is critical of self-identified racial categories (Nyborg, 2019). These categorizations are often imprecise and are sometimes politically constructed, such as in the case of the American category of "Asian," which groups ancestrally distinct East and South Asians together.

Seeking a firmer foundation for use in research, Nyborg has attempted to replace "the controversial and much disputed (self)descriptive race categorisation with a neutral, quantitative, ecologically relevant measure" that links groups to "multi-generational geo-bio-climatic ecozones of origin" (Lynn, 2022). Nyborg has called researchers to "redefine race in terms of thermodynamic Eco-types" (Nyborg, 2017). Explaining his reasoning, he notes that "current racial classifications are problematic" and that the "obvious solution is a complete genome scan of all people." Until this has been done, Nyborg argues that we should "begin to classify people by the climate and the ecological niche they have survived in for multiple generations" (Nyborg, 2017).

Nyborg takes a global ecozone-ecotypic approach to the origin of population differences. This approach aligns well with the genecology research program inaugurated by Swedish evolutionary botanist Göte Wilhelm Turesson, who invented the term ecotype (Turrill, 1946; Ortiz, 2020). According to Turesson (1922): "The term ecotype is proposed here as ecological unit to cover the product arising as a result of the genotypical response of an ecospecies to a particular habitat."

This is similar to the current commonly used definition of "a genetically differentiated population within a species that is adapted for a particular habitat" (Breed & Moore, 2014).

The ectopic approach is not inconsistent with ones based on the geographic race concept. As Merrell (1994) points out, "geographical races and ecotypes merely represent different ways of viewing the same biological entities, the natural populations that comprise species, and are as inextricably intertwined as morphology and function in an individual organism."

This genecological approach is clearly suited to the study of behavioral adaptations. To see this, one can compare Nyborg's (2019) research on behavioral differences between human ecotypes to that on ecotypes of other species. Breed and Moore (2016), for example, compared "European origin" and "Africanized" ecotypes of honeybee (Table 3.1). In contrast with the Africanized one, the European ecotype is characterized by high honey storage, low aggression, and reproductive restraint.

While we agree that this is a fruitful approach to studying human hereditary variation, in this chapter we follow up on Nyborg's (2019) suggestion to use genotypic data and "correlated allelic DNA" (Nyborg, 2019): "The recent explosion in Genome Wide Association Studies (GWAS) promises to soon lay bare the molecular DNA foundation of evolutionary and developmental differences in terms of identifying correlated allelic DNA structures guiding the development of individual, sex, family, and population phenotypic similarities and differences."

Using a new, nationally representative longitudinal sample, we show how correlated allelic DNA, in the form of continental genetic ancestry, can also be used as a neutral, quantitative measure to circumvent problems inherent with self-identified racial categories. Moreover, we show that the socially constructive aspects of self-identified racial categories, in conjunction with genetic ancestry, can be leveraged to decompose between group variance into genetic and environmental components. This admixture-based method does not, unlike Nyborg's approach, provide information about the ultimate cause of evolved differences (e.g., drift vs. selection and the ecological source of selective pressure). As such, we interpret it as a complementary approach that also addresses Nyborg's concern about the problems with self-identified race.

2. Admixture Regression Analysis

Racial/ethnic group identities such as Black, White, Hispanic, Native American, East Asian and South Asian show empirically strong linkages to medical and behavioral traits such as obesity (Wang & Beydoun, 2007), type 2 diabetes (Cheng et al., 2013), hypertension (Lackland, 2014), asthma (Choudhry et al., 2006), neuropsychological performance (Llibre-Guerra et al., 2018), smoking behaviors (Choquet, Yin, & Jorgenson, 2021), and sleep disorders (Halder et al., 2015). An important research question is to what degree any such observed trait variation arises from differences in the typical diets, cultural practices and other environmental particularities of the racial/ethnic groups, or from similarity in genetic pools within each group traceable to shared geographic ancestry. Many diverse national populations descend demographically from isolated continental groups within a few hundred years. Modern genetic technology can measure with high accuracy the proportion of an individual's ancestry associated with these continental groups. Also, in many culturally diverse nations, most individuals can reliably self-identify as members of one or more racial or ethnic groups. Admixture regression leverages these two data sources, self-identified race or ethnicity (SIRE) and genetically measured admixture proportions, to decompose trait variation correspondingly. Admixture regression has been widely applied to medical and behavioral traits including asthma (Salari et al., 2005), body mass index (Klimentidis, Miller, & Shriver, 2009), type 2 diabetes (Cheng et al., 2013), blood pressure (Klimentidis et al., 2012), neuropsychological performance (Llibre-Guerra et al., 2018), and sleep depth (Halder et al., 2015). It has particular value in the case of complex behavioral traits where reliably identifying genetic loci associated with trait variation is beyond the current reach of science. Admixture mapping is a more technically challenging methodology, often used in conjunction with admixture regression, which uses ancestral population trait differences to attempt to identify genetic loci associated with a trait. This paper focusses exclusively on admixture regression.

This paper first develops a simple statistical framework for admixture regression of behavioral traits by linking it to the linear polygenic index model from behavioral genetics; this framework clarifies the key assumptions that are implicit in this simple and powerful statistical technique. The paper then extends the admixture regression methodology in several ways. We provide a new test statistic for identifying whether a given multi-racial identity differs in its trait impact from the average impact of its component single-SIRE categories. We examine the role of additional explanatory variables in the admixture regression and their interpretation with and without orthogonalization with respect to the core explanatory variables. We generalize the linear admixture regression specification to a partially linear semiparametric form.

We apply our methodology to neuropsychological performance data from the Adolescent Brain Cognitive Development database. Neuropsychological performance is one of the most complex traits to which admixture regression analysis has been applied. Our findings corroborate existing evidence that genetic variation plays a statistically significant role in explaining neuropsychological performance differences across racial identities (Lasker, Pesta, Fuerst, & Kirkegaard, 2019). Using our new test statistic, we find that some multi-racial categories have an identifiably distinct impact relative to their component categories. We find that orthogonalization of additional variables can substantially change the interpretation of the core coefficients in the admixture regression. Our analysis also indicates (although not conclusively) that a partially linear semiparametric specification potentially adds empirical value.

3. A Statistical Framework for Admixture Regression Tests of Trait Variation

3.1. Variable Definitions

We assume that the database consists of n individuals indexed by $i = 1,...,n$ who have each self-identified their racial or ethnic group membership(s), recorded a score on a behavioral trait, S_i, and provided a personal DNA sample. The k racial or ethnic group self-identification choices are captured by a matrix of zero-one dummy variables $SIRE_{ij}$, $i = 1,...,n; j = 1,...,k$. We assume that every individual has self-identified as belonging to at least one and possibly more of the k groups.

We assume that a set of m geographic ancestries covered in the study have been chosen, such as African, European, Amerindian, South Asian, and East Asian, indexed by $h = 1,...,m$. The genotyped DNA samples are carefully decomposed into admixture proportions of geographic ancestry, as discussed in Section 4 below. For each individual, the ancestry proportions across the chosen geographic ancestries, A_{ih}, $i=1,...,n; h=1,...,m$, are all between zero and one, and they sum to one for each i.

In most applications of admixture regression, individuals' racial or ethnic group identities will have statistical relationships with individuals' genetically identified geographic ancestries and also with the observed trait s_i. The objective of admixture regression is to decompose trait variation into linear components due to genetic ancestries and linear components due to racial/ethnic group-related effects.

3.2. Ancestry Proportions as a Statistical Proxy for Ancestry-Linked Genetic Trait Variation

Admixture regression is an indirect method of analyzing group-related trait variation. In this subsection, we provide a foundation for admixture regression by considering a more direct, but empirically much more challenging, alternative approach based on a linear polygenic index model. We show that the admixture regression model can be viewed as a statistically feasible simplification of this linear polygenic index model, in which proportional ancestries serve as statistical proxies for ancestry-related genetic differences.

The human genetic code contains a very large number of genetic variants (the alleles on the genome which vary between individuals) called single nucleotide polymorphisms or SNPs. Consider hypothetically a complete list of all genetic variants with any impact on variation in the observed trait. Assign a value of 0, 1 or 2 to each SNP for individual i depending upon the number of minor alleles for that SNP. Let $SNP_{iz\,i} = 1,\ldots, n$; denote the number of minor alleles on the zth SNP of the ith individual in the sample.

The biochemical process linking human genetic variation to behavioral trait variation is highly complex, and scientific understanding of the full biochemical process is very limited. Genome-wide association studies (GWAS) have made slow but steady progress in statistically modeling these linkages, although precise biochemical linkages are beyond the contemporary scientific frontier for most behavioral traits. A standard, admittedly highly simplified, model of the gene variation/trait variation nexus is the linear polygenic index model, in which the genetic component of a trait is a simple linear function of a relevant subset of the individual's genetic variants. The linear polygenic index model has been applied to a wide range of medical and behavioral traits including body mass index (Yengo et al., 2018), neuroticism (Nagel et al., 2018), depression susceptibility (Wray et al., 2018), suicidal ideation (Mullins et al., 2014), schizophrenia (Mistry, Harrison, Smith, Escott-Price, & Zammit, 2018), educational attainment (Lee et al., 2018), neuropsychological test performance (Savage et al., 2018), and risk-taking (Clifton et al. 2018). The linear admixture regression model can be derived elegantly by invoking this standard linear polygenic index model, and hence we impose it, in order to provide a statistical underpinning for our admixture regression model.

Let p_i denote the genetic potential of individual i regarding the observable trait s_i. We assume that p_i is a linear function of a large number of genetic variants SNP_{iz} with associated linear coefficients β_z and constant term c_1:

$$p_i = c_1 + \sum_z \beta_z SNP_{zi}; i = 1, \ldots, n.$$

(1)

The key difference in the admixture regression methodology compared to GWAS is that there is no attempt to estimate the linear polygenic index (1). Rather, admixture regression uses the natural experiment of subpopulation mixing to infer differences in the conditional expected value of (1) arising from differences in the frequency distribution of genetic variants across ancestries. The assumed linearity of the polygenic index model (1), together with an assumption of random mating across ancestral populations, allows us to derive a linear regression model using admixture as a statistical proxy variable for the conditional expected value of p_i.

The frequency distributions of many SNPs depend notably upon geographic ancestries. Consider a hypothetical individual with single-origin ancestry h, that is, an individual with $A_h = 1$. Note that this also implies that $A_{h'} = 0$ for all $h' \neq h$ since the ancestral proportions are non-negative and sum to one. Consider the expected value of p conditional on an individual having this single-origin ancestry. The expectation of (1) using a single-origin frequency distribution for each SNP_z defines the average genetic trait potential of a single-origin ancestry:

$$E[p|A_h=1] = c_1 + \sum_z \beta_z E[SNP_z|A_h=1], h=1, \ldots, m.$$

(2)

In admixture regression there is no attempt to measure (2) directly, but instead differences between (2) across $h = 1,\ldots, m$ will be inferred indirectly using regression methods.

A key assumption of the admixture regression model is that admixture arises from recent random mating between the previously geographically isolated ancestral groups. Assuming recent random mating between ancestral lines, it follows from the fundamental processes of sexual reproduction that the expected value of any SNP for an admixed individual is the convex combination of the single-origin expected values, with linear coefficients equal to the individual's admixture proportions. (The relationship between the multivariate distributions of the SNPs is more complicated, but the multivariate distributions do not impact the expected trait given the linear polygenic index assumption.)

We assume that mating across geographic ancestries is recent and random, and therefore, in particular, that the univariate frequency distribution of each SNP for any individual is the convex combination of the single-origin frequency distributions:

$$E\left[SNP_{iz}\middle|A_{i\cdot}\right]=\sum_{h=1}^{m} A_{ih}\,E[SNP_z \vee A_h=1]$$

(3)

The linearity of genetic potential in the SNPs (1) and the random mixing assumption (3) imply that expected genetic potential of an admixed individual is a convex combination of the individual's admixture proportions. Taking the expectation of (1) using (2) and (3) the conditional expected value of genetic potential for an individual with admixture proportions $Ai.$ is the convex combination of the unobserved values $E[p|\,A_h = 1]$ with observed linear coefficients A_{ih}:

$$E\left[p_i\middle|A_{i\cdot}\right]=\sum_{h=1}^{m} A_{ih}\,E[SNP_z \vee A_h=1]$$

(4)

Equation (4) is a fundamental identification condition for the admixture regression methodology. As we discuss below, it allows differences between the single-origin expected values of genetic potential, $E[p| A_h = 1]$, $h = 1,..., m$, to be inferred by regression methods.

3.3. Adjusting for Ancestry-Related Environmental Influences on the Trait

Define the environmental component of the trait, e_i, as the observed trait minus genetic potential:

$$s_i = p_i + e_i,$$

(5)

where e_i is defined as all trait variation not captured by p_i. Equation (5) is only definitional; later we will impose various conditions on e_i to enable statistical identification of the model. Define p_i as the genetic component of the trait for each i which is not explained by ancestry proportions: $p_i = p_i - E[p_i \vee A_i]$; by simple substitution into (5) this gives:

$$s_i = c_1 + \sum_{h=1}^{m} A_{ih} E[SNP_z \vee A_h = 1] + p_i + e_i$$

(6)

Recall that the ancestry proportions sum to one for each i, so that one term in the sum in (6) is redundant for the purposes of creating a regression model. Dropping the $h=1$ term from the sum and rewriting (6) without the redundant term gives:

$$s_i = c_2 + \sum_{h=2}^{m} A_{ih} b_{Ah} + p + e_i$$

(7)

where $b_{Ah} = (E[p|A_h = 1] - E[p|A_1 = 1])$; $h = 2,..., m$, and $c_2 = c_1 + E[p|A_1 = 1]$.

Equation (7) is still not well-specified as a regression model since the error term $p_i + e_i$ will not be mean zero conditional on A_i, due to racial and ethnic group-related effects in e_i. In order to transform (7) into a regression model it is necessary to add explanatory terms to the regression model to remove the expected value of e_i conditional on A_i. This is accomplished by assuming that the differences in e_i conditional on A_i are dependent on the group self-identification choices, but otherwise not dependent upon admixture proportions.

For expositional simplicity, in this subsection we assume that every individual included in the sample has self-identified as belonging to exactly one from the pre-specified set of k racial or ethnic groups. In this case, the $n \times k$ matrix of racial/ethnic group explanatory variables used in the admixture regression, denoted G, is simply set equal to the SIRE matrix: $G_{ij} = SIRE_{ij}$ for $i = 1,\ldots, n$; $j = 1,\ldots, k$. Multi-racial individuals (those who have self-identified as belonging to two or more groups) will be introduced into the analysis in the next subsection.

We assume that after adjusting for the influence of the group identifiers G_{ij}, the remaining error term in (7) is independent of the ancestry proportions:

$$e_i = c_3 + \sum_{j=2}^{k} b_{Gj} G_{ij} + e_i,$$

(8)

where b_{Gj} captures the environmental component associated with membership in group j relative to the reference group $j = 1$, and e_i is assumed to be independent of A_i, G_i, and p_i, and c_3 is a constant term. Combining (7) and (8) produces the key linear admixture regression specification:

$$s_i = c_4 + \sum_{j=2}^{k} b_{Gj} G_{ij} + \sum_{h=2}^{m} A_{ih} b_{Ah} + \varepsilon_i$$

(9)

where $\varepsilon_i = e_i + p_i$ and c_4 is a constant term. Note that ε_i has zero mean and constant variance and is independent of A_i and G_i. Equation (9) is a well-specified linear regression model.

In many applications, the analyst also has information on the sampling substructure of the data, such as its division into site-specific subsamples. In this case, a linear mixed effects model can be used for estimating (9) rather than ordinary least squares. This involves partially decomposing the residual term ε_i in (9) into linear random effects components linked to data collection site identifiers and/or other subsample identifiers; see Heeringa and Berglund (2020).

3.4. Adding Multi-Racial Individuals to the Regression

Recall that $SIRE$ is the $n \times k$ matrix of race/ethnicity self-identifications. A key assumption of the admixture regression technique is that the environmental influences associated with racial/ethnic group membership are captured by these group membership self-identification choices. Many individuals self-identify as belonging to two or more racial or ethnic groups, and the group variables used in the regression must be adapted to this reality. In the context of our statistical framework, there are essentially three approaches: evenly splitting the individual's affiliation across their chosen groups, creating a new group for one or more particular multi-racial combinations, or deleting particular multi-racial observations where neither of the other two approaches seem appropriate.

We now allow that some individuals choose more than one category, so that the dummy variable $SIRE_{ij}$ can have more than one unit entry for some i. The simplest regression specification in this case is to assume that the group environment faced by a multi-racial individual is the average of the component group environments:

$$G_{ij} = SIRE_{ij} \sum_{j*i1}^{k} SIRE_{ij*i} \, i$$

/ (for all i,j. (10)

Although (10) is a reasonable specification, it is restrictive. It is possible to replace (10) with a more general specification at some loss of parsimony. Suppose that we are concerned about imposing the restrictive condition (10) for some common multi-racial choice (such as, for example, Black-White biracial in a US dataset). Let V_1 denote a k-vector with ones for the included race/ethnicity groups in this particular multi-racial combination and zeros elsewhere. We can supplement (10) by adding a $k + 1''$ group and using a different rule for this subset of multi-racials:

$$G_{ij} = 0 \, for \, j = 1, \ldots, k \, if \, SIRE_{i.} = V_1$$

$$G_{ik+1} = 1 \, if \, SIRE_{i.} = V_1 \, \text{(11)}$$

$$G_{ik+1} = 0 \, if \, SIRE_{i.} \neq V_1$$

where $SIRE_{i.} = V_1$ denotes vector equality between these two k-vectors. There are now $k + 1$ groups: the originally specified $SIRE$ groups and a new group for the selected multiracial combination. G becomes a $n \times (k + 1)$ matrix, and the regression (9) described in the previous subsection applies exactly as before but with one extra dimension to G. Any small number of defined multi-racial groups can be appended in this way. The only change to the regression methodology is that G becomes a $n \times k^*$ matrix (with an associated increase in the set of estimated parameters) where $k^* - k$ is the number of multiracial combinations added as new categories.

It is not feasible to use rule (11) for all race/ethnicity choice combinations due to lack of parsimony; there are $2^k - k$ potential multi-racial combinations and each one added requires an additional parameter in the regression. It can only be used for the common multi-racial choices where there is sufficient data of that combination in the sample. For all others, it is necessary to stick with the restrictive assumption (10) or drop the observations from the sample. This will be illustrated in the empirical application in Section 5.

Once a regression model is estimated using (11), it is possible to test the accuracy of restrictive assumption (10) for that multi-racial group. The restrictive assumption implicit in (10) requires that the average of the coefficients of the components equals the added-group coefficient in the unrestricted model:

$$\frac{1}{¿j*¿} \sum_{j*¿b_{G_{j*¿}}=b_{G,k+1}¿¿} ¿¿$$

(12)

where $\#j^*$ denotes the number of components in the multiracial category (typically either two or three) and the sum runs over these elements only. This is a linear restriction on the vector of coefficients, or multiple linear restrictions for $k^* - k$ greater than one, which can be tested with a t-test (for each group coefficient singly) or a Wald test for all them, as detailed below.

Let b denote the $(m + k^* - 1)$-vector of all the coefficients in the admixture regression (9): $b=[c_4,b_G,b_A]$ and let Cov_b denote the estimated $(m + k^* - 1) \times (m + k^* - 1)$-covariance matrix of these estimates.

First consider the case $k^* - k = 1$. Let R denote the $(m + k^* - 1)$-vector expressing restriction (12) imposed on b. For example, if the group combination consists of individuals who choose all three of the first, second, and third SIRE categories (recalling that the first SIRE category is not included in the regression), the restriction vector is:

$$R=\left[0,-\frac{1}{3},-\frac{1}{3},0,..,0,1,0,...,0\right]$$

where the 1 is element k^* in the vector. Any other restriction of type (12) is easily stated in this way. In the case of one group, this gives rise to a standard t-test of the one coefficient restriction, and in particular:

$$\frac{\left(\overset{\iota}{b}{}'R\right)}{R'Cov_bR}\quad t\left(n-m-k^{\iota}+1\right)$$

(13)

For the case $k^* - k > 1$ it is possible to test each multi-racial group equality individually as above using (13) or perform a joint Wald test on all of them. Let R denote the $(m + k^* - 1) \times (k^* - k)$– matrix of all the linear restrictions, giving the standard Wald test:

$$\left(\overset{\iota}{b}{}'R\right)\left(R'(Co\overset{\iota}{v}_b^{-1})R\right)(R\overset{\iota}{\iota}\overset{\iota}{}'\overset{\iota}{b})\quad \chi^2(k^{\iota}-k)\overset{\iota}{}$$

(14)

where   denotes the approximate distribution for large n. In the case of estimation by linear mixed effects modeling, both test statistics (13) and (14) are large–n asymptotic distributions rather than exact finite-sample distributions, but they remain valid tests.

4. Extensions of the Linear Admixture Regression Model

4.1. Additional Explanatory Variables with and without Orthogonalization

It is straightforward to include additional explanatory variables in the admixture regression model. Let $x_{i_1}, x_{i_2}, \ldots, x_{i_l}$ denote a set of explanatory variables that help to linearly explain the trait along with the ancestry proportions and group identities. We modify specification (9) to include these:

$$s_i = c_5 + \sum_{j=1}^{k} b_{Gj} G_{ij} + \sum_{h=2}^{m} b_{Ah} A_{ih} \sum_{d=1}^{l} b_{xd} X_{id} + \varepsilon_i$$

(15)

and keep all the other assumptions as before. The estimation theory for (15) is essentially identical to that of (9) as discussed above.

In some cases, the admixture regression model with additional explanatory variables (15) can be made more useful and informative by orthogonal rotation of one or more of the explanatory variables, in order to aggregate the full effects of proportional ancestries and group identities into their associated coefficients. To understand why such an orthogonal rotation might be useful, consider the hypothetical case of an admixture regression model of Body Mass Index (BMI) in which waist measurement is one of the explanatory variables. Waist measurement has such strong explanatory power for BMI that its presence in an admixture regression model like (15) will diminish the direct explanatory power of proportional ancestries and group identities; their total impact will be partly hidden within the waist measurement variable. This can be remedied by orthogonalizing the waist measurement variable with respect to the proportional ancestry and group identity variables before estimating the admixture regression, as explained next.

Suppose that variable x_l in (15) has strong explanatory power for s and substantial correlation with proportional ancestry and/ or group identity variables, and therefore the analyst wishes to orthogonalize it with respect to G_{ij} and A_{ih}, $j = 2,..., k$; $h = 2,..., m$. In a first step, the analyst can perform a simple least square regression decomposition of x_1 into the component linearly explained by these variables, and the residual, orthogonal component x_1^o:

$$x_1 = c_6 + \sum_{j=2}^{k} b_{Gj} G_{ij} + \sum_{h=2}^{m} b_{Ah} A_{ih} + x_1^o$$

(16)

Since all the explanatory variables are deterministic (that is, conditionally fixed variables rather than random variables in the regression model), this orthogonalization step is interpreted as a matrix transformation of fixed vectors and does not alter any statistical assumptions of the main regression model. It merely serves to linearly rotate the deterministic explanatory variables used in the actual, second-stage, admixture regression. Replacing x_1 with x_1^o in (15) changes the interpretation of the coefficients b_{Gj} and b_{Ah}, $j = 2,\ldots, k$; $h = 2,\ldots, m$ since they now include the G_{ij} and A_{ih} related explanatory power from x_1. An illustrative example will be provided in Section 5 below.

4.2. A Semiparametric Extension of the Admixture Regression Model

The linear dependence of the trait on admixture proportions in our regression model is in part an artefact of the assumption of a linear polygenic index (1). It is possible to weaken this linearity assumption using nonparametric regression methods. We replace the restrictive assumption of a linear polygenic index (1) with a very general description of genetic potential as a function of the full vector of genetic variants: $p_i = p(SNP_i)$ and instead of linearity as in (1) only require smoothness conditions on the conditional expectation of $p(\cdot)$ as a function of the ancestral proportions vector, as delineated below.

As in earlier subsections, we consider p_i as a stochastic function of the ancestral proportions vector $A_{i\cdot}$, but now without imposing the strict linearity (4) arising from the linear polygenic index assumption: $f(A_{i\cdot}) = E[p(SNP_{i\cdot})|A_{i\cdot}]$. Define the unexplained component of p_i as before; $\tilde{p}_i = p_i - f(A_{i\cdot})$ and we assume that $\tilde{p}_i = N(0, \sigma_p^2)$ and independent of $A_{i.}$ and $G_{i.}$. We impose the same assumptions on ε_i as in Section 2, giving:

$$s_i = \sum_{j=1}^{k} b_{Gj} G_{ij} + f(A_{i.}) + \varepsilon_i$$

(17)

where ε_i is assumed to be normally distributed with mean zero and constant variance and independent of $A_{i.}$ and $G_{i.}$. This equation (17) is a partially linear nonparametric regression model, see, e.g. Li and Racine (2007).

This model can be consistently estimated using the three-step procedure of Robinson (1988). We will impose Condition 7.1 from Li and Racine (2007) in order to justify this procedure within our framework (see the Technical Appendix for details).

For the case $m > 2$ the general specification (17) suffers from the curse of dimensionality and is unlikely to be estimable on moderate-sized datasets. A more restrictive specification is needed to give the model sufficient parsimony for estimation. One reasonable specification choice is to restrict the nonlinearity in the impact of ancestries on the trait to a single ancestral category, which we assume is ancestry category 2, giving rise to the specification:

$$s_i = \sum_{j=2}^{k} b_{Gj} G_{ij} + f_2(A_{i2}) + \sum_{h=3}^{m} b_{Ah} A_{ih} + \varepsilon_i,$$

(18)

and we will now rely on this more restrictive specification throughout the remainder of this subsection. We assume that the unconditional density $\Pr(A_2)$ is continuous and strictly positive everywhere on the

[0, 1] interval. Let $\overset{\iota}{Pr}\left(A_{i2}\right)$ denote the nonparametrically estimated unconditional density of A_{i2}:

$$\overset{\iota}{Pr}\left(A_{i2}\right)=\frac{1}{n}\sum_{i'=1}^{n}k\left(A_{i'2}-A_{i2}\iota\right)\iota$$

(19)

where $k(\bullet)$ is a kernel weighting function. In our empirical application in Section 5 we use the Gaussian kernel weighting function.

In the first step of the Robinson procedure, the conditional means of the dependent variable and linear-component explanatory variables are estimated nonparametrically as functions of the nonparametric-component explanatory variable, A_{i2}:

$$\overset{\iota}{f}_0\left(A_{i2}\right)\approx E[s_i \vee A_{i2}]$$

$$\overset{\iota}{f}_{Gj}\left(A_{i2}\right)\approx E\left[G_{ij}\middle|A_{i2}\right]; j=2,\ldots,k$$

and $\qquad \overset{\iota}{f}_{Ah}\left(A_{i2}\right)\approx E\left[A_{ih}\middle|A_{i2}\right]; h=3,\ldots,m$

that is: $\qquad \overset{\iota}{f}_0\left(A_{i2}\right)=\frac{1}{n}\sum_{i'=1}^{n}s_{i'}k\left(A_{i'2}-A_{i2}\iota\right)/\iota\iota$

$$\overset{\iota}{f}_{Gj}\left(A_{i2}\right)=\frac{1}{n}\sum_{i'=1}^{n}G_{i'j}k\left(A_{i'2}-A_{i2}\iota\right)/\iota\iota$$

and: $\qquad \overset{\iota}{f}_{Ah}\left(A_{i2}\right)=\frac{1}{n}\sum_{i'=1}^{n}A_{i'h}k\left(A_{i'2}-A_{i2}\iota\right)/\iota\iota$

In the second step, the linear parameters of the model (17) are estimated by ordinary least squares, replacing the dependent variable and linear-component explanatory variables with the deviations from their conditional mean functions:

$$\left(\overset{\iota}{b}_G, \overset{\iota}{b}_A\right) = \left(X'X\right)^{-1} X'y \quad \text{where:}$$

$$y_i = s_i - \overset{\iota}{f}_0(A_{i2})$$

$$X_{ij} = G_{ij} - \overset{\iota}{f}_{Gj}(A_{i2}); j = 2, \ldots, k,$$

$$X_{ih} = A_{ih} - \overset{\iota}{f}_{Ah}(A_{i2}); h = 3, \ldots, m.$$

Note that $\left(\overset{\iota}{b}_G, \overset{\iota}{b}_A\right)$ is a $(k + m - 3)$-vector and X is a $n \times (k + m - 3)$-matrix where the index first runs from 2 to k over j and then from 3 to m over h.

In the third step, the nonparametric component of the model is estimated by subtracting the predicted linear component from both sides of (17) and then applying standard nonparametric regression:

$$y_i^{\iota} = s_i - \left(\sum_{j=2}^{k} \overset{\iota}{b}_{Gj} G_{ij} + \sum_{h=3}^{m} \overset{\iota}{b}_{Ah} A_{ih}\right); i = 1, \ldots, n$$

and then:

$$f(A_{i2}) = \frac{1}{c_i} \sum_{i'=1}^{n} \overset{\iota}{\iota}$$

where:

$$c_i = \sum_{i=1}^{n} k(A_{i'2} - A_{i2}\overset{\iota}{}).\overset{\iota}{}$$

The partially linear nonparametric approach to admixture regression is more empirically challenging than the linear specification. Proper implementation of the technique involves a trade-off between parsimony, the generality of the specification used, and the distributional features of the available data. An example of (18) will be estimated in Section 5 below.

5. Materials and Methods

The Adolescent Brain and Cognitive Development (ABCD) study is the largest long-term study of brain development and child health in the United States, testing 11,000 children ages 9–10 at 21 testing sites; see Karcher and Barch (2021) for an overview.

Our sample consists of age and gender-adjusted scores and geno-typed DNA samples of the 9,972 children in the ABCD study who met our sample selection criteria, along with questionnaire responses of their parent(s)/guardian(s). The dependent variable in our model is the composite neuropsychological performance score based on the NIH Toolbox (NIHTBX) neurocognitive battery provided in the ABCD database; this consists of tasks measuring attention, episodic memory, language abilities, executive function, processing speed, and working memory. Age-corrected composite scores, based on the seven tasks, were provided by ABCD. We regressed out sex from these age-corrected composite scores. The residuals were then standard-ized and serve as the dependent variable in our empirical analysis in Section 5 below. Our core explanatory variables are seven SIRE variables, White, Black, Hispanic, Native American, East Asian, South Asian, and Other (and including multiple SIRE choices from among these) and five genetic ancestry proportions of European, African, Amerindian, East Asian and South Asian background obtained from the genotyped DNA samples.

Children whose parent(s)/guardian(s) identified the child as belonging to Pacific Islander racial groups were excluded from our analyses owing to a lack of corresponding ancestry category in our chosen five categories. The ABCD Version 3 database provides 516,598 genotyped SNP variants for each individual's DNA sample. After quality control, filtering, and pruning, we were left with 99,642 SNP variants to determine the five ancestry proportions, employing the Admixture 1.3 software package (Alexander, Shringarpure, Novembre, & Lange, 2015). The ABCD database includes site identifiers for the data collection sites (in most 268 cases, elementary schools) and fam-ily household identifiers (identifying multiple individuals in the sam-ple from the same family household, usually twins). As recommended by Heeringa and Berglund (2020) for regression analysis using the ABCD database, we include random effects in our regression models to account for any site-specific and family-specific error correlation.

We use the linear regression mixed effects estimate routine *lmer* from the R programming language library, see Bates et al. (2015). The one exception is regression Model 3 (see below), in which we estimate a semiparametric partially linear model. In that case, we use the *npplr* routine in the R programming subroutine library *NP*, written and maintained by Hayfield and Racine (2020), and do not correct for site-specific and family-specific error correlation.

See the Supplemental Materials for more detailed descriptions of the ABCD database, our sample selection procedure, and the construction of the variables that we use.

6. Results

In this section, we apply our admixture regression techniques to neuropsychological performance using the ABCD database. Table 1 shows means and standard deviations of the regression dependent variable on data subsets sorted by SIRE choice. On the full sample, by construction, the dependent variable has a mean of zero and standard deviation of one. There is considerable dispersion in the subsample means sorted by SIRE; for example, the means differ by 1.02 standard deviations (using the full-sample standard deviation for simplicity) between two of the largest SIRE categories shown, White-only SIRE and Black-only SIRE. The considerable variation in means for SIRE-based subsamples provides an initial justification for performing admixture regression analysis. This is a table of descriptive statistics; the standard errors shown are not appropriate for formal hypothesis testing since there is no adjustment for potential site-linked and family-linked correlations, particularly relevant in the case of the smaller subsample categories.

Table 1. Neuropsychological Performance Scores Sorted
by Self-identified Race or Ethnicity (SIRE).

Within-Category Means and Standard Deviations	Individuals with Single-SIRE Identities						
	White Only	Black Only	Native American Only	East Asian Only	South Asian Only	Other Only	All Hispanic
Mean	0.25	-0.77	-0.42	0.57	0.45	-.22	-.23
Standard Deviation	0.92	0.87	0.79	1.02	1.02	1.12	0.96
Number of Observations	5593	1434	31	107	43	97	1869
	Individuals with Selected Multiple-SIRE Identities						
	Black-White	Hispanic-White	Native American -White	East Asian - White	South Asian - White	Hispanic - Black	Hispanic - Other
Mean	-0.13	-0.19	0.01	0.58	0.83	-0.34	-0.45
Standard Deviation	0.95	0.96	0.86	0.98	0.84	0.93	0.92
Number of Observations	302	1171	131	249	40	84	411

Notes: The table shows means and standard deviations of neuropsychological performance scores for individuals sorted into categories by self-identified race and ethnicity (SIRE). The categories used are: individuals who choose only one of the six race categories (White, Black, Native American, East Asian, South Asian, and Other), all individuals selecting Hispanic ethnicity along with any of the six race categories, and individuals choosing the seven most common two-SIRE choices. By construction the mean and standard deviation of the full sample are zero and one; there are 9,972 individuals in the full sample.

Table 2 displays empirical results from three specifications of the admixture regression methodology. Recall that one SIRE variable and one ancestry proportion variable must be left out as an identification condition of the admixture regression: we leave out the White SIRE variable and the European ancestry proportion variable. Model 1 uses a linear regression specification and singleton SIRE categories for the group-identity variables G; individuals who choose multiple SIRE categories have G exposures equally divided between the chosen

SIRE categories. Three of the four ancestral proportion variables and one of the six group-identity variables have statistically significant coefficients. Model 2 adds a selected set of multiple-SIRE composite categories to the G specification.

We include the seven two-category choices with the largest number of observations in our sample. Individuals with one of these two-category choices has unit exposure to the associated explanatory variable, and no exposure to the weighted single-SIRE variables (see Equation 11 above). The same three of four ancestral proportion variables as in Model 1 are significant in Model 2, with similar coefficients to Model 1. None of the single-SIRE group identity variables is significant. Three of the seven selected two-SIRE group identity variables have significantly different coefficients from that implied by equal weightings of the component single-category coefficients. One of these (Hispanic-Other) has a statistically significant coefficient; the other two are not significantly different from zero, but are significantly different from the value implied by the composite single-category coefficients. Random effects are included in all models except Model 3 to capture any common variation associated with the individual data collection sites in the ABCD study or associated with those households having multiple individuals in the sample.

We use the *lmer* maximum likelihood mixed effects model estimation routine from the R language library, Bates, Maechler, and Bolker (2015), for all models except Model 3. See Nakagawa and Schielzeth (2013) for the definition and interpretation of conditional and marginal R^2 in a linear mixed effects model. The marginal R^2 (which does not include the explanatory power associated with site-specific and family-specific random effects) is approximately 0.16 in both model specifications. The African, Amerindian, and East Asian proportional ancestry variables have strong and significant explanatory power in Models 1 and 2. For single-SIRE individuals, the SIRE-based group identity variables are mostly indistinguishable from zero, but some of the multiple-SIRE group variables are significantly different from zero.

Table 2. Admixture Regression Results for Neuropsychological Performance: Linear Specifications with and without Composite Groups and a Partially Linear Semiparametric Specification.

Core Explanatory Variables

	Intercept	% African	% Amerindian	% East Asian	% South Asian	Black SIRE	Hispanic SIRE	Native American SIRE	East Asian SIRE	South Asian SIRE	Other SIRE
Model 1	0.3010	-1.0242	-1.3804	0.6439	0.4867	-0.1420	-0.0940	-0.1428	-0.2120	-0.0735	-0.1967
t-statistic	9.0640	-8.3330	-11.3700	3.1850	1.4910	-1.4050	-1.1150	-1.3340	-1.2060	-0.2820	-2.5210
Model 2	0.2949	-1.0238	-1.3358	0.6602	0.5439	-0.1503	0.3390	-0.1856	-0.3523	-0.2679	-0.1796
t-statistic	8.9330	-8.2250	-10.7830	3.2530	1.6590	-1.4620	1.7250	-1.3720	-1.9280	-0.9930	-1.7640
Model 3	N/A	Figure 3	-1.1914	0.6924	0.7377	-0.1289	-0.1202	-0.2578	-0.1369	-0.1523	-0.0761
t-statistic			-9.9517	3.4772	2.3109	-1.3291	-1.4464	-2.5228	-0.7736	-0.5955	-0.9088

Multiple-SIRE-Composite Explanatory Variables

	Black-White SIRE	Hispanic-White SIRE	Native America-White SIRE	East Asian-White SIRE	South Asian-White SIRE	Hispanic-Black SIRE	Hispanic-Other SIRE	Wald Test Statistic	Wald Test p-value
Model 2 [cont.]	0.0533	-0.0813	-0.0999	0.0043	0.3361	0.0361	-0.1657		
t-statistic	0.7110	-1.7890	-1.1850	0.0420	1.8000	0.2940	-2.4000		
Test 2	2.2835	-2.5520	-0.0689	0.9357	1.5102	-0.4236	-2.0061	27.0810	0.0003

Conditional R2 — Model 1: 0.550; Model 2: 0.550; Model 3:NA

Marginal R2 — Model 1: 0.157; Model 2: 0.160; Model 3:NA

Note: Model 1 uses single-SIRE categories with multiple-SIRE choices allocated evenly across them; Model 2 adds seven multiple-SIRE categories. Model 4 uses semiparametric estimation and single-SIRE categories as in Model 1. Group Component test gives the z-statistic for testing if the multiple-SIRE group coefficient equals the average of the component coefficients; the Wald statistic provides a joint test of all the group component test restrictions.

Model 3 implements a partially linear nonparametric specification. This specification requires that the highlighted ancestry proportion (whose impact is estimated nonparametrically) has observations throughout the [0, 1] range. For each of the five ancestry categories, Table 3 gives the number of sample observations of proportional ancestry in decile bins of percent ancestry for each of the five genetic ancestry categories. We use African proportional ancestry as the highlighted variable since it fulfils the requirement for observations throughout the [0, 1] interval, and therefore partially linear nonparametric estimation is feasible. Figure 1 shows the probability density of African ancestry for the full sample population; Figure 2 shows the density restricted to those individuals having measured African ancestry greater than 0.5%, this provides greater detail in the graph by excluding observations with near-zero ancestry. Interestingly, this density has three local peaks, at approximately 5%, 40% and 80% African ancestry.

Table 3. Number of Observations in Deciles of Proportional Ancestry for Each Ancestry Category.

	Interval	$A_{1i} \le 10\%$	$10\% < A_{1i} \le 20\%$	$20\% < A_{1i} \le 30\%$	$30\% < A_{1i} \le 40\%$	$40\% < A_{1i} \le 50\%$
European	Number of Obs.	298	908	425	346	461
	Interval	$50\% < A_{1i} \le 60\%$	$60\% < A_{1i} \le 70\%$	$70\% < A_{1i} \le 80\%$	$80\% < A_{1i} \le 90\%$	$90\% < A_{1i}$
	Number of Obs.	700	406	462	514	5452
African	Interval	$A_{2i} \le 10\%$	$10\% < A_{2i} \le 20\%$	$20\% < A_{2i} \le 30\%$	$30\% < A_{2i} \le 40\%$	$40\% < A_{2i} \le 50\%$
	Number of Obs.	7557	2935	286	125	165
	Interval	$50\% < A2i \le 60\%$	$60\% < A2i \le 70\%$	$70\% < A2i \le 80\%$	$80\% < A_{2i} \le 90\%$	$90\% < A_{2i}$
	Number of Obs.	88	130	406	787	149
Amerindian	Interval	$A_{3i} \le 10\%$	$10\% < A_{3i} \le 20\%$	$20\% < A_{3i} \le 30\%$	$30\% < A_{3i} \le 40\%$	$40\% < A_{3i} \le 50\%$
	Number of Obs.	8364	443	329	301	282
	Interval	$50\% < A_{3i} \le 60\%$	$60\% < A_{3i} \le 70\%$	$70\% < A_{3i} \le 80\%$	$80\% < A_{3i} \le 90\%$	$90\% < A_{3i}$
	Number of Obs.	156	75	18	0	4
East Asian	Interval	$A_{4i} \le 10\%$	$10\% < A_{4i} \le 20\%$	$20\% < A_{4i} \le 30\%$	$30\% < A_{4i} \le 40\%$	$40\% < A_{4i} \le 50\%$
	Number of Obs.	9455	74	84	20	225
	Interval	$50\% < A_{4i} \le 60\%$	$60\% < A_{4i} \le 70\%$	$70\% < A_{4i} \le 80\%$	$80\% < A_{4i} \le 90\%$	$90\% < A_{4i}$
	Number of Obs.	18	4	8	10	74
South Asian	Interval	$A_{5i} \le 10\%$	$10\% < A_{5i} \le 20\%$	$20\% < A_{5i} \le 30\%$	$30\% < A_{5i} \le 40\%$	$40\% < A_{5i} \le 50\%$
	Number of Obs.	9796	55	30	29	17
	Interval	$50\% < A_{5i} \le 60\%$	$60\% < A_{5i} \le 70\%$	$70\% < A_{5i} \le 80\%$	$80\% < A_{5i} \le 90\%$	$90\% < A_{5i}$
	Number of Obs.	4	11	9	21	0

Note: For each of the five geographic ancestries, the table shows the number of the 9,972 total observations within each of the deciles of proportional ancestry.

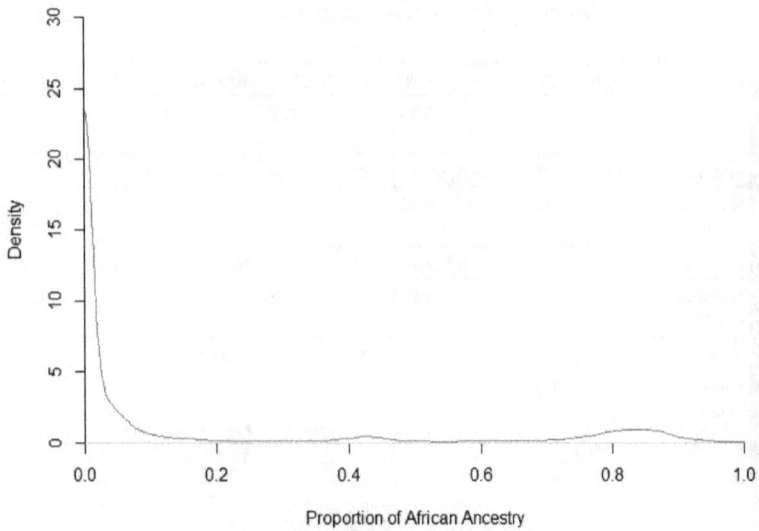

Figure 1. Estimated Density of African Ancestry for the Full Sample.

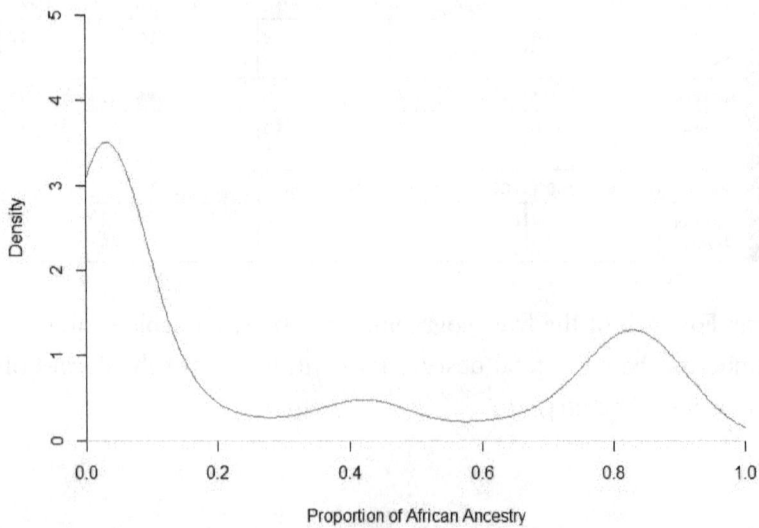

Figure 2. Estimated Density of African Ancestry for
a Restricted Sample (Ancestry > 0.5%).

Partially linear semiparametric Model 3 (18) is estimated using the *npplr* routine in the R programming language subroutine library *NP*, written and maintained by Hayfield and Racine (2020). We use the simple average SIRE specification of G as in Model 1. We use the Gaussian kernel throughout, and all bandwidths are chosen by iterated least-squares cross-validation. The linear coefficient estimates in Model 3 do not differ notably from those in Model 1. Figure 3 displays the nonparametric estimate of the impact of African ancestry on the performance variable along with the corresponding linear impact estimate from Model 1, that is, $\hat{f}(A_2) - \hat{f}(0)$ and $A_2 b_2$ for $A_2 \in [0, 1]$. There is some graphical evidence for an uptick in the nonlinear gradient for ancestry proportions above 90%. We now briefly examine this further.

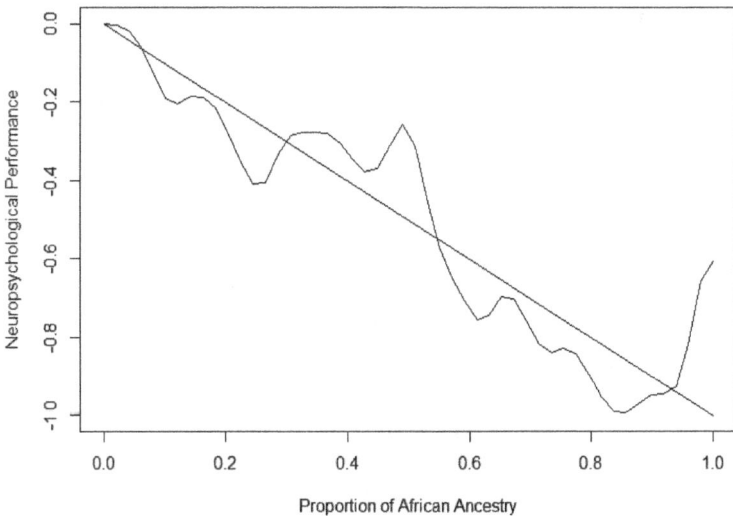

Figure 3. Linear and Nonlinear Gradients Measuring the Impact of African Ancestry.

Model 3 does not capture the efficiency gain and test statistic bias reduction from the mixed effects modeling used in the estimation of the other models. Figure 3 of Model 3 is estimated in the second stage of a two-stage semiparametric estimation process and this weakens its empirical reliability. To examine more carefully the graphical pattern observed in Figure 3, but with single-stage estimation and the advantage of mixed effects modeling, we estimate a piecewise linear specification for $A_{i2} \geq 0.9$. This was chosen in order to mimic the observed nonlinear uptick seen in Figure 3 within a linear regression functional form. Recall that African ancestry proportion is ancestry variable 2, giving the formulation:

$$s_i = c + \sum_{j=2}^{7} b_{Gj} G_{ij} + \sum_{h=2}^{5} b_{Ah} A_{ih} + b^{kink} A_{i2} D\left[A_{i2} \geq 0.9\right] + \varepsilon_i,$$

(20)

where $D[\bullet]$ is a zero-one dummy variable and b^{kink} is the added coefficient. The results are shown as Models 4 and 5 in Table 4. In Model 4 we use the simple average SIRE specification of G as in Model 1; Model 5 adds the same seven two-SIRE combination groups as in Model 2. The coefficient b^{kink} is significantly positive in one of the two models; the significance of this finding must be treated with caution since the particular kink specification (20) is based on examination of Figure 3 using the same data.

Table 4. Piecewise Linear Admixture Regression Results with and without Composite Groups.

Core Explanatory Variables

	Intercept	% African	% Amerindian	% East Asian	% South Asian	Black SIRE	Hispanic SIRE	Native American SIRE	East Asian SIRE	South Asian SIRE	Other SIRE
Model 4	0.3017	-1.0791	-1.3897	0.6365	0.4776	-0.1132	-0.0819	-0.1351	-0.2049	-0.0668	-0.1882
t-statistic	9.1120	-8.5290	-11.4390	3.1480	1.4630	-1.1060	-0.9690	-1.2610	-1.1650	-0.2560	-2.4080
Model 5	0.2956	-1.0949	-1.3437	0.6501	0.5316	-0.1163	0.3501	-0.1712	-0.3418	-0.2584	-0.1650
t-statistic	8.9890	-8.4750	-10.8440	3.2030	1.6220	-1.1160	1.7810	-1.2650	-1.8700	-0.9580	-1.6170

Multiple-SIRE-Composite Explanatory Variables

Piecewise Linear Variable	$D[A_2 \geq 0.9]A_2$	Black-White SIRE	Hispanic-White SIRE	Native America-White SIRE	East Asian-White SIRE	South Asian-White SIRE	Hispanic-Black SIRE	Hispanic-Other SIRE	Wald Test	Wald Test p-value
Model 4 [cont.]	0.1598	0.0782	-0.0749	-0.0997	0.0085	0.3401	0.0700	-0.1566		
t-statistic	1.8050	1.0300	-1.6450	-1.1820	0.0830	1.8220	0.5650	-2.2650		
Model 5 [cont.]	0.1809									
t-statistic	2.0370									
Test 2	2.4182	-2.5439	-0.1354	0.9303	1.5081	-0.3414	-2.0366		27.9764	0.0002

Conditional R2	Model 4: 0.550; Model 5: 0.549
Marginal R2	Model 4: 0.157; Model 5: 0.160

Note: Model 4 uses single-SIRE categories with multiple-SIRE choices allocated evenly across the categories; Model 5 adds seven multiple-SIRE categories. Both models include a kinked-linear explanatory variable for African ancestry above 90\%. Composite group test gives the z-statistic for testing if the multiple-SIRE group coefficient equals the average of the component coefficients; the Wald test provides a joint test of all the composite group test restrictions.

Table 5 and Table 6 add two new variables, US-born child and socioeconomic status (SES), to the admixture regression model. The US-born child variable equals one if the child was born in the US, and zero if born elsewhere. SES is a factor-analytic composite of underlying variables from the ABCD database, including neighborhood SES, subjective SES as determined from a set of questionnaire answers by the parent(s)/guardian(s) of the child on financial adversity, parental/guardian marital status, parental/guardian employment status, the completed level of parental/guardian education, reported neighborhood safety, and family income. See the Supplementary Materials for a more detailed discussion.

Table 5. Admixture Regression Results Including Raw Social-Economic Status (SES) and US-Born Child Variables.

	Core Explanatory Variables										
	Intercept	% African	% Amerindian	% East Asian	% South Asian	Black SIRE	Hispanic SIRE	Native American SIRE	East Asian SIRE	South Asian SIRE	Other SIRE
Model 6a	0.0799	-0.6299	-0.8208	0.6222	0.4300	-0.0959	-0.0313	-0.0340	-0.2179	-0.1140	-0.0763
t-statistic	1.2930	-5.0730	-6.8700	3.1690	1.3550	-0.9660	-0.3830	-0.3270	-1.2760	-0.4510	-1.0020
Model 7a	0.0846	-0.6503	-0.7828	0.6306	0.4709	-0.0978	0.3782	-0.05166	-0.3176	-0.2841	-0.0443
t-statistic	1.3710	-5.1320	-6.4300	3.1990	1.4780	-0.9670	1.9840	-0.3930	-1.7890	-1.0860	-0.4460

	Socio-Economic Variables		Multiple-SIRE-Composite Explanatory Variables								
Piecewise Linear Variable: D[A2≥0.9]A2	Socio-Economic Status	US Born	Black-White SIRE	Hispanic-White SIRE	Native America-White SIRE	East Asian - White SIRE	South Asian - White SIRE	Hispanic - Black SIRE	Hispanic - Other SIRE		Wald test and p-value
Model 6a [cont.]	0.0209	0.2800	0.1005	0.1186	-0.0427	-0.0584	-0.0318	0.2839	0.0645	-0.0764	
t-statistic	0.2420	23.7280	1.7650	1.6110	-0.9700	-0.7150	-0.3200	1.5700	0.5370	-1.1380	
Model 7a [cont.]	0.0447	0.2796	0.0897								
t-statistic	0.5170	23.7100	1.5730	3.0659	-2.4324	-0.3236	0.6783	1.4097	-0.5685	-2.0497	26.7141
Test 2											0.0004

Table 6. Admixture Regression Results Including Orthogonalized Social-Economic Status (SES) and US-Born Child Variables.

	Core Explanatory Variables					Multiple-SIRE-Composite Explanatory Variables					
	Intercept	% African	% Amerindian	% East Asian	% South Asian	Black SIRE	Hispanic SIRE	Native American SIRE	East Asian SIRE	South Asian SIRE	Other SIRE
Model 6b	0.1987	-1.1179	-1.3590	0.7182	0.6229	-0.1191	-0.0851	-0.2412	-0.2140	-0.1180	-0.1740
t-statistic	3.2310	-9.1130	-11.5960	3.6570	1.9630	-1.1990	-1.0430	-2.3260	-1.2530	-0.4670	-2.2900
Model 7b	0.2037	-1.1327	-1.3132	0.7316	0.6759	-0.1236	0.3584	-0.2698	-0.3505	-0.3147	-0.1593
t-statistic	3.3170	-9.0400	-10.9810	3.7120	2.1220	-1.2230	1.8800	-2.0530	-1.9730	-1.2030	-1.6040

	Piecewise Linear Variable $D|A2{\geq}0.9|A2$	Socio-Economic Variables		Multiple-SIRE-Composite Explanatory Variables							Wald test and p-value
		Socio-Economic Status	US Born	Black-White SIRE	Hispanic-White SIRE	Native America-White SIRE	East Asian-White SIRE	South Asian-White SIRE	Hispanic-Black SIRE	Hispanic-Other SIRE	
Model 6b [cont]		0.2055	0.2800	0.1005	0.0735	-0.0796	-0.1618	-0.0036	0.3184	0.0807	
t-statistic		2.3920	23.7280	1.7650	0.9990	-1.8180	-1.9790	-0.0360	1.7610	0.6710	
Model 7b [cont]	-0.1492	0.2267	0.2796	0.0897							
t-statistic	-2.2240	2.6310	23.7100	1.5730							
Test 2		2.4780		-2.7217	-0.2665	0.9170	1.5735	-0.2750	-2.0961		30.5889 / 0.0001

Conditional R2	Models 6a,b: 0.546; Models 7a,b: 0.546
Marginal R2	Models 6a,b: 0.218; Models 7a,b: 0.220

Note: Models 6a,b use single-SIRE categories with multiple-SIRE choices allocated evenly among them; Models 7a,b add seven multiple-SIRE categories. All models include a kinked-linear explanatory variable for African ancestry above 90%, a dummy variable for a child born in the US, and a composite variable measuring social-economic status. In Models 6a and 7a the social-economic status variable is in raw form whereas in Models 6b and 7b it is orthogonalized with respect to the other explanatory variables (except US-born). Composite group test gives the z-statistic for testing if the multiple-SIRE group coefficient equals the average of the component coefficients; the Wald statistic provides a joint test of all the composite group test restrictions.

Models 6 and 7 are identical to Models 4 and 5 (respectively) from Table 3, except for the addition of these two variables. As discussed in Section 3 above, including additional explanatory variables complicates the interpretation of an admixture regression model in terms of the implied decomposition of trait variation into linear components linked to group identities and components linked to genetic ancestries. The SES variable covaries strongly with both genetic and environmental components of neuropsychological performance scores. To retain the standard interpretability of the admixture regression, it is important to orthogonalize SES with respect to the group identity and ancestry variables before running the regression. For completeness, Models 6 and 7 are shown with and without the orthogonalization of SES; versions a and b of each model in Table 5 and Table 6, respectively. If the purpose of the estimation is to identify the total impact of SES on the trait, the regression with raw SES is more appropriate (version a). For admixture analysis intended to capture the total effects of group identity and genetic ancestry on the trait, orthogonalized SES is more appropriate (version b).

Adding SES to the admixture regression model increases the marginal R^2 from approximately 0.16 to 0.22. If SES is used in its raw form, the coefficients associated with proportional ancestries tend to decrease in magnitude, but the coefficients on African, Amerindian, and East Asian proportional ancestry remain strong and significant. There is no clear and reliable impact on the SIRE-based group-identity coefficients from using SES, in either its raw or orthogonalized form.

7. Discussion and Limitations

Many behavioral traits covary strongly with racial/ethnic self-identities, but it is often ambiguous whether this covariance reflects environmental causes associated with racial/ethnic identity groups or reflects underlying genetic similarity among group members arising from shared geographic ancestry. Admixture regression relies on the natural experiment of the recent genetic admixture of previously geographically isolated ancestral groups to measure the explanatory power arising from racial/ethnic group identities and that arising from ancestry-based similarities of genetic background. The admixture regression methodology, in various formulations, has been applied to a wide range of medical and behavioral traits, including asthma, obesity, type 2 diabetes, hypertension, neuropsychological performance, and sleep depth.

This paper provided a statistical framework for admixture regression based on the linear polygenic index model of behavioral genetics, and developed refinements and extensions of the methodology within this framework. We provided a simple new test procedure for determining whether multiple-SIRE categories have independent explanatory power not captured by the individual component categories. We considered additional explanatory variables in the admixture regression and their interpretation with and without orthogonalization with respect to core variables. We weakened the linearity assumption and developed a partially linear semiparametric regression specification.

We applied our methodology to neuropsychological performance test data from the Adolescent Brain Cognitive Development database. We confirmed existing findings that genetic variation plays a role in neuropsychological performance differences across self-identified races (Lasker et al., 2019). We found mixed evidence regarding the independent explanatory power of multi-racial identities relative to their component single-race categories. We found that when socio-economic status (SES) is included as an explanatory variable in the admixture regression, pre-regression orthogonalization of SES has a substantial impact on the measured magnitude of the ancestry proportion coefficients. We found that the proportional ancestry variable associated with African ancestry shows some evidence of nonlinearity in its impact on neuropsychological performance.

The techniques that we proposed for admixture regression studies have broad applicability, but they do have some limitations. We described three approaches to accommodating multiple-identity individuals in admixture regression studies (equal weighting, adding new groups, and deletion of some observations), but none of the three methods are fool-proof in terms of correctly capturing identity-related environmental influences in a parsimonious way. We described how to orthogonalize additional explanatory variables in order to accommodate them in an admixture regression while still capturing the full effect of ancestry-related genetic variation in the ancestry proportions coefficients. A limitation of this orthogonalization procedure is that it does not fundamentally alter the underlying regression being estimated –it merely rotates the estimated coefficients to aid in their interpretation. The partially linear admixture regression method that we describe has the usual limitations of nonparametric and semi-parametric estimation methods. It cannot be applied with complete generality due to the curse of dimensionality, and is data-intensive due to the nonparametric estimation component of the procedure.

The following are available online, at https://www.biorxiv. org/content/10.1101/2021.05.14.444173v3.supplementary-material, Supplemental File 2: R Estimation Code Library.

Author contributions: Both authors contributed equally to this study.

Funding: This research received no external funding.

Acknowledgements: Data used in the preparation of this article were obtained from the Adolescent Brain Cognitive Development (ABCD) Study held in the NIMH Data Archive (NDA). The ABCD Study® is supported by the National Institutes of Health and additional federal partners under award numbers U01DA041048, U01DA050989, U01DA051016, U01DA041022, U01DA051018, U01DA051037, U01DA050987, U01DA041174, U01DA041106, U01DA041117, U01DA041028, U01DA041134, U01DA050988, U01DA051039, U01DA041156, U01DA041025, U01DA041120, U01DA051038, U01DA041148, U01DA041093, U01DA041089, U24DA041123, U24DA041147. ABCD consortium investigators designed and implemented the study and or provided data but did not necessarily participate in the analysis or writing of this report. This manuscript reflects the research results and interpretations of the authors alone and may not reflect the opinions or views of the NIH or ABCD consortium investigators. The ABCD data repository grows and changes over time. The ABCD data used in this report came from Version 2.01 for phenotypic data and Version 3.01 for genotypic data. Additional support for this work was made possible from supplements to U24DA041123 and U24DA041147, the National Science Foundation (NSF 2028680), and Children and Screens: Institute of Digital Media and Child Development Inc.

This study relies exclusively upon archival data from the Adolescent Behavior Cognitive Development (ABCD) database and hence was not subject to institutional review.

Technical Appendix

In this technical appendix we re-state condition 7.1 from (Racine and Li 2007, p. 224) in the context of our partially linear admixture regression model (18).

We assume that the $(k + m - 1)$-vector of observations (s_i, G_{ij}, A_{ih}) $j = 2,\dots, k$; $h = 2,\dots, m$ has an i.i.d. distribution over observations $i = 1,\dots, n$ and that the conditional mean functions $E\,[G_{ij}|A_{i2}]$

and $E[A_{ih}|A_{i2}]$ are twice differentiable throughout the interior of the domain of A_2, the closed unit interval. Let $m(\bullet)$ denote any of these conditional mean functions or their first or second derivative functions. As in Racine and Li, we impose the following Lipschitz-type smoothness condition on these conditional mean functions and their first and second derivatives:

$$¿ m\left(A_2\right) - m\left(A_2{'}\right) \vee \leq H\left(z\right) \vee A_2 - A_2{'} \vee ¿$$

where $H(\bullet)$ is some continuous function such that $E[H(A_2)^2]$ is finite. The expectation of $H(A_2)^2$ is over the probability distribution of A_2.

We continue to assume that ε_i is mean-zero normally distributed with constant variance. Since G_{ij} only takes the values of zero and one and A_{ih} is confined to the unit interval, it necessarily follows that both have bounded fourth moments. We assume that $k(\bullet)$ is a bounded second-order kernel.

To formally derive the limiting distribution of the Robinson estimator, it is necessary to define a trimming parameter which ensures that the estimates $\overset{¿}{Pr}\left(A_{i2}\right)$ are bounded away from zero. Let t denote a trimming parameter and consider the estimator described in the text but where observations such that $\overset{¿}{Pr}\left(A_{i2}\right) < t$ in (19) are dropped from the subsequent estimation steps. Let ϕ denote the kernel bandwidth for sample size n. Assume that the trimming parameter obeys the following two limiting conditions as $n \to \infty$: $n\phi^2 t^4 \to \infty$ and $nt^{-4}\phi^8 \to 0$.

Under these conditions we have from (Robinson 1988) that:

$$d \lim \sqrt{n}\left[\left(\overset{¿}{b_{G\cdot}}, \overset{¿}{b_A}\right) - \left(b_G, b_A\right)\right] \ N ¿$$

where the matrix X is defined in the main text of the paper above, in step two of the Robinson procedure.

References

Alexander, D. H., Shringarpure, S. S., Novembre, J., & Lange, K. (2015). Admixture 1.3 software manual. Simon Laboratory, University of Wisconsin, Bioinformatics Programs, Madison, WI.

Bates, D., Maechler, M., & Bolker, B. (2015). Walker., S. Fitting linear mixed-effects models using lme4. J Stat *Softw*, 67(1), 1-48.

Breed, M. D., & Moore, J. (2016). *Animal behavior* (2nd ed.). Academic Press.

Cheng, C. Y., Reich, D., Haiman, C. A., Tandon, A., Patterson, N., Elizabeth, S., ... & Kao, W. L. (2012). African ancestry and its correlation to type 2 diabetes in African Americans: a genetic admixture analysis in three US population cohorts. *PloS One*, 7(3), e32840.

Choquet, H., Yin, J., & Jorgenson, E. (2021). Cigarette smoking behaviors and the importance of ethnicity and genetic ancestry. *Translational Psychiatry*, 11(1), 1-10.

Choudhry, S., Burchard, E. G., Borrell, L. N., Tang, H., Gomez, I., Naqvi, M., ... & Risch, N. J. (2006). Ancestry–environment interactions and asthma risk among Puerto Ricans. *American Journal of Respiratory and Critical Care Medicine*, 174(10), 1088-1093.

Clifton, E. A., Perry, J. R., Imamura, F., Lotta, L. A., Brage, S., Forouhi, N. G., ... & Day, F. R. (2018). Genome–wide association study for risk taking propensity indicates shared pathways with body mass index. *Communications Biology*, 1(1), 1-10.

Halder, I., Matthews, K. A., Buysse, D. J., Strollo, P. J., Causer, V., Reis, S. E., & Hall, M. H. (2015). African genetic ancestry is associated with sleep depth in older African Americans. *Sleep*, 38(8), 1185-1193.

Hayfield, T., & Racine, J. S. (2008). Nonparametric econometrics: The np package. *Journal of Statistical Software*, 27(5), 1-32.

Hartmann, P., Kruuse, N. H. S., & Nyborg, H. (2007). Testing the cross-racial generality of Spearman's hypothesis in two samples. *Intelligence*, 35(1), 47-57.

Heeringa, S. G., & Berglund, P. A. (2020). A guide for population-based analysis of the Adolescent Brain Cognitive Development (ABCD) Study baseline data. BioRxiv. doi:10.1101/2020.02.10.942011.

Li, Q., & Racine, J. S. (2007). Nonparametric econometrics: theory and practice. Princeton University Press: Princeton, NJ, USA, 2007.

Karcher, N. R., & Barch, D. M. (2021). The ABCD study: understanding the development of risk for mental and physical health outcomes. *Neuropsychopharmacology*, 46(1), 131-142.

Klimentidis, Y. C., Dulin-Keita, A., Casazza, K., Willig, A. L., Allison, D. B., & Fernandez, J. R. (2012). Genetic admixture, social–behavioural factors and body composition are associated with blood pressure differently by racial–ethnic group among children. *Journal of Human Hypertension*, 26(2), 98-107.

Klimentidis, Y. C., Miller, G. F., & Shriver, M. D. (2009). The relationship between European genetic admixture and body composition among Hispanics and

Native Americans. *American Journal of Human Biology: The Official Journal of the Human Biology Association*, 21(3), 377-382.

Lackland, D. T. (2014). Racial differences in hypertension: implications for high blood pressure management. *The American Journal of the Medical Sciences*, 348(2), 135-138.

Lasker, J., Pesta, B. J., Fuerst, J. G., & Kirkegaard, E. O. (2019). Global ancestry and cognitive ability. *Psych*, 1(1), 431-459.

Lee, J. J., Wedow, R., Okbay, A., Kong, E., Maghzian, O., Zacher, M., ... & Cesarini, D. (2018). Gene discovery and polygenic prediction from a genome-wide association study of educational attainment in 1.1 million individuals. *Nature Genetics*, 50(8), 1112-1121.

Llibre-Guerra, J. J., Li, Y., Allen, I. E., Llibre-Guerra, J. C., Rodríguez Salgado, A. M., Peñalver, A. I., ... & Llibre-Rodríguez, J. J. (2021). Race, Genetic Admixture, and Cognitive Performance in the Cuban Population. *The Journals of Gerontology: Series A*.

Lynn, R. (2022). Helmuth Nyborg: Life and Work of a Controversial Psychologist. In R. Lynn (ed.). *Intelligence, Race and Sex: Some Controversial Issues: A Tribute to Helmuth Nyborg at 85*. Arktos Media.

Merrell, D. J. (1994). *The adaptive seascape: the mechanism of evolution*. U of Minnesota Press.

Mistry, S., Harrison, J. R., Smith, D. J., Escott-Price, V., & Zammit, S. (2018). The use of polygenic risk scores to identify phenotypes associated with genetic risk of schizophrenia: systematic review. *Schizophrenia Research*, 197, 2-8.

Mullins, N., Perroud, N., Uher, R., Butler, A. W., Cohen-Woods, S., Rivera, M., ... & Lewis, C. M. (2014). Genetic relationships between suicide attempts, suicidal ideation and major psychiatric disorders: A genome-wide association and polygenic scoring study. *American Journal of Medical Genetics Part B: Neuropsychiatric Genetics*, 165(5), 428-437.

Nakagawa, S., & Schielzeth, H. (2013). A general and simple method for obtaining R2 from generalized linear mixed-effects models. *Methods in Ecology and Evolution*, 4(2), 133-142.

Nagel, M., Jansen, P. R., Stringer, S., Watanabe, K., De Leeuw, C. A., Bryois, J., ... & Posthuma, D. (2018). Meta-analysis of genome-wide association studies for neuroticism in 449,484 individuals identifies novel genetic loci and pathways. *Nature Genetics*, 50(7), 920-927.

Nyborg, H. (2017, July 17). What Made Europe Great, and What Could Destroy it? [Conference Presentation.] Fifteenth American Renaissance Conference, Nashville, United States.

Nyborg, H. (2019). Race as social construct. *Psych*, 1(1), 139-165.

Nyborg, H., & Jensen, A. R. (2000). Black–white differences on various psychometric tests: Spearman's hypothesis tested on American armed services veterans. *Personality and Individual Differences*, 28(3), 593-599.

Nyborg, H., & Jensen, A. R. (2001). Occupation and income related to psychometric *g*. *Intelligence*, 29(1), 45-55.

Ortiz, R. (2020). Göte Turesson's research legacy to Hereditas: from the ecotype concept in plants to the analysis of landraces' diversity in crops. *Hereditas*, 157(1), 1-8.

Pritchard, J. K., Stephens, M., & Donnelly, P. (2000). Inference of population structure using multilocus genotype data. *Genetics*, 155(2), 945-959.

Robinson, P. M. (1988). Root-N-consistent semiparametric regression. *Econometrica: Journal of the Econometric Society*, 931-954.

Salari, K., Choudhry, S., Tang, H., Naqvi, M., Lind, D., Avila, P. C., ... & Ziv, E. (2005). Genetic admixture and asthma-related phenotypes in Mexican American and Puerto Rican asthmatics. *Genetic Epidemiology: The Official Publication of the International Genetic Epidemiology Society*, 29(1), 76-86.

Turesson, G. (1922). The species and the variety as ecological units. *Hereditas*, 3(1), 100-113.

Turrill, W. B. (1946). The ecotype concept. A consideration with appreciation and criticism, especially of recent trends. *The New Phytologist*, 45(1), 34-43.

Wang, Y., & Beydoun, M. A. (2007). The obesity epidemic in the United States — gender, age, socioeconomic, racial/ethnic, and geographic characteristics: a systematic review and meta-regression analysis. *Epidemiologic Reviews*, 29(1), 6-28.

Wray, N. R., Ripke, S., Mattheisen, M., Trzaskowski, M., Byrne, E. M., Abdellaoui, A., ... & Viktorin, A. (2018). Genome-wide association analyses identify 44 risk variants and refine the genetic architecture of major depression. *Nature Genetics*, 50(5), 668-681.

Yengo, L., Sidorenko, J., Kemper, K. E., Zheng, Z., Wood, A. R., Weedon, M. N., ... & GIANT Consortium. (2018). Meta-analysis of genome-wide association studies for height and body mass index in~ 700000 individuals of European ancestry. *Human Molecular Genetics*, 27(20), 3641-3649.

Savage, J. E., Jansen, P. R., Stringer, S., Watanabe, K., Bryois, J., De Leeuw, C. A., ... & Posthuma, D. (2018). Genome-wide association meta-analysis in 269,867 individuals identifies new genetic and functional links to intelligence. *Nature Genetics*, 50(7), 912-919.

*

Supplemental File 1. Supplementary material for "Linear and partially linear models of behavioral trait variation using admixture regression" in which the dataset, variables, and methods for the empirical analysis are detailed.

1. Materials and Methods

1.1 Dataset

The Adolescent Brain Cognitive Development Study (ABCD) is a collaborative longitudinal project between 21 sites across the US. Its goal is to further research into the psychological and neurobiological basis of development. At baseline, around 11,000 9–10 year old children were sampled, using a probabilistic sampling strategy, from public and private elementary schools and through non-school-based community outreach between 2016 and 2018, with the goal of creating a broadly representative sample of US children of this age. Children who were not fluent in English (or whose parents were not fluent in either English or Spanish) were excluded, along with those with severe medical, neurological, or psychiatric conditions. Informed consent was provided by parents.

For phenotypic data, ABCD 2.1 data release was used. For this analysis, we excluded individuals who did not have NIH Toolbox® results, who did not have admixture data, and who were identified as being a Pacific Islander. This left 9,972 individuals.

1.2 Variables

1.2.1. Admixture

Subjects were genotyped using Illumina XX, with 516,598 variants directly genotyped and surviving the quality control done by the data provider. We used (updated with) the 3.0 release of the genotypic dataset, which also includes an edition with imputed variants using

TOPMED and Eagle 2.4. Because we had very few samples from Pacific Islanders, we excluded these from further analysis to simplify the reference populations needed (n = 69). All our work was done on build 38. Files in hg17/37 were lifted to hg38 using liftOver (https:// github.com/sritchie73/liftOverPlink) and the GRC chain file at ftp:// ftp.ensembl.org/pub/assembly_mapping/homo_sapiens/ (GRCh37_ to_GRCh38.chain.gz).

Before global admixture estimation, we applied quality control using plink 1.9. We used only directly genotyped, bi-allelic, autosomal SNP variants (494,433, 493,196, before and after lifting). We pruned variants for linkage disequilibrium at the 0.1 R^2 level using plink 1.9 (--indep-pairwise 10000 100 0.1), as recommended in the admixture documentation (https://vcru.wisc.edu/simonlab/bioinformatics/programs/admixture/admixture-manual.pdf). This variant filtering was done in the reference population dataset to reduce bias from sample representativeness. After pruning, we were left with 99,642 variants. To ensure a reasonable balance in the estimation dataset, we merged the target samples from ABCD, with reference population data for the populations of interest. We desired a k=5 solution (European, Amerindian, African, East Asian, and South Asian), so we merged with relevant samples from 1,000 Genomes and from the HGDP. The following populations were excluded: Adygei, Balochi, Bedouin, Bougainville, Brahui, Burusho, Druze, Hazara, Makrani, Mozabite, Palestinian, Papuan, San, Sindhi, Uygur, Yakut. These reference populations were excluded because they were overly admixed or because, in the case of Melanesians and San, the individuals in the ABCD sample lacked significant portions of these ancestries.

Because the estimation sample would still be very skewed towards European ancestry using this joint sample, we used repeated subsetting to achieve balance. Specifically, we split the ABCD target samples into 50 random subsets, each with about 222 persons, and merged them one at a time with the reference data, followed by running admixture k=5 on each merged subset. We verified that these subsets produced stable results by examining the stability of the estimates for the reference samples. There was very little variation across runs, e.g. for the reference sample with the most variance (European, NA12342), the mean estimate was 98.3% with SD=0.17% across the 50 runs. Since Admixture does not label the resulting clusters, we used 5 reference samples to index the populations so the data would be merged correctly. In no case did this produce any inconsistencies.

1.2.2. Neuropsychological Performance

The NIH Toolbox® (NIHTBX) neuropsychological battery was designed to measure a broad range of cognitive abilities. It consists of seven tasks which index attention (Flanker Inhibitory Control and Attention Task), episodic memory (Picture Sequence Memory Task), language abilities (Picture Vocabulary Task & Oral Reading Recognition Task), executive function (Dimensional Change Card Sort Task & Flanker Inhibitory Control and Attention Task), processing speed (Pattern Comparison Processing Speed Task), and working memory (List Sorting Working Memory Task) (Akshoomoff et al., 2014; Weintraub et al., 2013). NIHTBX was normed for samples between ages 3 and 85; tasks correlate highly with comparable ability assessmnents (Weintraub et al., 2013). Moreover, this battery has been shown to be measurement invariant across American ethnic groups (Lasker, Pesta, Fuerst, & Kirkegaard, 2019).

Age-corrected composite scores, based on the seven tasks, were provided by ABCD. We regressed out sex from these age-corrected composite scores. The residuals were then standardized.

1.2.3. Self-identified Race and Ethnicity

Self-identified race was based on parental responses to 18 questions asking about the child's race ("What race do you consider the child to be? Please check all that apply"). From these questions, six broad racial categories were created: European ("White"), African ("Black/African American"), Native American ("American/Native American" and

"Alaska Native"), South Asian ("Asian Indian"), East Asian ("Chinese," "Filipino," "Japanese," "Korean," and "Vietnamese," "Other Asian,"), and Other ("Other race," "Refused to answer," "Don't know"). The Other Asian group (N = 66) was classified as "East Asian" because the Asian ancestry component was predominantly East (44%;) not South (7%) Asian; the remaining ancestry was predominantly European (40%). The Pacific Islander groups ("Native Hawaiian," "Guamanian," "Samoan," and "Other Pacific Islander") were excluded as we did not have a corresponding admixture component. Self-identified ethnicity was based on parental responses to 1 question asking about Latin American ethnicity ("Do you consider yourself Hispanic/Latino/ Latina?"). From this we created an additional ethnic category.

Descriptive statistics for the SIRE groups are shown in Table S1. Statistics are reported for single ethnic categories, i.e., individuals reported as being only White, Black, East Asian, Native American, or Other, with no combinations (e.g., Hispanic & White), Hispanics, the seven top double combinations (i.e., Hispanic & White, Hispanic & Black, Hispanic & Other, non-Hispanic Black & White, non-Hispanic East Asian & White, non-Hispanic Native American & White, and non-Hispanic South Asian & White) and finally all other remaining groups combined.

Table 1. Descriptive Statistics for the SIRE Groups.

	N	Age M	Eur. %	Afr. %	E. Asian%	S. Asian%	Amer. %	US Born N	Neuro-psy.	SES
Total Sample	9972	9.91 (0.63)	0.74 (0.31)	0.16 (0.29)	0.03 (0.12)	0.01 (0.06)	0.06 (0.13)	9703	0.00 (1.00)	0.00 (1.00)
NH White Only	5533	9.93 (0.63)	0.97 (0.05)	0.01 (0.02)	0.00 (0.02)	0.01 (0.02)	0.01 (0.03)	5459	0.25 (0.92)	0.40 (0.75)
NH Black Only	1434	9.91 (0.61)	0.18 (0.11)	0.80 (0.11)	0.00 (0.02)	0.00 (0.01)	0.01 (0.02)	1402	-0.77 (0.87)	-1.00 (0.95)
NH East Asian Only	107	10.02 (0.62)	0.14 (0.18)	0.01 (0.05)	0.82 (0.23)	0.02 (0.10)	0.01 (0.02)	88	0.57 (1.02)	0.60 (0.75)
NH South Asian Only	43	10.03 (0.68)	0.24 (0.13)	0.00 (0.00)	0.03 (0.07)	0.73 (0.14)	0.01 (0.01)	35	0.45 (1.02)	0.88 (0.46)

	N	Age M	Eur. %	Afr. %	E. Asian%	S. Asian%	Amer. %	US Born N	Neuro-psy.	SES
NH Native American Only	31	9.70 (0.60)	0.71 (0.30)	0.11 (0.26)	0.01 (0.02)	0.01 (0.01)	0.15 (0.19)	31	-0.42 (0.79)	-0.81 (0.72)
NH Other Only	97	9.96 (0.61)	0.55 (0.30)	0.28 (0.31)	0.06 (0.19)	0.04 (0.11)	0.07 (0.15)	87	-0.22 (1.12)	-0.53 (1.11)
Any Hispanic	1869	9.88 (0.63)	0.60 (0.20)	0.10 (0.14)	0.02 (0.06)	0.01 (0.02)	0.27 (0.18)	1755	-0.23 (0.96)	-0.41 (0.93)
White Hispanic	1171	9.89 (0.64)	0.67 (0.18)	0.06 (0.06)	0.01 (0.02)	0.01 (0.01)	0.26 (0.17)	1097	-0.19 (0.96)	-0.29 (0.91)
Black Hispanic	84	9.80 (0.64)	0.35 (0.13)	0.53 (0.17)	0.00 (0.01)	0.00 (0.01)	0.11 (0.09)	79	-0.34 (0.93)	-0.64 (0.98)
Other Hispanic	411	9.89 (0.63)	0.49 (0.15)	0.09 (0.11)	0.02 (0.03)	0.00 (0.01)	0.40 (0.17)	383	-0.45 (0.92)	-0.75 (0.88)
NH Black & White	302	9.88 (0.62)	0.58 (0.12)	0.41 (0.12)	0.00 (0.01)	0.00 (0.01)	0.01 (0.02)	301	-0.13 (0.95)	-0.45 (1.06)
NH East Asian & White	249	9.99 (0.64)	0.56 (0.12)	0.01 (0.01)	0.41 (0.14)	0.02 (0.04)	0.01 (0.01)	244	0.58 (0.98)	0.66 (0.67)
NH Native American & White	131	9.78 (0.60)	0.90 (0.10)	0.01 (0.03)	0.01 (0.02)	0.01 (0.01)	0.07 (0.09)	131	0.01 (0.86)	-0.09 (0.91)
NH South Asian & White	40	9.79 (0.54)	0.63 (0.11)	0.00 (0.00)	0.02 (0.08)	0.34 (0.12)	0.01 (0.01)	39	0.83 (0.84)	0.78 (0.77)
Any_ Other NH combination	136	9.87 (0.62)	0.37 (0.21)	0.46 (0.25)	0.13 (0.20)	0.02 (0.07)	0.02 (0.05)	131	-0.27 (1.06)	-0.63 (1.03)

Note: Euro.% = European ancestry percentage, Afr.% = African ancestry percentage, E.Asian% = East Asian ancestry percentage, S.Asian% = South Asian ancestry percentage, Neuropsy. = Neuropsychiatric performance, SES = general socioeconomic component score. NH = non-Hispanic. Hispanic & White, Hispanic & Black, and Hispanic & Other are subsets of the Any Hispanic category.

The racial and ethnic variables were then recoded to create interval categories for which individuals are assigned a percentage of each SIRE category based on the number of responses chosen (Liebler & Halpern-Manners, 2008; Kirkegaard et al., 2019). By this coding, if someone was marked as White and Hispanic, they were assigned scores of .5 for white and .5 for Hispanic and 0 for the other 5 categories. The correlations between these interval scores and genetic ancestry components are shown in Table S2 below ($N = 9972$). These associations are similar to those found by others (for example: Guo et al. 2014); self-identified race generally corresponds with genetic ancestry.

Table S2. Correlations between Interval Coded SIRE and Genetic Ancestry.

	European ancestry	African ancestry	East Asian ancestry	South Asian ancestry	Amerindian ancestry
White_SIRE	0.91	-0.74	-0.21	-0.05	-0.31
Black_SIRE	-0.76	0.96	-0.08	-0.09	-0.18
East_Asian_SIRE	-0.24	-0.08	0.92	0.02	-0.06
South_Asian SIRE	-0.11	-0.04	0.01	0.87	-0.03
Native_SIRE	-0.02	0.00	-0.01	-0.03	0.07
Hispanic_SIRE	-0.21	-0.10	-0.04	-0.06	0.77
Other_SIRE	-0.16	-0.01	0.00	0.00	0.38

1.2.4. Region of Birth (US-Born)

Region of birth was based on the parental response to the question, "In which country was the child born?". The response "United States" was recoded as 1 and all other responses were recoded as 0.

1.2.5. Socioeconomic Status

Socioeconomic status was based on seven indicators: financial adversity, area deprivation index, neighborhood safety protocol, parental education, parental income, parental marital status, and parental employment status. These are detailed below:

1.2.5.1. Financial Adversity (Reverse Coded)

Parents answered a seven-item Financial Adversity Questionnaire (PRFQ). They were asked: "In the past 12 months, has there been a time when you and your immediate family experienced any of the following:

(1) "Needed food but could not afford to buy it or could not afford to go out to get it?",

(2) "Were without telephone service because you could not afford it?"

(3) "Did not pay the full amount of the rent or mortgage because you could not afford it?",

(4) "Were evicted from your home for not paying the rent or mortgage?",

(5) "Had services turned off by the gas or electric company, or the oil company would not deliver oil because payments were not made?",

(6) "Had someone who needed to see a doctor or go to the hospital but did not go because you could not afford it?", and

(7) "Had someone who needed a dentist but could not go because you could not afford it?"

For each of the seven items they answered "yes" (1) or "no" (0). We summed responses. Thus the maximum was 7 and the minimum was 0.

This variable was reverse coded, so that higher scores indicated less financial adversity, and then standardized.

1.2.5.2. Area Deprivation Index (ADI) (Reverse Coded)

Parents completed a residential history questionnaire. They provided the residential addresses and the number of full years they lived at each residence. For each address an Area Deprivation Index (ADI) was computed by ABCD and the national percentile of the area's socioeconomic status was given. ADI was based on the following variables:

"Percentage of occupied housing units without complete plumbing (log)"

"Percentage of occupied housing units without a telephone"

"Percentage of occupied housing units without a motor vehicle"

"Percentage of single"

"Percentage of population below 138% of the poverty threshold"

"Percentage of families below the poverty level"

"Percentage of civilian labor force population aged >=16 y unemployed (unemployment rate)"

"Percentage of occupied housing units with >1 person per room (crowding)"

"Percentage of owner"

"Median monthly mortgage"

"Median gross rent"

"Median home value"

"Income disparity defined by Singh as the log of 100 x ratio of the number of households with <10,000 annual income to the number of households with >50,000 annual income"

"Median family income"

"Percentage of population aged >=25 y with at least a high school diploma"

"Percentage of population aged >=25 y with <9 y of education"

Scores were provided in terms of national percentiles. We used scores for the most recent residence (variable: reshist_addr1_adi_perc). The resultant values were reverse coded to make higher values indicate better neighborhoods, and then standardized.

1.2.5.3. Neighborhood Safety Protocol

Parents were asked three Likert scale (1 = strongly disagree; 5 = strongly agree) questions about neighborhood safety: "I feel safe walking in my neighborhood, day or night," "Violence is not a problem in my neighborhood," and "My neighborhood is safe from crime." We used the precomputed summary scores for which the three scores were summed and then divided them by three.

1.2.5.3. Education

Parents were asked: "What is the highest grade or level of school you have completed or the highest degree you have received?" To create an interval variable, we recoded parental education as 0 to 18: Never attended/Kindergarten only = 0, 1st grade = 1, 2nd grade = 2, 3rd grade = 3, 4th grade = 4, 5th grade = 5, 6th grade = 6, 7th grade = 7, 8th grade = 8, 9th grade = 9, 10th grade = 10, 11th grade = 11, 12th grade = 12, High school graduate = 12, GED or equivalent Diploma General = 12, Associate degree: Occupational Program = 14, Associate degree: Academic Program = 14, Bachelor's degree = 16, Master's degree = 18, Professional school = 18, Doctoral degree = 18. We standardized the scores for each educational scores for both parents and standardized the average scores.

1.2.5.4. Income

Family was an interval variable which reflected the parents' total combined family income in the past 12 months. The variable was recoded as follows: 1.00 = less than $5,000 (recode: 4,500); 2.00 = $5,000 to 11,999 (recode: 5,000); 3.00 = $12,000 to 15,999 (recode: 12,000); 4.00 = $16,000 to 24,999 (recode: 16,000); 5.00 = $25,000 to 34,999 (recode: 25,000); 6.00 = $35,000 to 49,999 (recode: 35,000); 7.00 = $50,000 to 74,999 (recode: 50,000); 8.00 = $75,000, to 99,999 (recode: 75,000); 9.00 = $100,000 to 199,999 (recode: 100,000); 10.00 = $200,000 and greater (recode: 200,000).

1.2.5.5. Marital Status

Parental marital status was coded as 1 if married and 0 for any other arrangement.

1.2.5.6. Employment Status

Parental employment was coded as 1 if at least one parent was working now either full or part time and 0 for all other cases.

3.2.5.7. General SES

Missing data for the seven economic indicators were imputed using the mice package (df, m=5, maxit = 50, method = 'pmm', seed = 500). Descriptive statistics for the imputed SES indicators are provided in Table S3, while the correlation matrix for the imputed variables (N = 9972), along with neuropsychiatric performance, is shown in Table S4.

Table S3. Descriptive Statistics & Correlation Matrix for the SES indicators (N = 9972 in all cases).

Variable	M	SD	1	2	3	4	5	6	7	8
1. Financial Adversity	0.00	1.00								
2. ADI	0.00	1.00	.21**							
			[.19, .23]							
3. Neighborhood Safety Protocol	0.00	1.00	.24**	.25**						
			[.22, .26]	[.23, .27]						
4. Education	0.00	1.00	.28**	.28**	.28**					
			[.27, .30]	[.26, .30]	[.27, .30]					
5. Income	0.00	1.00	.34**	.34**	.31**	.57**				
			[.33, .36]	[.33, .36]	[.29, .33]	[.56, .58]				
6. Marital Status	0.68	0.47	.27**	.23**	.23**	.33**	.46**			
			[.25, .29]	[.21, .25]	[.21, .25]	[.31, .35]	[.44, .47]			
7. Employment Status	0.91	0.28	.16**	.13**	.15**	.26**	.27**	.28**		
			[.14, .18]	[.11, .15]	[.13, .17]	[.25, .28]	[.25, .28]	[.27, .30]		
8. General SES	0.00	1.00	.56**	.54**	.55**	.73**	.80**	.66**	.48**	
			[.55, .58]	[.53, .56]	[.53, .56]	[.72, .74]	[.79, .81]	[.64, .67]	[.46, .49]	
9. Neuropsy.	0.00	1.00	.20**	.21**	.18**	.40**	.35**	.27**	.18**	.43**
			[.18, .22]	[.19, .23]	[.16, .20]	[.39, .42]	[.33, .37]	[.26, .29]	[.16, .20]	[.41, .44]

Note. M and SD are used to represent mean and standard deviation, respectively. Values in square brackets indicate the 95% confidence interval for each correlation. The confidence interval is a plausible range of population correlations that could have caused the sample correlation (Cumming, 2014). * indicates $p < .05$. ** indicates $p < .01$.

We then submitted the seven SES indicators to Principal Component Analysis (PCA). For this, we used the R package PCAmixdata, which handles mixed categorical and continuous data (Chavent, Kuentz-Simonet, & Saracco, 2014). The first unrotated component explained 39% of the variance. The PCA_1 loadings for the seven SES indicators were as follows: financial adversity (.317), area deprivation index (.296), neighborhood safety protocol (.298), parental education (.529), parental income (.641), parental marital status (.431), and parental employment status (0.230). The vector of PCA_1 loadings correlated with the vector of SES indicator effects on Neuropsychiatric Performance at $r = .91$ ($N=7$). Similarly, the vector of PCA_1 loadings strongly correlated with the vectors of genetic ancestry, with absolute values of $r = .62$ to $r = .95$ ($N=7$). Table S4 shows the correlations between SES indicators and genetic ancestry for all five ancestry components. These results indicate that the better measures of general SES have stronger correlations with both Neuropsychiatric Performance and genetic ancestry.

Table S4. General SES loadings and the Correlations between SES Indicators and Genetic Ancestry within the Full Sample.

	General SES Loadings	rEurope	rAfrican	rAmerindian	rEast Asian	rSouth Asian
Financial Adversity	0.317	0.24	-0.26	-0.07	0.05	0.05
ADI	0.296	0.26	-0.32	0.00	0.06	0.04
Neighborhood Safety Protocol	0.298	0.30	-0.28	-0.12	0.02	0.04
Education	0.529	0.38	-0.29	-0.39	0.10	0.12
Income	0.641	0.38	-0.36	-0.23	0.09	0.11
Marital Status	0.431	0.37	-0.40	0.09	0.07	0.07
Employment Status	0.230	0.21	-0.20	-0.08	0.02	0.03
r(SES loadings x ancestry correlations)		0.89	-0.62	-0.73	0.87	0.95

Note: Of relevance is the magnitude, not direction, of the correlations between the vector of SES loadings and the vectors of ancestry correlations.

PCA_1 scores correlated with Neuropsychological Performance at $r = .43$ in the full sample. Among non-Hispanic Whites, non-Hispanic Blacks, and Hispanics, the correlations between PCA_1 and Neuropsychological Performance was $r = .25$ ($N = 5533$), $r = .31$ ($N = 1434$), and $r = .31$ ($N = 1869$), respectively. These magnitudes of child-parental SES correlations are consistent with those previously reported (Flores-Mendoza, Ardila, Gallegos, & Reategui-Colareta, 2021; Sirin, 2005). The congruence coefficients for the SES component loadings were greater or equal to $r = .97$ for the largest three SIRE groups (non-Hispanic Whites, non-Hispanic Blacks, and Hispanics), indicating identical structures across groups.

2. Methods

A series of regression models were run with NIHTBX as the dependent variable. The NIHTBX and socioeconomic variables were standardized (based on the subsample of 9,972 retained). The ancestry variables were left unstandardized, thus the coefficients from ancestries can be interpreted as a change in 100% ancestry over a change in one standardized unit of NIHTBX scores. European ancestry and White SIRE were selected as reference values and thus not included as independents. For the regression analyses, following the recommendations of Heeringa and Berglund (2021), we used a three-level (site, family, individual) multi-level mixed effects model. This model was applied to the pooled twin and regular ABCD baseline sample. This specification approximates the ABCD Data Exploration and Analysis Portal (DEAP) specification (Heeringa and Berglund, 2021).

References

Akshoomoff, N., Newman, E., Thompson, W. K., McCabe, C., Bloss, C. S., Chang, L., ... & Jernigan, T. L. (2014). The NIH Toolbox Cognition Battery: results from a large normative developmental sample (PING). *Neuropsychology*, 28(1), 1.

Chavent, M., Kuentz-Simonet, V., & Saracco, J. (2014). Multivariate analysis of mixed data: the PCAmixdata R package. arXiv. arXiv preprint arXiv:1411.4911.

Flores-Mendoza, C., Ardila, R., Gallegos, M., & Reategui-Colareta, N. (2021) General Intelligence and Socioeconomic Status as Strong Predictors of Student Performance in Latin American Schools: Evidence From PISA Items. *Front. Educ.* 6:632289. doi: 10.3389/feduc.2021.632289

Guo, G., Fu, Y., Lee, H., Cai, T., Harris, K. M., & Li, Y. (2014). Genetic bio-ancestry and social construction of racial classification in social surveys in the contemporary United States. *Demography*, 51(1), 141-172.

Heeringa, S. G., & Berglund, P. A. (2020). A guide for population-based analysis of the Adolescent Brain Cognitive Development (ABCD) Study baseline data. *BioRxiv.*

CHAPTER 5

SEX DIFFERENCES IN SELF-ESTIMATED INTELLIGENCE

ADRIAN FURNHAM

NORWEGIAN BUSINESS SCHOOL

A Word about Helmut

I MET HELMUT IN the psychology department in Oxford where I was doing my DPhil (PhD) and he was a visitor. The department was dominated by experimental cognitive psychologists with a rather dismissive attitude to those interested in individual differences, which they always thought of as simply error variance. I remember him talking loudly and enthusiastically about hormonal effects on behaviour, which was intriguing and somehow dangerous, particularly if one proposed experimental work.

He was, and remains, well-read, articulate and not afraid of confronting taboo topics. He remains always curious, controversial, and where necessary confrontational.

We subsequently met at ISSID conferences. He was always a good raconteur with a very broad range of interests in individual differences. I also became aware of all the trouble he had with his university, and I, like many others, wrote to the Vice Chancellor in support of his work, and the now frequently challenged concept of academic freedom.

Over the years he has become more controversial as the socio-political environment has changed. You need courage and conviction to stay the course with sex differences, and this is surely what he has done. He has become one of a small band of elite survivors: researchers, like the editor of this book, who keep working into what used to be called "old age" with no signs of cognitive decline or fatigue.

My interests, which I review in this chapter, are related, but different. They refer to sex differences in *perceived or estimated* intelligence: essentially what people think about their own and other's intelligence levels. Self-assessed characteristics (ability, personality) is interesting and related to actual (psychometrically assessed) characteristics. However, we know there are systematic differences in both, which are worth exploring. I shall leave the discussion of "actual" sex differences in cognitive ability to the editor and his colleagues, who have researched this area for many years.

However, it is important to clarify Helmut's position.He is very clear in his analysis of sex differences in IQ, comparing those theorists like Jenson who suggest minimal differences and Lynn who notes a developmental trend in puberty leading to clear sex differences. For instance, he concluded that, following rigorous methodology, there is a male advantage in g that increases exponentially at higher levels, relates to brain size, and partly explains the universal male dominance in society (Nyborg, 2005). In his extensive analysis investigating sex differences in IQ, he concluded, ... sex differences in general intelligence first appear robustly around puberty across (three) race(s). They show that Male/Female IQ ratios, calculated at puberty, predict substantial sex differences in educational and occupational achievements with fair accuracy, even if they obviously do not identify the cause(s)." (p55)

This area of research has been greatly stimulated by what is now called the *Dunning–Kruger effect*, which is considered a cognitive bias describing how people with low cognitive ability at a task (and probably in general) overestimate their own ability while people with high ability at a task underestimate their own ability. It has been argued that this bias results from an error about the self, whereas the miscalibration of the highly competent stems from an error about others (Kruger, 1999; Kruger & Dunning, 1999).

Further, studies on lay people's beliefs about their own and others' intelligence consistently shows that everybody believes they are "above average", which is called the Lake Woebegon Effect. As we shall see, females, of all ages and from all cultures, think they are less intelligent than men, specifically their spatial and mathematical intelligence, but they do think they are higher on emotional intelligence. Certainly, lay people believe these differences are actually greater than most of the scientific literature has shown.

The topic has received a great deal of attention and critique but kept alive a great interest in self-assessed intelligence and self-perceived intelligence (Gignac & Zajenkowski, 2020; Schlösser et al., 2013). Many reseachers have become interested in the causes, correlates and consequences of self-beliefs about abilities (Beyer at al., 1997; Cooper et al, 2018; Heck et al., 2018; Halpern, 2011; McCarty et al, 2005)

There also remain in those interested in empirically exploring sex differences seeking to establishing whether and, more importantly, why any differences exist (Colom, & García-López,,2002; Hines, 2011; 2015; Reilley et al., 2016; Reilly, & Neumann, 2013; Svedholm-Häkkinen et al., 2018)

Introduction

Over the past three decades, there has been a sustained and vicious attack on scientists from various backgrounds (mainly the biological and social sciences) for the work they do, and the theories they attempt to test, on predominantly race and sex differences. If the scientists take a contrarian view or one which opposes the current socio-political *zeitgeist*, they tend to get attacked more and more from a variety of quarters, including their own universities. In modern terminology, they get "cancelled." Thus, the President of Harvard University, who suggested that it was women's (relative) lack of mathematical ability that explained the sex differences in the Science Faculty at universities, was forced to resign. Many others have been cancelled, vilified and various awards and positions retracted. Many are well known to authors in this book.

Researchers in biology, psychology and sociology often have to be courageous, naïve or unwise to research or write about sex differences (Furnham, 2018). However, political agendas and the threat of litigation have reduced the quality and quantity of research in the area of gender and sex differences. There remains a great deal of popular debate about such things as the sex-linked differences in business success, the glass ceiling, cliff, escalator and the "sticky" floor, all of which imply career opportunities are quite different for men and women.

Helmut Nyborg has been at the forefront on research in this area for nearly half a century. He has pioneered a number of very specific areas of research, which are discussed by other authors in this volume.

Popular vs Scientific conclusions

A particular curiosity in the area of sex differences is the apparent contradiction between *popular* and *scientific* writers. There are many popular books that portray a simple evolutionary perspective that describe, and even rejoice in, sex differences in almost all human behaviour but particularly communication, relationships and work. Many of these "popular" books are just that, and sell in very large numbers proving the popularity of the socio-biological view on sex differences. They seem to chime with what people observe and provide an explanation for them. They argue which is in fact an essentialist argument for sex differences (Skewes et al, 2018).

These are contrasted with the measured and cautious academic books and papers that note how complex some of these seemingly simply questions are and how all the answers require numerous qualifiers (Hyde, 2014; Pezzuti et al., 2020).

All the academics in this area are super-sensitive to radical claims made on the basis of poor studies: bad research design, invalid measures and small, unrepresentative populations. They know how important and difficult it is to do good research that leads to clear, unequivocal answers to these most sensitive questions.

One "check-list" has been offered by Diane Halpern, whose standard book on this topic has been through four editions. She suggests a number of questions be asked which help correctly evaluate research claims. For example: *Who were the participants and how were they selected? What are their ages and background and representativeness in the population? Which measures are used and why? Why were they chosen and what known properties do they have? Are the results both statistically significant vs practically significant, and how big is the difference? Are the results consistent with other studies and any theory of sex differences? If not, why not? Could the results have been influenced by how and who and where the testing took place?*

Good scientific research is difficult, time-consuming and complex. We know that all sorts of factors regarding the people studied, the tests used and the testing condition can affect the results. In this area, more than others, it seems essential that research methods are very carefully examined. Fortunately, some researchers have found data sets, often initiated by government educational institutions, to assess intelligence. This has proved a great asset to many researchers in the area, like the editor of this volume.

Inevitably, there are two strongly competing, opposite forces: those who stress the *biology of difference* and those who stress the *sociology of similarity*. The former often suggest that these differences are immutable, though we know that all innate traits can be changed with experience of many sorts.

Whilst nearly everyone acknowledges that we are *biopsychosocial* beings, there are those who see us more as BIOpsychosocial as opposed to biopsychoSOCIAL. This all concerns explaining how and why observed differences occur. Slogans like "biology is destiny" have been banded about by both sides whose theories and research are often very different.

There are therefore those who want to argue that well-established, actual, biologically based sex differences in abilities, personality and values inevitably lead to both different occupational choices as well as adaptation to those jobs. Others want to stress social forces that, for a variety of ideological reasons, have pre- or pro-scribed gender differences at work that do not exist. They argue that any evident sex differences are learned and therefore can be unlearned. It could be argued that both are selective regarding the papers and theories they quote.

At the heart of the issue is the quality and quantity of differences, their cause and consequence. Though the focus has always been on differences, the trend has been to talk of similarities, which is what a great deal of the literature suggests. Indeed, it has been argued that the word difference is too easily confused with deficiency.

Interestingly, many researchers are interested in gender differences in *personality,* which appears to be much less controversial. There are questions about both the effect sizes of any differences encountered, and, more importantly, trying to explain them.

Furnham and Treglown (2021) noted the difference between *maximizers vs minimizers.* Maximizers are happy to find and explain the (many large) differences between the sexes while the minimizers want to emphasize how few real and meaningful differences there are (Furnham, 2017). Much depends on the data (measures, populations) and also the interpretation of Cohen's d: none, trivial, small, medium, large and very large. This means that if two groups' means do not differ by $d < 0.2$, the difference is trivial, even if it is statistically significant. However, these cut-off points have been disputed. Thus, there may be many differences, but they are essentially trivial, versus a few differences which are large and merit further research and explanation.

In their study of six personality tests, Furnham and Treglown (2021) concluded that "accepting that there are some real, biologically based, stable sex differences, as opposed to socialised gender differences, in personality traits, the question arises as to why they occur. Results such as these cannot inform the nature-nurture debate, with (most) evolutionary psychologists offering a cohesive (and for some convincing) argument as to why there are replicable, consistent, and cross-cultural findings. Minimizers who reject the 'biology as destiny' approach attempt to explain all these differences in terms of primary and secondary socialisation."

Overall, the research on sex differences in estimated and actual personality suggests three things. First, there are consistent cross-national and age differences in personality traits but most of the differences are not large. Second, people are "reasonably good" at predicting their own personality score being better at more familiar traits like Extraversion. Third, there are small but significant and predictable sex differences in personality (females tend to score higher on Agreeableness and Neuroticism) which people tend to be aware of. These findings are relevant to sex differences in intelligence, which is the focus of this chapter.

Five Different Positions on Sex Differences in Intelligence

Over the past century, there have been periods where both the "difference" and "non-difference" view was in favour. The growth of environmentalism and feminism from the 1960s onwards perpetuated the idea that any observable differences between the sexes were the result of socialization. The pendulum may have temporarily swung the other way towards a more biological and evolutionary perspective, which recognised and explained sex differences. However, it is very clear from academics working in the area that the pendulum has swung violently towards the "sociological" end, where the word gender not sex is used and the idea is that gender is flexible, fluid and a matter of choice rather than a binary biological fact.

It is possible to detect five positions when it comes to sex differences in intelligence:

1. There are no sex differences at all for one of two reasons. First, there are no good evolutionary or environmental theories or reasons to suppose there should be. Second, the early tests were so developed to show no difference. That is, certain tests were included and excluded so that neither sex was advantaged or disadvantaged. The argument is that any empirical evidence of cognitive ability variables is associated with measurement errors, or else differences are so small they are not worth investigating.

2. There are no mean or average differences between the sexes, but there are differences at the extremes. Thus, men tend to be over-represented at both the extremes of the Bell Curve. The most brilliant are men and so are the most challenged, meaning the average is the same but the distribution is wider for men. This explains the Nobel Prize phenomenon, as well as eminence in many other aspects of human endeavour which are dominated by males. It also "explains" the less discussed observation that often it is men who sink to the bottom of the social strata because of low ability.

3. There are numerous demonstrable and replicable sex differences in a whole range of abilities that make up overall intelligence. They may be small, but they are definitely there and possibly explicable in terms of evolutionary psychology. Thus, females score higher on tests of story recall and fine-motor co-ordination (precision tasks) while males score higher at mathematical reasoning and mental rotation tasks. Overall, however, when looking at "g" or general intelligence there is essentially no difference: facets might differ slightly but the mean indicates no difference.

4. Sex differences that do emerge are not real. They occur for three reasons. Females are taught humility and males hubris, and this social message leads them to approach tests (and other aspects of social life like job interviews) differently. That is, lower self-confidence and increased test anxiety lead to lower scores in test-taking rather than revealing real differences. Next, it is less of a social requirement (particularly in mate selection) for females to be intelligent so they invest less in education and skill development (i.e. crystalised intelligence). Third, females are less emotionally stable than males and thus anxiety reflects that test performance. That is, IQ results reflect established and agreed personality differences and not actual differences. Therefore, any differences that emerge do not reflect underlying reality: it is all about attitude toward and experience in test-taking.

5. There are real differences between the sexes with males having a 4–8 point advantage, which becomes noticeable after the age of 15. Before adolescence, females in fact have an advantage. The difference between the sexes is greatest for spatial intelligence. The difference is reflected in the brain size difference (corrected for body size) between men and women. Further, this "real" difference also "explains" male superiority in arts, business, education and science. Both the editor of this volume and Helmut appear to support this position. They tend to opt for five arguments: (1) similar differences are observed across time, culture and species (hence unlikely to be learned), (2) specific differences are predictable on basis of evolutionary specialisation (hunter/warrior vs gatherer/nurse/educator), (3) brain differences are established by prenatal sex hormones — later on, hormones affect ability profiles (e.g. spatial suppressed by oestrogen, HRT maintains verbal memory), (4) sex-typed activity appears before gender-role awareness — at age 2, girls have better communication; boys are better at construction tasks; this is not learned, (5) environmental effects

(e.g. expectations, experience, training) are minimal; they may exaggerate (or perhaps reduce) differences.

It should be pointed out that people who favour these positions often rely on, and quote, very different literature. Further, these views are very passionately held and appear to relate to a number of other philosophic positions.

Self-estimated intelligence

What do people think about their own intelligence? How do they estimate their own intelligence and that of their relatives? What determines their self-estimates? Are males more accurate than females? What are the consequences of self-belief in intelligence?

It seems the first paper published in this area was Hogan (1978), but the field grew rapidly (Bennett, 1996), particularly in the first decade of this century, leading to a meta-analysis of studies a decade ago (Freund & Karsten, 2012).

Furnham and Grover (2020) argued that self-estimated intelligence (SEI) is a topic of considerable current interest for various reasons (Gignac, 2018; Herreen & Zajac, 2018; Howard & Cogswell, 2018; Keefer, 2015). *First,* to help people with poor insight into their performance, notably people whose self-estimates are very different from their objective scores (Schlösser et al., 2013; Chan & Martinussen, 2015; Zell & Krizan, 2014). *Second,* to look at the individual differences and processes (like social desirability, hubris, and ability test experience) that lead to (in)accurate insight about abilities (Paulhus et al., 1998). *Third,* to assist in self-awareness as it relates to career choice (Ackerman & Wolman, 2007).

There is overwhelming evidence that demonstrates stable and universally consistent gender differences in SEI (Furnham & Shagabutdinova, 2012; von Stumm, Chamorro-Premuzic, & Furnham, 2009), also known as the 'hubris-humility effect' (HHE) (Beloff, 1992; Storek & Furnham, 2012; Storek & Furnham, 2013).

The following causes have been suggested to play a role: diverse child rearing and socialisation practices, social and gender-role normative stereotyping and self-stereotyping (Guimond, et al. 2006), self-enhancement and self-derogatory evaluation biases (Furnham, 2001; Kwan, John, Robin, & Kuang, 2008), lack of confidence and/ or overconfidence (Sleeper & Nigro, 1987), gender differences in self-concept and inaccurate self-estimates (Mirjalili, et al., 2011; Pallier, 2003), personality traits and male superiority in certain areas of cognition (Chamorro-Premuzic & Furnham, 2005).

It is possible that 'humility' is an erroneous 'label' for female ability to provide more accurate self-estimates of ability than males (Rammstedt & Rammsayer, 2002). It seems males are overconfident about their math performance, whilst females report low math confidence (Carr, Hettinger-Steiner, Kyser, & Biddlecomb, 2008).

A meta-analytical study (Szymanowicz, & Furnham, 2011) assessing the extent of gender differences in mathematical/logical, spatial, overall and verbal SEI demonstrated the biggest weighted mean effect sizes for mathematical/logical, $(d = .44)$, followed by spatial $(d = .43)$, overall $(d = .37)$ and verbal $(d = .07)$ intelligences, with males providing higher estimates in all but verbal intelligence. 'Domain-Masculine Intelligence Type' (DMIQ), which is a composite of mathematical/logical and spatial intelligences, has been shown as the best predictor of HHE and gender differences in SEI (Storek & Furnham, 2012; Storek & Furnham, 2013).

Early Work

The work from the last decade of the last century and the first of this was stimulated by Beloff (1992) who provoked a great deal of interest into sex differences in self-estimated intelligence. She found, among her Scottish undergraduates, a six-point difference with males estimating their score significantly higher than females. She noted "The young women see themselves as intellectually inferior compared to young men ... Women see equality with their mothers, men with their fathers and men superior to their mothers. Mothers therefore come out as inferior to fathers. The pattern has been consistent each year." (p.311). Beloff argued that the modesty training girls receive in socialization accounts for these data. This was the first assertion of what has become known as the hubris-humility effect.

The "feminist" position was clearly articulated by Beloff (1992) in her first study, where she suggested that the self-estimate differences are erroneous and simply due to attribution errors. Men deny negative feedback while women do not. "On the whole, women are more rational, men more rationalizing" (Beloff, 1992: 3 10). She believes men are more ambitious. "Modesty-training is given to girls. Modesty and humility are likely to be connected to the overestimates of women and for women" (Beloff, 1992: 3 10). She also notes that, as IQ is correlated with occupational grade and men tend to occupy certain occupations more than women (for political rather than ability reasons), females tend to believe (erroneously) that they are less intelligent than males.

In an early cross-cultural study, Furnham et al. (1999) found Slovakian females (as opposed to an equivalent Belgian and British student group) awarded themselves higher overall (g) and verbal scores. This shows a unique group of confident females, and the authors offered the following possible explanation. It may well be that under the pressure of socialist governments of Eastern Europe the role of females in society was somewhat different from that in capitalist Western Europe, where they took a more active role in the economy and were socialized differently in school. Slovakia had a consistent effort to improve the position of women in society; there was a mandatory percentage of women in the parliament; the state propagated the employment of women in non-traditional occupations; women were encouraged to obtain educational qualifications. Overall, in Slovakian society, education was held in high prestige. Another explanation might be that the Slovakian women had the most experience in taking intelligence tests and were therefore presumably more likely to be aware of the very small differences between the sexes (Furnham et al., 1999: 137).

Soon others attempted to replicate this effect. Furnham (2000) reported on eight studies, all but one of which showed significant sex differences in self-rated overall IQ, ranging from 3.9 to 8.6 points. Student groups tend to believe their IQ is about one-and-a-half standard deviations above the mean (Furnham, Clark & Bailey, 1999a) (around 120) whereas non-student British adults believe they are around a half standard deviation above the norm (Furnham, 2000).

Starting from Beloff (1992), a number of these studies looked at estimates of respondents' blood relations (Furnham, Fong & Martin, 1999). They showed that people believed there are clear *generational effects* in IQ. People tend to believe they are a little brighter than their mothers but certainly much brighter than their grandparents. Parents also tend to believe their children are brighter than they are. There does seem a trend that people believe there is a half standard deviation (6–8 points) difference in IQ between the generations. Thus, people believe their grandfathers brighter than their grandmothers, their fathers brighter than their mothers, their brothers brighter than their sisters, and their sons brighter than their daughters. Indeed, the findings of Flynn (1984, 1999) suggest this observation may be true. Interestingly for parents estimating their children the results were stronger for first-borns, compared to those born later indicating the possible working of the principle of primogeniture.

Furthermore, these results have been shown to be cross-culturally robust as the sex difference effect has been demonstrated in Asia (Japan, Hong Kong), Africa (Uganda, South Africa), Europe (Belgium, Britain, but not Slovakia) and America (Furnham, Hosoe & Tang, 2001).

Indeed, studies have been done cross-culturally from Austria (Stieger et al., 2010) to Spain (Perez et al., 2010), Switzerland (Proyer, 2011), and Wales (Workman, 2004). Recent studies continue to be done in many countries, including Pakistan (Shahzada et al., 2014),

Russia (Kornilova & Novikova, 2012), and Tanzania (Dixon et al., 2016). Gender and cultural differences in self-estimates of ability have also been examined (Ivcevic & Kaufman, 2013). One study compared sex differences in self-estimated intelligence across 12 countries (von Stumm et al., 2009). With no exceptions, all the above studies show a significant sex difference, with males giving higher estimates than females. However, there are more dramatic differences between countries, with both sexes from African countries giving higher self-estimates than those not from African countries.

Thus, there does seem to be a robust and cross-culturally valid finding that, when asked to rate their overall intelligence, there is a clear, consistent sex difference with males rating themselves and their male relations higher than females rate themselves and their female relations. It is also worth noting that it is very rare for people to rate their scores, or indeed those of relations as below average (< 100 IQ points).

Self-estimated Multiple intelligence

Gardner's (1983) multiple intelligence theory is highly disputed and challenged in academic circles but proved an interesting impetus to the self-estimated literature. There are now well over a dozen studies that have examined sex differences on Gardner's multiple intelligences (Neto, 2019; Neto et al., 2016, 2017).

This has led to a number of studies on self-estimated multiple intelligence (Kaufman, 2012; Storek & Furnham, 2012; 2013; 2014; 2016). The results of self-estimates of the seven multiple intelligences have been consistent and give an important clue into sex differences in overall performance. Most people rate their own interpersonal and intrapersonal intelligence as very high (about 1 SD above the mean). They also rate their musical and body kinetic intelligence as strictly average, around 100. This leaves the other types of intelligence, according to the Gardner model: verbal, mathematical and spatial intelligence. Sex differences are found only in mathematical and spatial intelligence, but particularly spatial intelligence, where females typically estimate six to ten points lower than males. There were no sex differences on the verbal score (Furnham, 2001).

Results from many studies show strongest on the mathematical–logical and spatial intelligences, followed by overall (g) and then verbal intelligences; with men significantly overestimating, and women significantly underestimating, their abilities relative to each other. This consistent gender difference has been referred to as the Hubris-Humility Effect (HHE; Storek & Furnham, 2012).

Some studies have asked participants to estimate their overall (g) score first, followed by their scores on the seven specific multiple intelligences. This has made it possible to regress simultaneously the seven multiple intelligence scores on to the overall intelligence estimate. Studies show that what people believe really contributes to a high overall "g" IQ score is mathematical (logical), then spatial, then verbal intelligence. This has allowed for the testing of the hypothesis that lay conceptions of intelligence are male normative in the sense that those abilities that men tend to be better at are those that most people consider to be the essence of intelligence. Thus, lay people conflate mathematical/spatial and overall intelligence, so explaining the consistent sex differences in overall score but relatively few when measuring multiple intelligence. It may be that the often-observed and debated spatial difference in IQ between the sexes accounts for the overall IQ difference score (Lynn & Kanazawa, 2011).

Correlations between Self-estimated and Test-measured IQ

Are self-estimates accurate? In other words, is the correlation between (valid) IQ test and self-estimates high? Some psychologists have even suggested that if the scores are highly correlated, self-estimates may serve as useful measures at a fraction of time, money and administrative costs.

Various studies have found that the correlations are around $r = .30$ and that therefore self-reports will not serve as proxy measures at all well (Paulhus, Lysy and Yık, 1998). One study, however, inspected the problem of outliers in the analysis and concluded that if removed, most raters exhibit 90% to 100% reliability. Reilly and Mulhern (1995) note that IQ-estimates research should not be based on the "assumption that gender differences at group level represent a generalized tendency on the part of either sex to either overconfidence or lack of confidence with regard to their own intelligence" (Reilly & Mulhern, 1995, p.189).

Other studies have shown similar results. For instance, Furnham (2009) tested 150 young bankers who estimated their IQ (Academic/Cognitive Intelligence) and EQ (Emotional Intelligence) before taking an IQ test. Pearson correlations were $r = .40$ and $.41$ between IQ test (Wonderlic Personnel Test) scores and IQ estimates and EQ estimates, respectively. He found females' mean self-estimated IQ was significantly lower than men's.

Furnham and Robinson (2022) reported in a similar analysis in five different on-line studies (total N=2280) and using different intelligence tests. Overall, they found correlations between intelligent test scores and estimates to be around r=.20

Some researchers have tried to understand (and improve) the size of the correlation between self-estimates and test scores by using more tests on bigger populations, yet the size of the correlations remains the same, around the $r = .30$ mark. Results do show a tendency for males to overestimate and females to underestimate their score but this, in part, is related to the actual IQ test used. There may well be important motivational factors at play in the self-estimation of intelligence, which may lead to serious distortions in the scores. Thus, a close examination of the conditions and instructions under which participants make self- estimations of intelligence may give us a clue as to how they make their self-estimate. If social norms and conventions in part dictate how people respond, then under particular circumstances (anonymously) it may be that the effects of these perceived requirements are reduced.

A summary of this literature

First, males of all ages and backgrounds tend to estimate their (overall) general intelligence about 5 to 15 IQ points higher than do females. Those estimates are nearly always above average and usually around one standard deviation above the norm.

Second, when judging "multiple intelligences", males estimate their spatial and mathematical (numerical) intelligence higher, but emotional intelligence lower, than do females. On some multiple intelligences (verbal, musical, body-kinaesthetic), there is little or no sex difference.

Third, people believe these sex difference occur across generations: people believe their grandfather was/is more intelligent than their grandmother, their father more than their mother, their brothers more than their sisters, and their sons more than their daughters. That is, throughout the generations, in one's family, males are judged more intelligent than females.

Fourth, sex differences are consistent cross-culturally. While Africans tend to give higher estimates, and Asians lower estimates, there remains a sex difference across all cultures. Differences seem to lie in cultural definitions of intelligence as well as norms associated with humility and hubris.

Fifth, the correlation between self-estimated and test-generated IQ is positive and low in the range of $r = .2$ to $r = .5$, suggesting that you cannot use test scores as a proxy for actual scores. This relationship is affected by an individual's experience of IQ, which itself appears to be related to intelligence.

Sixth, with regard to outliers, those who score high on IQ but give low self-estimates tend nearly always to be female, while those with the opposite pattern (high estimates, low scores) tend to be male.

Thus, there appear to be super-humble females and super-hubristic males.

Seventh, most people say they do not think there are sex differences in intelligence, but those who have taken tests and received feedback seem to get better scores.

Eighth, these differences are observable in early adolescence and continue into old age, though it is unclear whether there are any noticeable generational effects

Conclusion

The sex/gender similarity vs difference debate has important consequences. For some people, there is a monstrous and totally unacceptable discrimination against women in (every) society as a function of false beliefs and assumptions. Others argue that various sex differences are well established and explicable in terms of evolutionary processes. The issue at stake would then be one of social policy. An important question is, should educational institutions and businesses take this into consideration? If so, how and to what extent? Yet again, a fierce debate exists between those who want to attempt "correcting" or downplaying the differences and those who want to exploit them as much as possible.

In short, sex difference research on group differences has become extremely politicized and scared away numerous researchers from the field.

The results on self-estimated intelligence also call for an explanation. Some would argue that overall the sex differences that exist are a function of reality: that is, that so-called female humility is a reflection of reality as there are actual sex differences that both males and females know about. Others argue that they are the result of socialisation, which takes us back to the beginning of this chapter. There are also consequences to "whether you believe you can, and whether you believe you can't — you are right" in the sense that these beliefs are self-fulfilling (Furnham, 2018). Certainly, it would appear for all concerned that people had an accurate appraisal of all their abilities, including cognitive ability.

Helmut Nyborg and others in this volume have literally spent a lifetime investigating a number of these problems. It is, as the philosophers say, an interesting time to be alive for those interested in sex differences.

References

Ackerman, P., & Wolman, S. (2007). Determinants and validity of self-estimates of ability and self-concept measures. *Journal of Experimental Psychology: Applied*, *13*(2), 57-78.

Beloff, H. (1992). Mother, father and me: Our IQ. *The Psychologist*, *5*, 309-311.

Bennett, M. (1996). Men's and women's self-estimates of intelligence. *Journal of Social Psychology*, *136*(3), 411-412.

Beyer, S., & Bowden, E. M. (1997). Gender differences in self-perceptions: Convergent evidence from three measures of accuracy and bias. *Personality and Social Psychology Bulletin*, *23*(2), 157-172.

Carr, M., Hettinger-Steiner, H., Kyser, B., & Biddlecomb, B. (2008). A comparison of predictors of early emerging gender differences in mathematics competency. *Learning and Individual Differences*, *18*, 61-75.

Chamorro-Premuzic, T., & Furnham, A. (2005). *Personality and Intellectual Competence*. New Jersey: Laurence Erlbaum Associates.

Chamorro-Premuzic, T., Moutafi, J., & Furnham, A. (2005). The relationship between personality traits, subjectively-assessed and fluid intelligence. *Personality and Individual Differences*, *38*, 1517-1528.

Chamorro-Premuzic, T., Ahmetoglu, G., & Furnham, A. (2008) Little more than personality: Dispositional determinants of test anxiety (the Big Five, core self-evaluations, and self-assessed intelligence). *Learning and Individual Differences*, *18*(2), 258-263.

Chan, T., & Martinussen, R. (2015). Positive illusions? The accuracy of academic self-appraisals in adolescents with ADHD. *Journal of Pediatric Psychology*, *41*(7), 799-809.

Cooper, K., Krieg, A., & Brownell, S. (2018). Who perceives they are smarter? *Advances in Physiology Education*, *42*(2), 200-208.

Colom, R., & García-López, O. (2002). Sex differences in fluid intelligence among high school graduates. *Personality and Individual Differences*, *32*(3), 445-451.

Dixon, P., Humble, S., & Chan, D. (2016). How children living in poor areas of Dar Es Salaam, Tanzania, perceive their own multiple intelligence. *Oxford Review of Education, 42*(2), 230-248.

Flynn, J. R. The mean IQ of Americans: Massive gains 1932–1978. *Psychological Bulletin.* 1984A;95(1):29–51.

Flynn, J. R. *Are We Getting Smarter? Rising IQ in the Twenty-First Century.* Cambridge: Cambridge University Press, 2012

Freund, P. A., & Kasten, N. (2012). How smart do you think you are? A meta-analysis on the validity of self-estimates of cognitive ability. *Psychological Bulletin, 138*(2), 296-321.

Frome, P. M., & Eccles, J. S. (1998). Parents' influence on children's achievement-related perceptions. *Journal of Personality and Social Psychology, 74*(2), 435-452. doi:10.1037/0022-3514.74.2.435

Furnham, A. (2000). Parents' estimates of their own and their children's multiple intelligences. *British Journal of Developmental Psychology, 18*(4), 583-594.

Furnham, A. (2001). Self-estimates of intelligence: culture and gender difference in self and other estimates of both general (g) and multiple intelligences. *Personality and Individual Differences, 31*(8), 1381-1405.

Furnham, A. (2009). Sex, IQ, and Emotional Intelligence. *Psychological Reports.* 105(3):1092-1094.

Furnham, A. (2017). Sex differences in self-estimated intelligence, competiveness and risk-taking. *Mankind Quarterly, 58*(1), 109-111.

Furnham, A. (2017), "Whether you think you can, or you think you can't — you're right." Differences and consequences of beliefs about your ability. In Robert Sternberg, Susan Fiske, and Don Foss (2017) *Scientists Making a Difference: The Greatest Living Behavioral and Brain Scientists Talk about Their Most Important Contributions.* Cambridge: Cambridge University Press.

Furnham, A. (2018). Personality and Occupational Success. In V. Zeigler-Hill & T. K. Shackelford (eds.), *The SAGE Handbook of Personality and Individual Difference* (pp. 537-551). New York: Sage.

Furnham, A., Clark, K., & Bailey, K. (1999). Sex differences in estimates of multiple intelligences. *European Journal of Personality, 13*(4), 247-259.

Furnham, A., Fong, G., & Martin, N. (1999). Sex and cross-cultural differences in the estimated multi-faced intelligence quotient score for self, parents and siblings. *Personality and Individual Differences, 26*, 1025-1034.

Furnham, A., Rakow, T., Sarmany-Schuller, I., & De Fruyt, F. (1999). European differences in self-perceived multiple intelligences. *European Psychologist, 4*, 131-138.

Furnham., A., & Robinson, C. (2022). Sex Difference in estimated intelligence, emotional intelligence and IQ scores. *Journal of Genetic Psychology.*

Furnham, A., & Gasson, L. (1998). Sex difference in parental estimates of their children's intelligence. *Sex Roles, 38*(1-2), 151-162.

Furnham, A., & Grover, S. (2020). Correlates of self-estimated intelligence. *Journal of Intelligence, 8*, 6.

Furnham, A., Hosoe, T., & Tang, T. (2001). Male hubris and female humility? A cross-cultural study of ratings of self, parental, and sibling multiple intelligence in America, Britain, and Japan. *Intelligence, 30*(1), 101-115.

Furnham, A., & Rawles, R. (1995). Sex differences in the estimation of intelligence. *Journal of Social Behavior & Personality, 10*(3), 741-748.

Furnham, A., & Shagabutdinova, K. (2012). Sex differences in estimating multiple intelligences in self and others: A replication in Russia. *International Journal of Psychology, 47*, 1-12.

Furnham, A., & Treglown, L. (2021). Sex Differences in Personality scores on Six Scales: Many significant, but mostly small, differences. *Current Psychology*, 1-11.

Furnham, A., Reeves, E., & Budhani, S. (2002). Parents think their sons are brighter than their daughters: Sex differences in parental self-estimations and estimations of their children's multiple intelligences. *Journal of Genetic Psychology, 163*(1), 24-39.

Furnham, A., Shahidi, S., & Baluch, B. (2002). Sex and Culture Differences in Perceptions of Estimated Multiple Intelligence for Self and Family. *Journal of Cross-Cultural Psychology, 33*(3), 270-285.

Gardner, H. (1983). *Frames of Mind: The Theory of Multiple Intelligences.* London, UK: Fontana Press.

Gardner, H. (1999). *Intelligence Reframed: Multiple Intelligences for the 21st Century.* New York: Basic Books. Gentile, B.,

Greven, C. U., Harlaar, N., Kovas, Y., Chamorro-Premuzic, T., & Plomin, R. (2009). More than just IQ. *Psychological Science, 20*(6), 753-762.

Gignac, E. (2018). Socially desirable responding suppresses the association between self-assessed intelligence and task based intelligence. *Intelligence, 69*, 50-58.

Gignac, G. E., & Zajenkowski, M. (2020). The Dunning-Kruger effect is (mostly) a statistical artefact: Valid approaches to testing the hypothesis with individual differences data. *Intelligence, 80*, 101449.

Guimond, S., Martinot, D., Chatard, A., Crisp, R. J., & Redersdorff, S (2006). Social comparison, self-stereotyping, and gender differences in self-construals. *Journal of Personality and Social Psychology, 90,* 221-242.

Halpern, D. F. (2011). *Sex Differences in Cognitive Abilities* (4th ed.). Mahwah, NJ: Erlbaum.

Herreen, D., & Zajac, T. (2018). The reliability and validity of a self-report measure of cognitive abilities in older adults. *Journal of Intelligence, 6*(1), 1-15

Heck, P., Simons, D., & Chabris, C. (2018). 65% of Americans believe they are above average in intelligence. *Plos One, 13*(7).

Hines, M. (2011). Gender development and the human brain. *Annual Review of Neuroscience, 34,* 69-88.

Hines, M. (2015). Early androgen exposure and human gender development. *Biology of Sex Differences, 6*(1), 1-10.

Hogan, H. W. (1978). IQ self-estimates of males and females. *The Journal of Social Psychology, 106*(1), 137-138.

Hyde, J. S. (2014). Gender similarities and differences. *Annual Review in Psychology,* 65:373–98.

Howard, M., & Cogswell, J. (2018). The "other" relationships of self-assessed intelligence. *Journal of Research in Personality, 77,* 31-46.

Ivcevic, Z., & Kaufman, J. C. (2013). The can and cannot do attitude: How self-estimates of ability vary across ethnic and socioeconomic groups. *Learning and Individual Differences, 27,* 144–149.

Kwan, V. S., John, O., Robin, R., & Kuang, L. (2008). Conceptualizing and assessing self-enhancement bias: A componential approach. *Journal of Personality and Social Psychology, 94,* 1062-1077.

Kaufman, J. (2012). Self-estimates of general, crystallised, and fluid intelligences in an ethnically diverse population. *Learning and Individual Differences, 22,* 118–122.

Keefer, K. (2015). Self-Report assessments of emotional competencies. *Journal of Psychoeducational Assessment, 33*(1), 3-23.

Kornilova, T., & Novikova, M (2012). Self-Assessed Intelligence, Personality and Psychometric Intelligence. *Psychology in Russia, 2,* 34-47.

Kruger, J. (1999). Lake Wobegon be gone! The "below-average effect" and the egocentric nature of comparative ability judgments. *Journal of Personality and Social Psychology, 77*(2), 221-232.

Kruger, J., & Dunning, D. (1999). Unskilled and unaware of it: How difficulties in recognizing one's own incompetence lead to inflated self-assessments. *Journal of Personality and Social Psychology, 77*(6), 1121-1134.

Lynn, R. & Kanazawa, S. (2011) A longitudinal study of sex differences in intelligence at ages 7, 11, and 16 years. *Personality and Individual Differences, 51,* 321-324.

McCarthy, M.M., & Konkle, A.T. (2005).When is a sex difference not a sex difference? *Frontiers in Neuroendocrinology.* 26(2):85–102.

Mirjalili, R. S., Farahani, H. A., & Akbari, Z. (2011). Self-esteem as moderator of the relationship between self-estimated general intelligence and psychometric intelligence. *Procedia-Social and Behavioral Sciences, 30,* 649-653.

Neto, F. (2019). Sex differences in estimates of lay views about reversal motivational intelligences for self and others. *Annals of Psychology, 35*(1), 68-74.

Neto, F., Mullet, E., & Furnham, A. (2016). Self-estimated correlates of lay views about reversal multiple intelligences. *Imagination, Cognition and Personality, 35*(4), 380-396.

Neto, F., Pinto, M. C., Mullet, E., & Furnham, A. (2017). Estimates of reversal multiple intelligences for self and others: Sex and cross-cultural comparisons. *International Journal of Psychology, 52*(6), 436-444.

Nyborg, H. (2005). Sex-related differences in general intelligence g, brain size, and social status. *Personality and Individual Differences, 39,* 497-509

Nyborg, H. (2015). Sex differences across different racial ability levels: Theories of origin and societal consequences. *Intelligence, 52,* 44-62

Pallier, G. (2003). Gender differences in the self-assessment of accuracy on cognitive tasks. *Sex Roles, 48,* 265-276.

Paulhus, D. L., Lysy, D. C., & Yik, M. S. M. (1998). Self-report measures of intelligence: Are they useful as proxy IQ tests? *Journal of Personality, 66*(4), 525-554.

Perez, L. F., Gonzales, C., & Beltran. J. A. (2010). Parental estimates of their own and their relatives' intelligence: A Spanish replication. *Learning and Individual Differences, 20,* 669–676.

Pezzuti, L., Tommasi, M., Saggino, A., Dawe, J., & Lauriola, M. (2020). Gender differences and measurement bias in the assessment of adult intelligence: Evidence from the Italian WAIS-IV and WAIS-R standardizations. *Intelligence, 79,* 101436.

Proyer, R. T. (2011). Being playful and smart? The relations of adult playfulness with psychometric and self-estimated intelligence and academic performance. *Learning and Individual Differences, 21,* 463-467.

Rammstedt, B., & Rammsayer, T. H. (2002). Gender differences in self-estimated intelligence and their relation to gender role orientation. *European Journal of Personality, 16*(5), 369-382.

Reilly, J. & Mulhern, G. (1995). Gender difference in self-estimated IQ: The need for care in interpreting group data. *Personality and Individual Differences, 18*, 189-192.

Reilly, D., & Neumann, D. L. (2013). Gender-role differences in spatial ability: A meta-analytic review. *Sex Roles, 68*(9), 521-535.

Reilly, D., Neumann, D. L., & Andrews, G. (2016). Sex and sex-role differences in specific cognitive abilities. *Intelligence, 54*, 147-158.

Schlösser, T., Dunning D., Johnson, K. L., & Kruger, J. (2013). How unaware are the unskilled? Empirical tests of the "signal extraction" counterexplanation for the Dunning–Kruger effect in self-evaluation of performance. *Journal of Economic Psychology, 39*, 85–100.

Skewes. L., Fine, C., & Haslam, N. (2018). Beyond Mars and Venus: The role of gender essentialism in support for gender inequality and backlash. *PLoS ONE 13*(7): e0200921.

Sleeper, L. A., & Nigro, G. N. (1987). It's not who you are but who you're with: Self-confidence in achievement settings. *Sex Roles, 16*, 57-69.

Shahzada, G., Khan, U., Noor, A., & Rahman, S. (2014). Self-estimated multiple intelligences of urban and rural students. *Journal of Research and Reflections in Education, 8*(2), 116-124.

Stieger, S., Kastner, C., Voracek, M., von Stumm, S., Chamorro-Premuzic, T., & Furnham, A. (2010). Independent effects of personality and sex on self-estimated intelligence: Evidence from Austria. *Psychological Reports, 107*, 553–63.

Storek, J., & Furnham, A. (2012). Gender and gender role differences in domain-masculine intelligence and beliefs about intelligence: A study with Mensa UK members. *Personality and Individual Differences, 53*(7), 890-895.

Storek, J., & Furnham, A. (2013). Gender, g, gender identity concepts, and self-constructs as predictors of the self-estimated IQ. *Journal of Genetic Psychology, 174*(6), 664-676.

Storek, J., & Furnham, A. (2014). Gender and task confidence as predictors of the Domain-Masculine Intelligence Type (DMIQ). *Personality and Individual Differences, 69*, 43-49.

Storek, J., & Furnham, A. (2016). The role of gender, task success probability estimation and score as predictors of the Domain-Masculine Intelligence type (DMIQ). *Learning and Individual Differences, 50*, 23-29.

Svedholm-Häkkinen, A. M., Ojala, S. J., & Lindeman, M. (2018). Male brain type women and female brain type men: Gender atypical cognitive profiles and their correlates. *Personality and Individual Differences, 122*, 7-12.

Szymanowicz, A., & Furnham, A. (2011). Gender differences in self-estimates of general, mathematical, spatial and verbal intelligence: Four meta analyses. *Learning and Individual Differences, 21*(5), 493-504.

Yuen, M., & Furnham, A. (2006). Sex differences in self-estimation of multiple intelligences among Hong Kong Chinese adolescents. *High Ability Studies, 16*(2), 187-199. doi:10.1080/13598130600618009.

Zhang, Y., & Gong, Y. (2001). Self-estimated intelligence and its related factors. *Chinese Journal of Clinical Psychology, 9*, 193-195.

von Stumm, S. (2014). Intelligence, gender, and assessment method affect the accuracy of self-estimated intelligence. *British Journal of Psychology, 105*(2), 243-253.

von Stumm, S., Chamorro-Premuzic, T., & Furnham, A. (2009). Decomposing self-estimates of intelligence: Structure and sex differences across 12 nations. *British Journal of Psychology, 100*(2), 429-442.

Workman, L. (2004). Self-perception of intelligence in male and female undergraduates in old and new Welsh Universities. *Psychology, Learning and Teaching, 4*(1), 22-26.

Zell, E., & Krizan, Z. (2014) Do people have insight into their abilities? *Perspectives in Psychological Science, 9*(2), 111-125.

CHAPTER 6

GENDER, ETHNICITY, RACE, AND PHYSICAL FIGHTING: THE ROLE OF PRENATAL TESTOSTERONE

ANTHONY W. HOSKIN*

IDAHO STATE UNIVERSITY

*Department of Sociology, Social Work, and Criminology, Idaho State University, S. 8th Avenue, Stop 8114, Pocatello, ID 83209, USA. Email address: hoskanth@isu.edu

Abstract

Purpose: Mainstream criminology explains gender, ethnic, and racial differences in physical fighting in terms of social conditions experienced during adolescence and young adulthood. This study investigates the possibility that differences in prenatal testosterone exposure might help explain differential rates of violence.

Methods: Self-reported data and a measure of the 2D:4D digit ratio — a proxy of prenatal testosterone exposure — were collected on 294 college students — a mix of African Americans, Hispanics, and non-Hispanic whites. A bootstrapping approach to mediation analysis was conducted to assess the degree to which prenatal testosterone explains the relationships between gender, ethnicity, and race on the one hand and two types of physical fighting — individual and group — on the other.

Results: For both types of fighting, 2D:4D partially mediated the effect of gender. For ethnicity, individual fighting did not differ between Hispanics and whites, but digit ratio fully mediated the effect of ethnicity on group fighting. Digit ratio mediated fully the relationship between race and individual fighting, and it did so partially for group fighting.

Conclusions: This study provides some tentative support for the hypothesis that prenatal testosterone mediates, in part, the associations between demographics and physical fighting. Study limitations, explanations, and suggestions for future research are also discussed.

Keywords: Gender, Ethnicity, Race, Prenatal Testosterone, Violence, Crime, Delinquency

Gender, Ethnicity, Race, and Physical Fighting: The Role of Prenatal Testosterone

Introduction

Mainstream criminology has carefully documented the large sex difference in violent offending (Moffitt et al., 2001) but explanations for the gap are not fully understood. Criminologists also explain ethnic and racial differences in physical fighting in terms of social conditions experienced by adolescents and young adults. A classic example is Wolfgang and Ferracuti's subcultural theory of violence (1967). They posited that poor minorities are often embedded in a value system that embraces aggression. In another formulation that emphasizes culture, Elijah Anderson (2000) documented the need for African American youths, especially males, to maintain a fearless reputation in order to navigate the dangers posed by living in a high-crime, inner-city neighborhood. According to general strain theory, higher rates of violence by minority youths are caused by circumstances that generate intense levels and unique types of aversive emotions which are managed through physical aggression (Kaufman, Rebellon, Thaxton, & Agnew, 2008). In a similar vein, structural theories point to race-based economic inequality as an important determinant of racial differences in violent crime (Blau & Blau, 1982). Other macro-level theories have emphasized community disadvantage (Sampson & Wilson, 1995).

What these perspectives have in common is the claim that the critical source of interpersonal violence lies in social conditions experienced during adolescence, and gender and ethnic disparities emerge as juveniles encounter social barriers and attitudes conducive to crime. While there is empirical evidence for these perspectives, the current study investigates the possibility that gender and ethnic differences in violence emerge much earlier than in adolescence, as do the causes of such violence. This study specifically tests the hypothesis that gender and ethnic differences in fetal testosterone (FT) exist and that these differences help explain predispositions toward fighting.

Prenatal Androgens, Gender, Ethnicity, and Crime

There has been accumulating evidence in recent years that males and females and various ethnic groups differ in their average *in utero* exposure to androgens. Using the 2D:4D digit ratio as a proxy measure of FT, many studies have documented the sex difference in prenatal testosterone (Hönekopp & Watson, 2010). Manning and colleagues (2004) found that the 2D:4D ratio was lower in males than in females, and that Oriental Han subjects had the highest mean 2D:4D, followed by Caucasian Berbers and Uygurs, with the lowest mean ratios found among Afro-Caribbean Jamaicans. A study of an American sample reported higher mean 2D:4D for whites and lower means for Hispanics and Asians (Lippa, 2003). A meta-analysis conducted by a Chinese research team reported highest-to-lowest FT exposure levels as follows:

blacks, Han Chinese, Hispanics, and whites (Xu & Zheng, 2014). A similar pattern was observed in a BBC Internet survey of more than 250,000 participants (Manning, Churchill, & Peters, 2007).

Gender and ethnic difference in digit ratios are observed in children as well as adults, consistent with the view that 2D:4D reflects prenatal and early child environments, not adolescence. Wong and Hines (2016) found a moderate sex difference among toddlers. According to a study by Manning et al. (2004), Jamaican children had lower mean finger ratios (i.e., had higher FT levels) than Berber, Uygur, or Han Chinese children.

Recent research suggests a link between prenatal androgens and crime. Two studies by the same authors found significant associations between the 2D:4D digit ratio and involvement in interpersonal violence, property crime, and victimless crime (Ellis & Hoskin, 2013; Hoskin & Ellis, 2015). According to a study of German men, those with lower finger ratios had more traffic violations (Schwerdtfeger & Heer, 2008). A UK study of men found that those with at least one criminal conviction had a lower mean 2D:4D ratio than those with no conviction (Hanoch, Gummerum, & Rolison, 2012). In a sample of intimate partner violence (IPV) perpetrators, more masculine digit ratios were associated with more anger expression and IPV recidivism (Romero-Martínez, Lila & Moya-Albiol, 2017).

At least two studies have examined the link between FT and aggression among children. In a study of Chinese elementary school children, digit ratio predicted aggression and attention problems among boys but not girls (Liu, Portnoy, & Raine, 2012). Russian data revealed a significant negative correlation between 2D:4D and self-ratings on physical aggression in male children as well as adolescents (Butovskaya, Veselovskaya, & Prudnikova, 2010). A significant association between masculinized digit ratios and hostility and physical aggression among boys (but not girls) was reported for four different ethnic groups (Butovskaya, Burkova, Karelin, & Filatova, 2019).

Research on children has revealed that racial divergence in aggression emerges before adolescence. A study of nine countries revealed that physical aggression among 7–10 year-olds went from high to low as follows: Kenya, Jordan, Italy, Philippines, the United States, Colombia, Sweden, Thailand, and China (Lansford et al., 2012). According to Hetherington (1966), black boys are more likely than white boys to engage in competitive activities that involve force. Among children ages 5 to 16, blacks are, on average, more antisocial than whites (Conners, 1970). In a study of elementary school children, African-Americans had significantly higher peer-nominated aggression scores than white and Latino children (Guerra, Huesmann, Tolan, Van Acker, & Eron, 1995). A sample of elementary school children revealed the highest proactive rates of aggression among blacks, medium levels among Hispanics, and low average rates among whites and Asians (Baker, Raine, Liu, & Jacobson, 2008). Among children ages 9 to 12, those from minority groups were more likely to exhibit proactive aggression (Fite et al., 2010).

No studies conducted thus far have focused specifically on physical fighting, but there are good reasons for such focus, especially in the context of the study of ethnicity and crime. Research has revealed that while blacks in the United States do not necessarily engage in higher rates of theft or consensual crime than whites, higher rates of physical fighting seem well-established (Felson & Kraeger, 2015). According to Jencks (1991), higher rates of violence among blacks have been observed since at least the 1950s. This long-observed pattern motivated the race-difference theories described above. More recent research has reported a similar pattern. According to Elliot and Ageton (1980), blacks commit more self-reported acts of violence than whites. Analyzing a national sample of adolescents, McNulty and Bellair (2003a) found higher rates of serious violence among blacks, Latinos, and Native Americans. The authors report similar findings based on data from another national survey of adolescents (McNulty and Bellair 2003b). A study of Chicago youths revealed that compared to whites, blacks had higher odds of committing violence, but Latinos had a lower risk (Sampson, Morenoff, & Raudenbush, 2005). Although the evidence is weaker, international data also suggests racial differences in violent behavior (Neapolitan, 1998).

While researchers have not investigated the possibility that differential prenatal testosterone exposure might help explain racial differences in violent offending among adults, there is evidence to suggest that racial groups differ in levels of circulating testosterone, and that this might mediate racial differences in antisocial behavior. Booth and Osgood (1993) reported greater adult deviance among non-whites and that deviance was predicted by testosterone. Both Ellis and Nyborg (1992) and Booth and Osgood (1993) found significant racial differences in levels of testosterone. Compared to whites, native/metis subjects committed more violent offenses and had significantly higher serum testosterone levels (Brooks and Reddon,1996). Rada et al. (1979) failed to find racial differences in plasma testosterone among a sample of convicted rapists and child molesters, but the study lacked statistical power. Related to antisocial behavior, Nyborg (2004) found levels of psychoticism to be higher among black males compared to white males, and psychoticism was positively associated with plasma testosterone.

Using Digit Ratio as a Marker of Prenatal Testosterone

The prenatal testosterone studies cited above relied on proxy measures. Fetal testosterone (FT) levels are not easy to determine. The concentration of testosterone in the amniotic fluid can be measured from an amniocentesis, but the procedure carries with it certain risks and is generally done only if there is medical justification (van de Beek, Thijssen, Cohen-Kettenis, Goozen, & Buitelaar, 2004). Levels can also be estimated at birth from umbilical cord blood, but this is months after the critical period when high concentrations of testosterone masculinize the fetus.

Fortunately, a simple non-invasive method of measurement, the 2D:4D digit ratio, has been developed and used in recent years (Manning, 2008). It has been established that a sex difference in the ratio of the length of the index finger (numbered the 2nd digit) and the ringer finger (numbered the 4th digit) emerges during gestation, becomes nearly fixed early in childhood, and is relatively unaffected by puberty (McIntyre, 2006). Research on animals and humans suggests that this ratio reflects approximately the prenatal concentration of testosterone (Manning, 2008) or perhaps the balance of testosterone and estrogen (Lutchmaya, Baron-Cohen, Raggatt, Knickmeyer, & Manning, 2004).

The most convincing animal research has manipulated fetal hormone levels in order to observe the effects on digit ratio. In a study of rats, elevating testosterone during pregnancy lowered (i.e., masculinized) the 2D:4D ratio of the right paw of their offspring when measured in adulthood (Talarovičová, Kršková, & Blažeková, 2009). Zheng and Cohn (2011) demonstrated in mice that the fourth digit is particularly dense in androgen and estrogen receptors. When androgen receptors were deleted, mice developed high (i.e., feminine) 2D:4D digit ratios. Deleting estrogen receptors produced mice with low ratios.

The starting point for the finger ratio in humans is the sex difference. The lower male average has been well-documented (Manning, 2008) and the effect size suggests a moderate difference (Berenbaum, Bryk, Nowak, Quigley, & Moffat, 2009). There are factors other than sex hormones (e.g., the direct effect of sex chromosome genes) that could potentially cause the 2D:4D sex disparity, but research has provided little support for these alternatives (Breedlove, 2010). Relative finger length emerges in the first trimester of gestation (Garn, Burdi, Babler, & Stinson, 1975), and the difference between males and females emerges by the second trimester (Galis, Ten Broek, van Dongen, & Wijnaendts, 2010; Malas, Dogan, Hilal Evcil, & Desdicioglu, 2006). Coincident with sex hormone levels, digit ratio lies relatively dormant during childhood, but unlike sex hormones, it remains unchanged during adolescence (Manning et al., 1998) suggesting that the finger ratio is not a reflection of the actions of pubertal sex hormones (Trivers, Manning, & Jacobson, 2006).

Research on both general and clinical populations provides evidence for the fetal testosterone/2D:4D ratio connection. Female dizygotic twins growing next to males average lower finger ratios than those growing next to females, the assumption being that the twin is exposed to her brother's testosterone (van Anders, Vernon, & Wilbur, 2006; Voracek & Dressler, 2007b). A study based on hormone levels taken from amniocentesis showed that a high testosterone-to-estradiol ratio strongly predicts a low finger ratio in toddlers (Lutchmaya et al., 2004). In a similar study, testosterone concentrations sampled during mid-gestation revealed that amniotic testosterone levels were negatively related to the digit ratio of both hands, but this was true for females only (Ventura, Gomes, Pita, Neto, & Taylor, 2013).

Males with Klinefelter's syndrome (KS) have an extra X chromosome which reduces FT production. Men with KS have a much higher 2D:4D ratio than controls (Manning, Kilduff, & Trivers, 2013). Children with autism — a developmental disorder much more common in males and thought to be influenced by elevated levels of FT — have, on average, much more masculine finger ratios than controls (Manning et al., 2001). In addition, women with androgen insensitivity syndrome (AIS) carry a mutation that impairs the function of the androgen receptor gene. The mean digit ratio for these women is particularly high (i.e., feminine) (Berenbaum et al., 2009). In a meta-analysis of 12 studies, subjects with congenital adrenal hyperplasia (CAH), a suite of conditions characterized by elevated adrenal androgen, were found to have masculinized digit ratios (Richards et al., 2020).

Research shows a statistically significant association between FT and the 2D:4D digit ratio, but to serve as a good proxy, the correlation should be a strong one. According to the study by Lutchmaya et al.

(2004) among toddlers whose mothers had been given an amniocentesis, the correlation between the ratio of testosterone to estradiol taken from amniotic fluid and the right hand 2D:4D ratio at age two was -.52. This suggests the digit ratio serves as an approximate measure of the prenatal balance of testosterone and estradiol.

One important aspect of the digit ratio is that it seems to be more sexually dimorphic on the right hand than on the left hand in humans and other species (Johannes Hönekopp & Watson, 2010). Not surprisingly, studies that have compared the predictive utility of digit ratio obtained from both the left and the right hands on psychosocial variables have typically reported more reliable effects for the right hand (Manning, 2008).

The Present Study

This present study has three objectives: 1) to employ survey data and a measure of the right-hand digit ratio to investigate the possibility that there are gender, ethnic, and racial differences in fetal testosterone; 2) to examine the relationship between gender, ethnicity, and race on two types of physical fighting; and 3) to assess the mediating role of FT. The overall question addressed is, how much of the relationships between gender, ethnicity, and race and fighting are due to FT?

Data and Methods

Undergraduate students in criminology classes at a public university in Texas were offered extra credit points if they were willing to complete a short questionnaire and to have their digit ratios measured. Students were offered additional points if they successfully recruited other adults to participate in the study. A total of 310 subjects participated. Sixteen subjects were not black, Hispanic, or non-Hispanic white and were omitted from the present analysis, giving a net number of 294 cases. Participants were assured that the original data collected would be: 1) kept in a secure place, 2) identified by number and not by the respondent's name, 3) examined by the research team only, and 4) destroyed as soon as the information was coded and entered into an electronic data file.

Respondents were asked two questions about fighting: 1) how many times had they ever gotten into a physical fight, and 2) how many times had they ever gotten into a group fight. Answer choices ranged from 0 to 10, and answers over 10 were scored as 10. To measure each respondent's 2D:4D digit ratio, a desktop printer/scanner with a 600 × 600 dpi resolution was used. The subject's right hand was placed palm down on the glass and was held flat to make certain that fingers were equally extended and to ensure that the scanner captured a clear digital image of the entire right hand. GNU Image Manipulation Program (GIMP 2.8) software was used to measure digitally the length of the fingers. For both the second and the fourth digits, mouse-controlled calipers were placed on the basal crease of the finger and extended to the tip of the finger so that the lengths were measured in number of pixels rounded to one decimal place. The length of the second digit divided by the length of the fourth digit was recorded as the value for the right-hand finger ratio (hereafter referred to as 2D:4D). A similar methodology has been used by numerous other researchers (Allaway, Bloski, Pierson, & Lujan, 2009). If the two fingers are of approximately equal length (2D:4D ≈ 1) or if the index finger is longer (2D:4D > 1), then low FT is indicated. If the ring finger is noticeably longer than the index finger (2D:4D < 1), then the testosterone levels were high prenatally.

Gender was measured by asking respondents if they were male (1) or female (0). For both the ethnicity and race variables, non-Hispanic whites served as the reference category, so for ethnicity, those saying they are Hispanic were scored as a 1 and whites were scored as a 0. For race, African Americans were scored as 1, while whites were 0.

Analytic Strategy

In order to assess the degree to which digit ratio mediates the relationship between gender, ethnicity, and race on the one hand and physical fighting on the other, a bootstrapping approach will be used. Preacher and Hayes (2004) demonstrated the limitations of using more traditional mediation techniques, such as those explained in Baron and Kenny (1986) and Sobell (1982).

Table 1. Descriptive Statistics, Tests of Mean Differences.

Variables	Minimum	Maximum	Mean	Standard Deviation	Cohen's d	T-statistic
2D:4D						
Males	0.87	1.02	0.95	0.04	(MF) .25***	-3.83
Females	0.86	1.07	0.96	0.04		
Whites	0.88	1.07	0.97	0.04		
Hispanics	0.86	1.04	0.95	0.03	(HW).57***	-3.99
Blacks	0.89	1.00	0.93	0.03	(BW) 1.13**	-3.55
Physical Fighting						
Males	0	10	3.31	3.80	(MF) .60***	5.43
Females	0	10	1.41	2.36		
Whites	0	10	1.92	3.11		
Hispanics	0	10	2.31	3.20	(HW) .12	1.02
Blacks	0	10	3.94	3.29	(BW) .63*	2.54
Group Fighting						
Males	0	10	1.49	2.45	(MF) .71***	6.74
Females	0	6	0.22	0.69		
Whites	0	10	0.49	1.35		
Hispanics	0	10	0.87	1.99	(HW) .22*	1.91
Blacks	0	7	1.65	2.15	(BW) .65**	3.12
* p < .05; ** p < .01; *** p < .001, two-tailed test						

Using gender as an example, the traditional approach to the questions of the current study is to estimate a series of models that establish whether or not gender predicts 2D:4D and violent behavior, and the degree to which the gender/violence association is reduced with the inclusion of 2D:4D in a multivariate model (Kenny & Baron, 1986). This approach suffers from having low statistical power, and the possible indirect effect of gender on violence via digit ratio is not directly tested for statistical significance (Preacher & Hayes, 2004).

Figure 1. Mediation of Gender/Physical Fighting, standardized coefficients estimated with bootstrapping—1,000 samples.

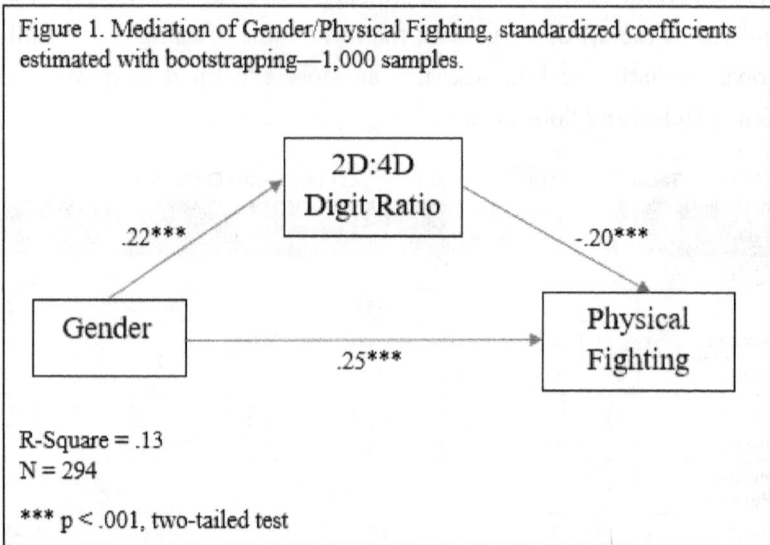

R-Square = .13
N = 294

*** p < .001, two-tailed test

A formal test of the statistical significance of the indirect effect is presented in Preacher and Hayes (2004). This alternative approach bootstraps the sampling distribution of the indirect effect coefficient. Bootstrapping is a non-parametric technique that tests the statistical significance of effect sizes without making assumptions about the distribution of the variables or the sampling distribution of the statistic (Efron & Tibshirami, 1994). Bootstrapping is conducted by taking a large number of samples from the data and calculating the indirect effect for each sample. The point estimate is simply the mean of all the coefficient estimates. The standard error is simply the standard deviation of all the estimates (Preacher & Hayes, 2004). The researcher chooses the number of samples to be taken. It was decided in the present analysis to request estimates for 1,000 samples.

Results

The gender split was 65 percent female and 35 percent male. The racial and ethnic composition of the sample was 37 percent Hispanic, 57 percent non-Hispanic white, and 6 percent African American. Table

1 lists the descriptive statistics for each demographic group, statistical significance tests of differences in means, and the size of the differences in terms of the Cohen's *d* statistic. Males average significantly lower digit ratios (i.e., more masculinized) than females, but the difference is not large. Compared to whites, Hispanics have a significantly more masculinized 2D:4D, and the difference is of moderate magnitude. Blacks average a lower digit ratio than whites, and the gap is large. These results are similar to those of other studies (Manning, Churchill, and Peters, 2007; Xu and Zheng, 2014). (Due to space limitations, black–Hispanic comparisons are not made.)

Turning to individual physical fighting, the mean for men is quite a bit higher than that for women. The Hispanic mean is higher than the white mean, but the difference falls slightly short of statistical significance. By contrast, mean fighting for blacks is significantly higher than that of whites, and the difference is moderately large. The pattern is a little clearer with group fighting. The frequency of males fighting in groups is quite a bit higher than for females. The Hispanic/white gap is not large, but this time it is statistically significant. The black mean is significantly higher than that of whites, and the magnitude of the difference is moderate.

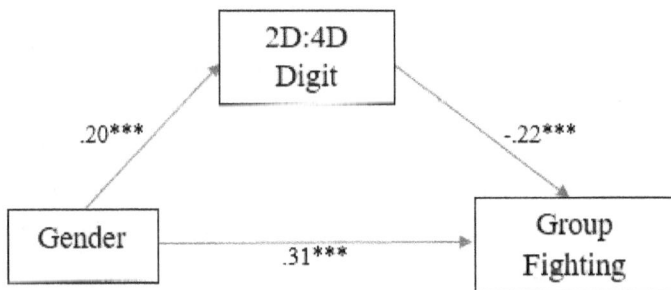

Figure 2. Mediation of Gender/Group Fighting, standardized coefficients estimated with bootstrapping—1,000 samples.

2D:4D Digit

.20***

-.22***

Gender

.31***

Group Fighting

R-Square = .16
N = 294

*** p < .001, two-tailed test

Figure 1 shows the results of the bootstrapping-based mediation analysis with the independent variable (gender), the mediator (digit ratio), and the dependent variable (physical fighting). Gender has a direct effect on fighting, and an indirect effect via 2D:4D digit ratio. The indirect effect is statistically significant (B = .32, SE = .12, p < .001, two-tailed). The direct and indirect effect of gender explains 13% of the variance in physical fighting. Since the direct effect is still significant after the indirect effect has been taken into account, this is a case of partial mediation. In other words, part of the reason why males engage in higher rates of fighting than females is because of greater prenatal testosterone exposure.

Figure 3. Mediation of Ethnicity/Physical Fighting, standardized coefficients estimated with bootstrapping—1,000 samples.

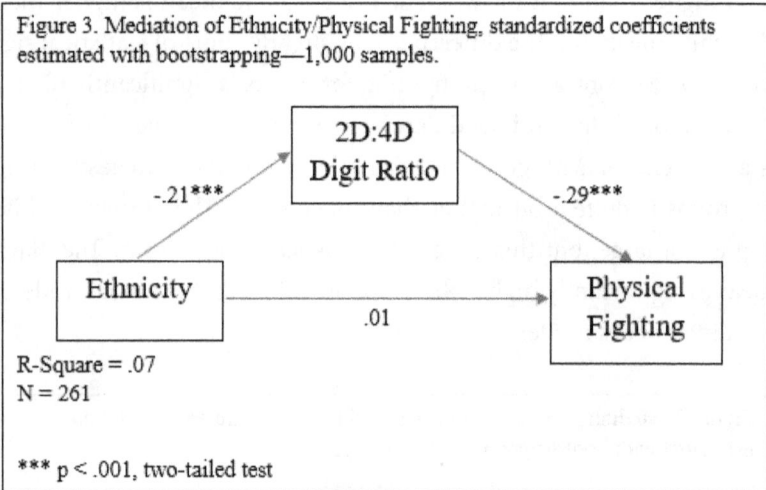

```
            ┌─────────────┐
            │   2D:4D     │
            │ Digit Ratio │
            └─────────────┘
   -.21***                   -.29***

┌───────────┐                      ┌───────────┐
│ Ethnicity │ ──────────────────→  │ Physical  │
└───────────┘         .01          │ Fighting  │
                                   └───────────┘
```

R-Square = .07
N = 261

*** p < .001, two-tailed test

The results are similar for group fighting (Figure 2). Gender has a significant direct effect on group fighting, and an indirect effect through 2D:4D. The indirect effect again is statistically significant (B = -.15, SE = .07, p < .05, two-tailed). R-square is .16. Again, the mediation is partial: Men are, in part, more likely than women to participate in group fights due to greater exposure to testosterone *in utero*.

Figure 4. Mediation of Ethnicity/Group Fighting, standardized coefficients estimated with bootstrapping—1,000 samples.

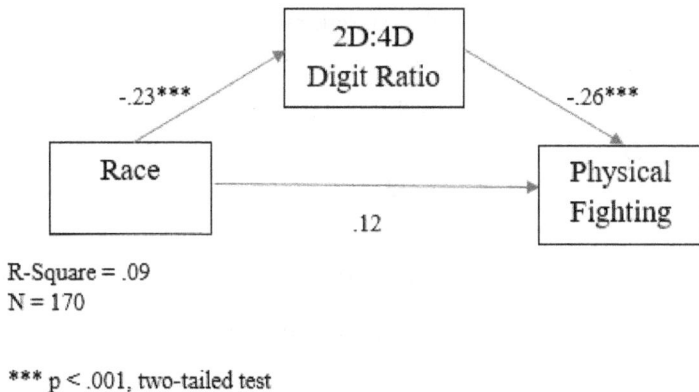

2D:4D Digit Ratio

-.21***   -.22***

Ethnicity   Group Fighting

.06

R-Square = .07
N = 261

*** p < .001, two-tailed test

Figure 5. Mediation of Race/Physical Fighting, standardized coefficients estimated with bootstrapping—1,000 samples.

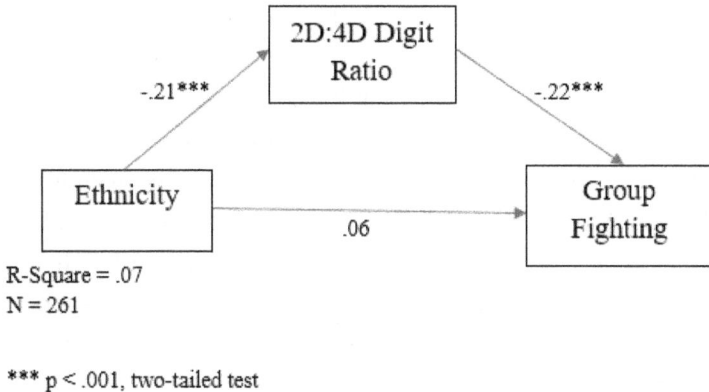

2D:4D Digit Ratio

-.23***   -.26***

Race   Physical Fighting

.12

R-Square = .09
N = 170

*** p < .001, two-tailed test

Results presented in Table 1 indicate that Hispanics and whites do not differ significantly in terms of rates of individual fighting, and when two groups do not differ on the dependent variable, there is no relationship to explain. The results shown in Figure 3 are consistent with this: the direct path from ethnicity to physical fighting is non-significant. On the other hand, a significant path is observable from ethnicity through digit ratio to fighting. This indirect pathway is statistically significant (B = .41, SE = .15, p < .01, two-tailed). Compared to whites, Hispanics average lower digit ratios, which in turn is associated with more individual fighting.

The pattern of results is different for group fighting. According to Table 1, the Hispanic mean for group fighting is significantly higher than the white men, yet the direct path in Figure 4 has fallen to non-significance. The indirect effect is statistically significant (B = .17, SE = .08, p < .05, two-tailed). Here we have full mediation: greater Hispanic group fighting is fully explained by more fetal testosterone exposure. Figure 5 also indicates full mediation for race and individual fighting. The significant race/fighting association seen in Table 1 drops to non-significance in the mediation analysis. Again, the indirect pathway through digit ratio is significant (B = .63, SE = .27, p < .05, two-tailed) and R-square is .09. As was seen in the Hispanic/white comparison of group fighting, the black/white difference in individual fighting is completely explained by the 2D:4D digit ratio.

The final mediation analysis is presented in Figure 6. This is a case of partial mediation. While the indirect pathway is statistically significant (B = .25, SE = .11, p < .05, two-tailed), the direct effect of race on group fighting remains significant even after modeling the indirect effect. According to the data, part of the reason for higher rates of black group fighting is exposure to higher concentrations of FT.

Conclusion/Discussion

The aim of the present study was to examine the extent to which a proxy of fetal testosterone mediates the relationships between gender, ethnicity, and race on the one hand and two forms of physical fighting on the other. The mediation analyses generally suggest that differential exposure to prenatal testosterone helps explain the demographic differences in fighting. For both types of fighting, 2D:4D partially mediated the effect of gender. For ethnicity, individual fighting did not differ between Hispanics and whites, but digit ratio fully mediated the ethnicity's effect on group fighting. Finally, 2D:4D mediated fully the relationship between race and individual fighting, and it did so partially for group fighting.

The present study has a number of limitations. While the total sample size is adequate, the number of minority participants in future studies needs to be increased. Results can be unstable with small sample sizes. Sampling was also based on convenience and consequently is not likely to be representative of the general population (although the inclusion of non-student recruits did diversify the sample). Digit ratio has been shown to be an imprecise proxy of prenatal androgen exposure (Lutchmaya et al., 2004). One should bear in mind that factors other than androgens affect digit growth (McIntyre, 2006). Furthermore, concentrations of testosterone in the fingers cannot be considered anything but roughly associated with androgen levels inside the nervous system during critical periods of fetal development (McIntyre, 2006). Also, it is worth noting that self-reports of offending provide only imperfect measures of violent behavior (Thornberry and Krohn, 2000). As a result of the limitations just described, the findings reported here should be considered tentative, and much more research in the area is warranted. On the other hand, this study does raise questions about the focus of theories that locate gender and ethnic differences in violence exclusively in the social conditions of adolescence and young adulthood. Knowledge on the emergence of early differences is thin and in need of development.

Much more research is needed concerning the determinants of fetal testosterone levels. According to a heritability study of twins, the best-fitting structural equation model indicated that all of the environmental portion of the variance in 2D:4D was of the non-shared type (Voracek & Dressler, 2007a). This suggests that researchers should focus on prenatal factors that might vary among siblings rather than structural factors which siblings experience in common.

Prenatal stress seems to be a promising line of research. A study of pregnant women who received an amniocentesis revealed that amniotic fluid cortisol levels — a hormone closely tied to stress — and levels of testosterone were positively correlated, suggesting that stressful conditions might elevate FT levels (Sarkar, Bergman, Fisk, O'Connor, & Glover, 2007). In a similar study, prenatal exposure to stressful life events was associated with higher FT in girls (Barrett & Swan, 2015).

At least two studies have identified cigarette smoking and alcohol consumption as possible causes of FT elevation and subsequent behavior problems. A sample of primary schools revealed that boys, but not girls, tended to have lower digit ratios if their mothers had smoked during pregnancy (Rizwan, Manning, & Brabin, 2007). In a study of preschoolers, finger-length ratios interacted with prenatal nicotine use to predict hyperactivity among boys (but not girls) (Roberts & Martel, 2013). FT also interacted with prenatal alcohol exposure to predict hyperactivity/impulsivity and oppositional defiance disorder in both sexes.

Diet could potentially influence hormone levels, even after the baby is born. Formula feeding was found to be associated with higher testosterone in infant girls (Thompson & Michelle, 2013). While research on the effects of environmental pollutants has suggested that normal fetal development is disrupted and FT *reduced* by toxins (Papadopoulou et al., 2013; Parks et al., 2000), this area of research is in its early stages and might prove fruitful. Other promising areas in prenatal research include maternal depression, birth complications, traumatic head injury, lead exposure, and child abuse (Liu, 2011). There remains a great deal to be learned about prenatal causes of androgen levels, but the importance of the prenatal environment for later child well-being justifies serious research commitment.

The findings reported here, while very tentative, suggest that gender, ethnic, and racial differences in violence might have roots in the prenatal environment. Theories that focus exclusively on later social conditions might present an inaccurate picture of the phenomenon and might motivate empirical research agendas that lack balance. If differences emerge early in development, early interventions might turn out to be the most effective (Liu, 2011). Models that omit important early factors might be misspecified. Theories of violence that incorporate important early factors will likely make gains in predictive power as well as empirical adequacy.

References

Allaway, H. C., Bloski, T. G., Pierson, R. A., & Lujan, M. E. (2009). Digit ratios (2D:4D) determined by computer-assisted analysis are more reliable than those using physical measurements, photocopies, and printed scans. *American Journal of Human Biology, 21*(3), 365–370. http://doi.org/10.1002/ajhb.20892.

Anderson, E. (2000). *Code of the street: Decency, violence, and the moral life of the inner city.* New York: WW Norton & Company.

Baker, L. a., Raine, A., Liu, J., & Jacobson, K. C. (2008). Differential genetic and environmental influences on reactive and proactive aggression in children. *Journal of Abnormal Child Psychology, 36*(8), 1265–1278. http://doi.org/10.1007/s10802-008-9249-1.

Baron, R. M., & Kenny, D. A. (1986). The moderator-mediator variable distinction in social psychological research: conceptual, strategic, and statistical considerations. *Journal of Personality and Social Psychology, 51*(6), 1173–1182.

Barrett, E. S., & Swan, S. H. (2015). Stress and androgen activity during fetal development. *Endocrinology, 156*, 1325–1335. http://doi.org/10.1210/en.2015-1335.

Berenbaum, S. A., Bryk, K. K., Nowak, N., Quigley, C. A., & Moffat, S. (2009). Fingers as a marker of prenatal androgen exposure. *Endocrinology, 150*(11), 5119–5124. http://doi.org/10.1210/en.2009-0774.

Blau, J. R., & Blau., P. M. (1982). The cost of inequality: Metropolitan structure and violent crime. *American Sociological Review, 47*(1), 114–129.

Booth, A., & Osgood, D. W. (1993). The influence of testosterone on deviance in adulthood: Assessing and explaining the relationship. *Criminology, 31*(1), 93-117.

Breedlove, S. M. (2010). Minireview: Organizational hypothesis: Instances of the fingerpost. *Endocrinology.* http://doi.org/10.1210/en.2010-0041.

Brooks, J. H., & Reddon, J. R. (1996). Serum testosterone in violent and nonviolent young offenders. *Journal of Clinical Psychology, 52*(4), 475-483.

Butovskaya, M., Burkova, V., Karelin, D., & Filatova, V. (2019). The association between 2D:4D ratio and aggression in children and adolescents: cross-cultural and gender differences. *Early Human Development, 137*, 104823.

Butovskaya, M. L., Veselovskaya, E. V., & Prudnikova, A. V. (2010). Models of man's biosocial adaptation in an industrial society. *Archaeology, Ethnology and Anthropology of Eurasia, 38*(4), 143–154. http://doi.org/10.1016/j.aeae.2011.02.012.

Conners, C. K. (1970). Symptom patterns in hyperkinetic, neurotic, and normal children. *Child Development, 41*(3), 667–682.

Efron, B., & Tibshirani, R. J. (1994). *An introduction to the bootstrap.* CRC press.

Elliott, D. S., & Ageton, S. S. (1980). Reconciling race and class differences in self-reported and official estimates of delinquency. *American Sociological Review, 45*(1), 95. http://doi.org/10.2307/2095245.

Ellis, L., & Hoskin, A. W. (2013). Criminality and the 2D:4D Ratio: Testing the prenatal androgen hypothesis. *International Journal of Offender Therapy and Comparative Criminology.* http://doi.org/10.1177/0306624X13503813.

Ellis, L., & Nyborg, H. (1992). Racial/ethnic variations in male testosterone levels: a probable contributor to group differences in health. *Steroids, 57*(2), 72-75.

Felson, R., & Kraeger, D. (2015). Group differences in delinquency: What is there to explain? *Race and Justice, 5*(1), 58–87.

Fite, P. J., Vitulano, M., Wynn, P., Wimsatt, A., Gaertner, A., & Rathert, J. (2010). Influence of preceived neighborhood safety on proactive and reactive aggression. *Journal of Community Psychology, 38*(6), 757–768. http://doi.org/10.1002/jcop.

Galis, F., Ten Broek, C. M. A., Van Dongen, S., & Wijnaendts, L. C. D. (2010). Sexual dimorphism in the prenatal digit ratio (2D:4D). *Archives of Sexual Behavior, 39*(1), 57–62. http://doi.org/10.1007/s10508-009-9485-7.

Garn, S. M., Burdi, a R., Babler, W. J., & Stinson, S. (1975). Early prenatal attainment of adult metacarpal-phalangeal rankings and proportions. *American Journal of Physical Anthropology, 43*(3), 327–332. http://doi.org/10.1002/ajpa.1330430305.

Guerra, N. G., Huesmann, L. R., Tolan, P. H., Van Acker, R., & Eron, L. D. (1995). Stressful events and individual beliefs as correlates of economic disadvantage and aggression among urban children. *Journal of Consulting and Clinical Psychology, 63*(4), 518–528. http://doi.org/10.1037/0022-006X.63.4.518.

Hanoch, Y., Gummerum, M., & Rolison, J. (2012). Second-to-fourth digit ratio and impulsivity: A comparison between offenders and nonoffenders. *PLoS ONE, 7*(10). http://doi.org/10.1371/journal.pone.0047140.

Hetherington, E. M. (1966). Effects of paternal absence on sex-typed behaviors in Negro and white preadolescent males. *Journal of Personality and Social Psychology, 4*(1), 87.

Hollier, L. P., Keelan, J. a., Jamnadass, E. S. L., Maybery, M. T., Hickey, M., & Whitehouse, A. J. O. (2015). Adult digit ratio (2D:4D) is not related to umbilical cord androgen or estrogen concentrations, their ratios or net bioactivity. *Early Human Development*, *91*(2), 111–117. http://doi.org/10.1016/j. earlhumdev.2014.12.011.

Hönekopp, J., Bartholdt, L., Beier, L., & Liebert, A. (2007). Second to fourth digit length ratio (2D:4D) and adult sex hormone levels: new data and a meta-analytic review. *Psychoneuroendocrinology*, *32*(4), 313–321. http://doi.org/10.1016/j. psyneuen.2007.01.007.

Hönekopp, J., & Watson, S. (2010). Meta-analysis of digit ratio 2D:4D shows greater sex difference in the right hand. *American Journal of Human Biology*, *22*(5), 619–630. http://doi.org/10.1002/ajhb.21054.

Hoskin, A. W., & Ellis, L. (2015). Fetal testosterone and criminality: Test of evolutionary neuroandrogenic theory. *Criminology*, *53*(1), 54–73. http://doi. org/10.1111/1745-9125.12056.

Jencks, C. (1991). Is violent crime increasing? 4 (1991): 98-109. *American Prospect*, *4*, 98–109.

Kaufman, J. M., Rebellon, C. J., Thaxton, S., & Agnew, R. (2008). A general strain theory of racial differences in criminal offending. *Australian & New Zealand Journal of Criminology*, *41*(3), 421–437.

Lansford, J. E., Skinner, A. T., Sorbring, E., Giunta, L. Di, Deater-Deckard, K., Dodge, K. a., … Chang, L. (2012). Boys' and girls' relational and physical aggression in nine countries. *Aggressive Behavior*, *38*(4), 298–308. http://doi. org/10.1002/ab.21433.

Lippa, R. a. (2003). Are 2D:4D finger-length ratios related to sexual orientation? Yes for men, no for women. *Journal of Personality and Social Psychology*, *85*(1), 179–188. http://doi.org/10.1037/0022-3514.85.1.179.

Liu, J. (2011). Early health risk factors for violence: Conceptualization, evidence, and implications. *Aggression and Violent Behavior*, *16*(1), 63–73. http://doi. org/10.1016/j.avb.2010.12.003.

Liu, J., Portnoy, J., & Raine, A. (2012). Association between a marker for prenatal testosterone exposure and externalizing behavior problems in children. *Development and Psychopathology*. http://doi.org/10.1017/S0954579412000363.

Loehlin, J. C., McFadden, D., Medland, S. E., & Martin, N. G. (2006). Population differences in finger-length ratios: Ethnicity or latitude? *Archives of Sexual Behavior*, *35*(6), 739–742.

Lutchmaya, S., Baron-Cohen, S., Raggatt, P., Knickmeyer, R., & Manning, J. T. (2004). 2nd to 4th digit ratios, fetal testosterone and estradiol. *Early Human Development, 77*(1-2), 23–28. http://doi.org/10.1016/j.earlhumdev.2003.12.002.

Malas, M. A., Dogan, S., Hilal Evcil, E., & Desdicioglu, K. (2006). Fetal development of the hand, digits and digit ratio (2D : 4D). *Early Human Development, 82*(7), 469–475. http://doi.org/10.1016/j.earlhumdev.2005.12.002.

Manning, J., Kilduff, L., & Trivers, R. (2013). Digit ratio (2D:4D) in Klinefelter's syndrome. *Andrology, 1*(1), 94–9. http://doi.org/10.1111/j.2047-2927.2012.00013.x.

Manning, J. T. (2008). *The finger book: Sex, behaviour and disease revealed in the fingers.* London: Faber and Faber.

Manning, J. T., Barley, L., Walton, J., Lewis-Jones, D. I., Trivers, R. L., Singh, D., … Szwed, A. (2000). The 2nd:4th digit ratio, sexual dimorphism, population differences, and reproductive success. *Evolution and Human Behavior.* http://doi.org/10.1016/S1090-5138(00)00029-5.

Manning, J. T., Baron-Cohen, S., Wheelwright, S., & Sanders, G. (2001). The 2nd to 4th digit ratio and autism. *Developmental Medicine and Child Neurology, 43*(3), 160–164. http://doi.org/10.1097/00004703-200110000-00019.

Manning, J. T., Churchill, A. J. G., & Peters, M. (2007). The effects of sex, ethnicity, and sexual orientation on self-measured digit ratio (2D:4D). *Archives of Sexual Behavior, 36*(2), 223–233. http://doi.org/10.1007/s10508-007-9171-6.

Manning, J. T., Scutt, D., Wilson, J., & Lewis-Jones, D. I. (1998). The ratio of 2nd to 4th digit length: a predictor of sperm numbers and concentrations of testosterone, luteinizing hormone and oestrogen. *Human Reproduction, 13*(11), 3000–3004. http://doi.org/10.1093/humrep/13.11.3000.

Manning, J. T., Stewart, A., Bundred, P. E., & Trivers, R. L. (2004). Sex and ethnic differences in 2nd to 4th digit ratio of children. *Early Human Development, 80*(2), 161–168. http://doi.org/10.1016/j.earlhumdev.2004.06.004.

McIntyre, M. H. (2006). The use of digit ratios as markers for perinatal androgen action. *Reproductive Biology and Endocrinology : RB&E, 4,* 10. http://doi.org/10.1186/1477-7827-4-10.

McNulty, T. L., & Bellair, P. E. (2003). Explaining racial and ethnic differences in serious adolescent violent behavior. *Criminology, 41*(3), 709–747.

McNulty, T. L., & Bellair., P. E. (2003). Explaining racial and ethnic differences in adolescent violence: Structural disadvantage, family well-being, and social capital. *Justice Quarterly, 20*(1), 1–31.

Menard, S. (2002). *Applied logistic regression analysis* (Vol. 106). Thousand Oaks, CA: Sage.

Moffitt, T. E., Caspi, A., Rutter, M., & Silva, P. A. (2001). *Sex differences in antisocial behaviour*. Cambridge, UK: Cambridge University Press.

Neapolitan, J. L. (1998). Cross-national variation in homicides: Is race a factor? *Criminology, 36*(1), 139–156. http://doi.org/10.1111/j.1745-9125.1998.tb01243.x

Nyborg, H. (2004). Multivariate modelling of testosterone-dominance associations. *Behavioral and Brain Sciences, 27*(1), 155-159.

Papadopoulou, E., Vafeiadi, M., Agramunt, S., Mathianaki, K., Karakosta, P., Spanaki, A., ... Kogevinas, M. (2013). Maternal diet, prenatal exposure to dioxins and other persistent organic pollutants and anogenital distance in children. *Science of the Total Environment, 461-462*, 222–229. http://doi.org/10.1016/j. scitotenv.2013.05.005

Parks, L. G., Ostby, J. S., Lambright, C. R., Abbott, B. D., Klinefelter, G. R., Barlow, N. J., & Gray, L. E. (2000). The plasticizer diethylhexyl phthalate induces malformations by decreasing fetal testosterone synthesis during sexual differentiation in the male rat. *Toxicological Sciences, 58*(2), 339–349. http://doi. org/10.1093/toxsci/58.2.339

Preacher, K. J., & Hayes, A. F. (2004). SPSS and SAS procedures for estimating indirect effects in simple mediation models. *Behavior Research Methods, Instruments, & Computers, 36*(4), 717-731.

Rada, R. T., Laws, D. R., & Kellner, R. (1976). Plasma testosterone levels in the rapist. *Psychosomatic Medicine, 38*(4), 257-268.

Richards, G., Browne, W. V., Aydin, E., Constantinescu, M., Nave, G., Kim, M. S., & Watson, S. J. (2020). Digit ratio (2D: 4D) and congenital adrenal hyperplasia (CAH): Systematic literature review and meta-analysis. *Hormones and Behavior, 126*, 104867.

Rizwan, S., Manning, J. T., & Brabin, B. J. (2007). Maternal smoking during pregnancy and possible effects of in utero testosterone: Evidence from the 2D:4D finger length ratio. *Early Human Development, 83*(2), 87–90. http://doi. org/10.1016/j.earlhumdev.2006.05.005

Roberts, B. A., & Martel, M. M. (2013). Prenatal testosterone and preschool disruptive behavior disorders. *Personality and Individual Differences, 55*(8), 962–966. http://doi.org/10.1016/j.paid.2013.08.002

Romero-Martínez, A., Lila, M., & Moya-Albiol, L. (2017). The 2D: 4D Ratio as a Predictor of the Risk of Recidivism after Court-mandated Intervention Program for Intimate Partner Violence Perpetrators. *Journal of Forensic Sciences, 62*(3), 705-709.

Sampson, R. J., Morenoff, J. D., & Raudenbush, S. (2005). Social anatomy of racial and ethnic disparities in violence. *American Journal of Public Health*, *95*(2), 224–232. http://doi.org/10.2105/AJPH.2004.037705

Sampson, R. J., & Wilson, W. J. (1995). Toward a theory of race, crime, and urban inequality. (1995): 177-190. In S. L. Gabbidon & H. T. Taylor (Eds.), *Race, Crime, and Justice: A Reader* (pp. 177–190). London: Routledge.

Sarkar, P., Bergman, K., Fisk, N. M., O'Connor, T. G., & Glover, V. (2007). Amniotic fluid testosterone: Relationship with cortisol and gestational age. *Clinical Endocrinology*, *67*(5), 743–747. http://doi.org/10.1111/j.1365-2265.2007.02955.x

Schwerdtfeger, A., & Heer, J. (2008). Second to fourth digit ratio (2D:4D) of the right hand is associated with nociception and augmenting-reducing. *Personality and Individual Differences*, *45*(6), 493–497. http://doi.org/10.1016/j.paid.2008.05.027

Talarovičová, A., Kršková, L., & Blažeková, J. (2009). Testosterone enhancement during pregnancy influences the 2D:4D ratio and open field motor activity of rat siblings in adulthood. *Hormones and Behavior*, *55*(1), 235–239. http://doi.org/10.1016/j.yhbeh.2008.10.010

Thompson, A. L., & Michelle, L. (2013). Prenatal and postnatal energetic conditions and sex steroids levels across the first year of life. *American Journal of Human Biology*, *25*(5), 643–654. http://doi.org/10.1002/ajhb.22424

Trivers, R., Manning, J., & Jacobson, A. (2006). A longitudinal study of digit ratio (2D:4D) and other finger ratios in Jamaican children. *Hormones and Behavior*, *49*(2), 150–156. http://doi.org/10.1016/j.yhbeh.2005.05.023

Van Anders, S. M., Vernon, P. a., & Wilbur, C. J. (2006). Finger-length ratios show evidence of prenatal hormone-transfer between opposite-sex twins. *Hormones and Behavior*, *49*(3), 315–319. http://doi.org/10.1016/j.yhbeh.2005.08.003.

Van de Beek, C., Thijssen, J. H., Cohen-Kettenis, P. T., Goozen, S. H. van, & Buitelaar., J. K. (2004). Relationships between sex hormones assessed in amniotic fluid, and maternal and umbilical cord serum: what is the best source of information to investigate the effects of fetal hormonal exposure? *Hormones and Behavior*, *46*(5), 663–669.

Ventura, T., Gomes, M. C., Pita, A., Neto, M. T., & Taylor, A. (2013). Digit ratio (2D:4D) in newborns: Influences of prenatal testosterone and maternal environment. *Early Human Development*, *89*(2), 107–112. http://doi.org/10.1016/j.earlhumdev.2012.08.009.

Voracek, M., & Dressler, S. G. (2007a). Digit Ratio (2D:4D) in twins: Heritability estimates and evidence for a masculinized trait expression in women from opposite-sex pairs. *Psychological Reports*, *100*(1), 115–126.

Voracek, M., & Dressler, S. G. (2007b). Digit ratio (2D:4D) in twins: heritability estimates and evidence for a masculinized trait expression in women from opposite-sex pairs. *Psychological Reports, 100*(1), 115–126. http://doi.org/10.2466/PR0.100.1.115-126.

Wong, W. I., & Hines, M. (2016). Interpreting digit ratio (2D: 4D)–behavior correlations: 2D: 4D sex difference, stability, and behavioral correlates and their replicability in young children. *Hormones and Behavior, 78*, 86-94.

Wolfgang, M. E., & Ferracuti, F. (1967). *The subculture of violence.* New York: Social Science Paperbacks.

Xu, Y., & Zheng, Y. (2014). The digit ratio (2D:4D) in China: A meta-analysis. *American Journal of Human Biology, 27*(3), 304–309.

Zheng, Z., & Cohn, M. J. (2011). From the cover: Developmental basis of sexually dimorphic digit ratios. *Proceedings of the National Academy of Sciences.* http://doi.org/10.1073/pnas.1108312108.

CHAPTER 7

INTELLIGENCE AND ANTI-NATALIST INTENTIONS ON DATING SITES: AN ANALYSIS OF THE OKCUPID DATASET

EMIL KIRKEGAARD AND EDWARD DUTTON

Abstract

A BODY OF RESEARCH indicates that people who are more intelligent tend to have fewer children than do those who are less intelligent, at least since around 1900 (Lynn, 2011). Nyborg (2012) has predicted that the consequent IQ decline will lead to the eventual decay of Western civilization. However, there is little research on fertility *intentions* and intelligence. Do smarter people end up with fewer children because they ideally desire fewer, or is it due to competing interests, such as a desire for money and status combined with more efficient use of contraception, as Nyborg (2012) observes? We analysed the OKCupid dataset of predominantly Western, English-speaking online users. Employing an ad hoc intelligence test composed of 14 questions on the dating service, we find that intelligence does indeed negatively relate to fertility intentions (β = -0.15, ordinal regression), even adjusting for age, sex, and race/ethnicity (β = -0.14). We also replicate the usual pattern of a negative association between intelligence and actual fertility, though the dataset was suboptimal for this analysis as fertility was only a binary outcome.

1. Introduction

There is a long-standing interest in the relationship between fertility and human capital traits and specifically the relationship between fertility and intelligence. Various scholars have come to the conclusion that throughout much of history, there was a positive association between socio-economic status and the number of surviving children, such that the partly-genetic traits that led to socioeconomic status were under positive selection (Clark, 2007; Lynn, 2011). Still, it has been found that starting sometime in the 1800s, these associations started to reverse such that people lower in these traits had more (surviving) children. This was later termed *dysgenics* as an antonym of *eugenics*. Nyborg (2012) observed that this 'Double Relaxed Darwinian Selection' — the collapse of conditions causing a positive IQ-fertility nexus and the rise of innovations, such as contraception, which cause a negative IQ-fertility nexus — will lead to the decay of civilization, due to the high heritability of IQ, of around 0.8 (Lynn, 2011, p.101).

Interest in the subject began in earnest with the work and discoveries of Francis Galton, a Victorian polymath and half-cousin of Charles Darwin (Galton, 1869; Jensen, 2002). While there has been some debate over the measurement, magnitude and consistency of dysgenic fertility patterns, a modern meta-analysis shows a fairly consistent pattern (Reeve et al., 2018). The overall effect size is weak, r = -.11. This varies with sexes; the pattern is almost always observed to be more negative for women than men. In their meta-analysis, for the samples with completed fertility and persons of at least 50 years of age, the correlations were -.14 and -.07, for women and men, respectively.

For men, sometimes in some developed countries, the pattern is observed to be slightly positive, though probably not positive enough to outweigh the female negative relationship. The best evidence of the positive associations comes from Nordic register data studies, which rely on near-complete population datasets from the army induction testing (Barclay & Kolk, 2020; Bjerkedal et al., 2007; Kolk & Barclay, 2019, 2021). As women are not forced to participate in Nordic military service, their intelligence data are rarer and of questionable representativeness. Women's fertility is not analyzed in the published studies of Nordic military data, so we do not know what the associations are.

There is uncertainty about the causes of these patterns, and their prevalence in poorer regions of the world. There is emerging evidence that dysgenic patterns are already visible outside of the Western world. One study in Libya found a correlation of -.42 between the number of siblings and scores on the Raven's test (Al-Shahomee & Lynn, 2018). Another study found correlations of -.16 for women and .06 for men in the Dominican Republic (Meisenberg et al., 2006). Of particular interest was that the correlation between the ideal number of children and actual number of children was only r = .15. Thus, the ideal number of children does not seem to have much to do with the actual number of children, at least for this country and time period. Furthermore, the correlation between the ideal number of children with intelligence was very weak, .01 for men and -.01 for women. It is unknown whether these values will generalize to Western countries. In recent decades, childlessness has gone from an unpopular rarity to being explicitly embraced. It is conceivable this has altered the correlations with intelligence, if smarter people tend to adopt popular ideas more or faster than duller people. In this regard, it has been shown that intelligence is associated with conformity to the dominant set of societal values. This may be because intelligent people are better able to understand what these values are, are better able to understand the future benefits of conformity, and have sufficient effortful control to force themselves to adopt the dominant set of values (Woodley of Menie & Dunkel, 2015).

The purpose of this study is to examine the relationship between the ideal number of children and intelligence in Western samples. The goal is to see whether a decrease in the ideal number of children may explain the decrease in the number of children among smarter people. A prior study, Kanazawa (2014), has shown a very weak association between childhood IQ and wishing to remain childless of about 0.02, though this did attain significance. Those who, at age 23, wished to have children had an IQ of 100, while those who wanted to be childless had an IQ of approximately 104. This was based on Britain's National Childhood Development Study, which interviewed people born in 1958 and 1969 at the age of 23. However, an examination of the US National Longitudinal Study of Youth, 1979, found no relationship between fertility intentions and intelligence (Meisenberg & Kaul, 2010). We aim to develop these analyses by drawing upon a new and substantial data set.

2. Method

Data

We used data from the OKCupid dataset, which was published as part of Kirkegaard and Bjerrekær (2016). This dataset was collected by scraping (automated downloading) of information from the then large dating service OKCupid (https://www.okcupid.com/). In total, the dataset contains data from 68,371 users across 2,620 variables. However, since all users only have partial data, and most users have only very little data, the effective sample size is often 10,000 to 20,000. In demographic terms, the dataset is mostly Western (~95%) and English-speaking (~85%), as well as 61% male. The age variation is extensive, skewed towards younger people as would be expected from a dating service.

The main functionality of the dating service was to allow users to create and fill out 1,000s of survey questions. Each of these allowed for between 2 to 4 answer options, and users could also assign them importance. The site's algorithm would then use the collected data in order to compute a match score with each other user, which is useful for dating purposes due to the very strong assortative mating in humans (Hur, 2003; Kirkegaard, 2021; Luo, 2017). Almost all users allowed their answers to be visible to other users of the site, which is what allowed the dataset to be collected. The questions on the site were mostly user-generated, but site staff had created the first 100 or so questions (out of many 1,000s). Since most people grow tired of filling out questions on a dating site, there is not full coverage for users and questions. The variety of questions is extreme compared to most surveys since there was apparently little oversight or quality control of the questions.

Some of the questions are intelligence questions. Prior studies of these questions have shown that they work as a primitive intelligence test (Kirkegaard, 2018; Kirkegaard & Bjerrekær, 2016; Kirkegaard & Lasker, 2020). The questions are shown below:

- Which is bigger, the earth or the sun?

- STALE is to STEAL as 89475 is to what?

- What is next in this series? 1, 4, 10, 19, 31, __

- If you turn a left-handed glove inside out, it fits on your left or right hand?

- In the line "Wherefore art thou Romeo?" what does "wherefore" mean?

- How many fortnights are in a year?

- Half of all policemen are thieves and half of all policemen are murderers. Does it follow logically that all policemen are criminals?

- Which is longer, a mile or a kilometer?

- When birds stand on power lines and don't get hurt, it's most likely because of what?

- Etymology is?

- If some men are doctors and some doctors are tall, does it follow that some men are tall?

- A little grade 10 science: what is the Ideal Gas Law?

- If you flipped three pennies, what would be the odds that they all came out the same?

- Which is the day before the day after yesterday?

3. Results

The intelligence data was scored using a single factor model using the mirt package as done in prior studies. We standardized the resulting scores to mean of 0 and standard deviation of 1. There are no norms for these data, so we are unable to convert to the familiar 100/15 scale. The sample is likely somewhat above average in the countries of collection as indicated by studies of who employs dating sites (e.g. Nam, 2017), so likely the mean IQ would be around 105 with a slightly reduced standard deviation, around 13. Due to the fact that most users did not provide answers to all of the 14 questions, the scores are based on the available data. This means the reliability is not as high as is desired. Using all the available data as is, the estimated empirical reliability is only .55, or .75 if we assume a normal distribution with full data. One solution to this is to subset the data by the number of filled out questions, thus making a quantity-quality trade-off. Figure 1 shows the effect of doing this on the test's estimated reliability.

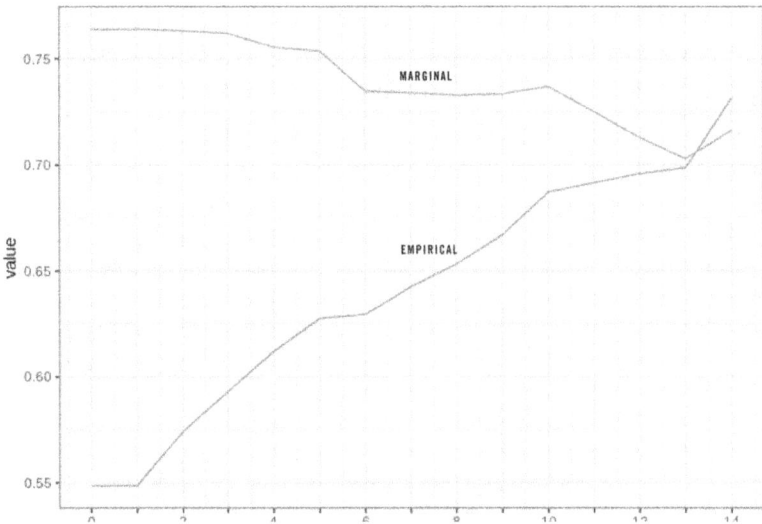

Figure 1. Estimated test reliability as function of restricting the sample size to subjects who have filled out at least a given number of intelligence items.

The marginal (theoretical) reliability declines somewhat across sample restrictions. This may seem odd, but it probably reflects the fact that as sample restrictiveness in terms of intelligence variation declines (because smarter people fill out more items), the g-loadings are deflated, and thus the reliability of the test is reduced. The empirical estimated reliability, however, increases with sample restrictiveness, as expected since each user provides more data.

In terms of fertility, there is no question about the number of children subjects currently have. The profile, however, required people to answer the question "Do you have a child or children?" (yes/no), thus providing a crude binary measure. There was a question about desired fertility: "How many children would you ideally like to have?" with options being: "None", "1-2", "3-4", "5 or more!". Figures 2 and 3 show the distributions of intelligence by responses to these questions.

We restricted our analysis of the dataset to subjects who were heterosexual, and who had filled out at least 8 items in the intelligence test. This provided a reasonable trade-off between the quality of the measure and ensuring sufficient sample size to detect effects of concern. This reduced the sample size to 18,219. Figure 2 displays intelligence by parenthood status, while Figure 3 displays the relationship between intelligence and desired number of children.

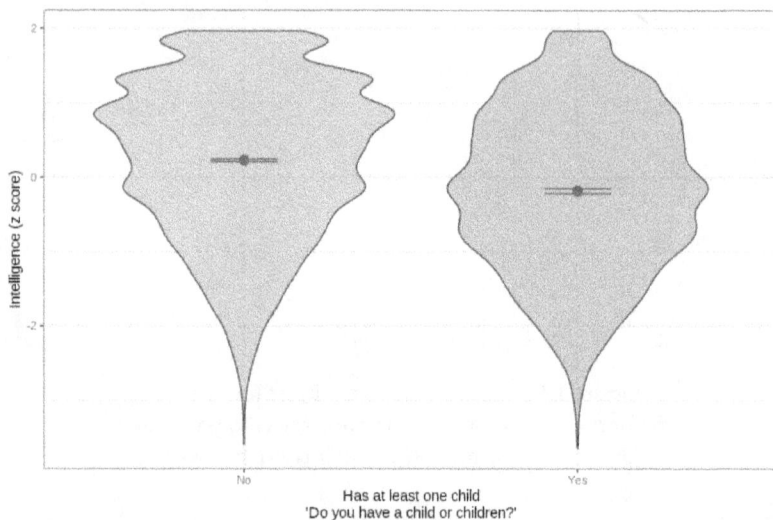

Figure 2. Violin plot of intelligence by parenthood status.

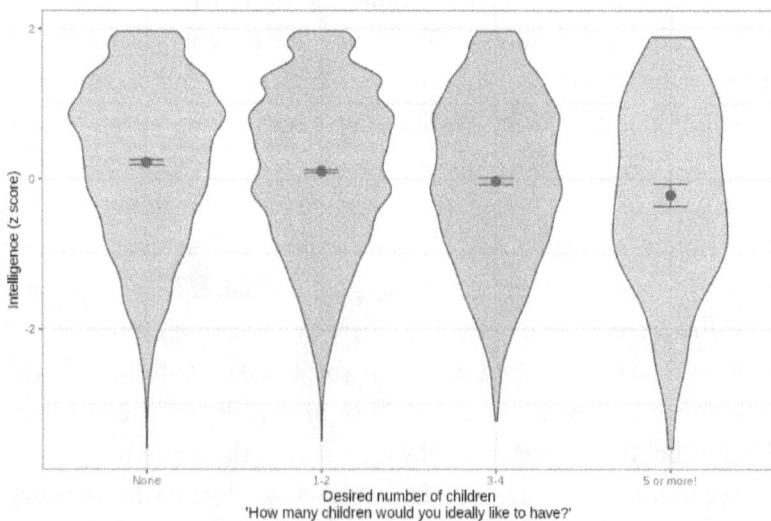

Figure 3. Violin plot of intelligence by ideal desired children number.

Due to the large sample size, all differences are much larger than expected purely by chance (i.e., very small p values). Table 1 shows the effect sizes in terms of Cohen's d.

Table 1. Intelligence differences between groups by ideal number of children (95% confidence intervals in brackets). Cohen's d values. Extended output with pairwise sample sizes can be found in the R notebook.

How many children would you ideally like to have?	None	1-2	3-4	5 or more
None		-0.11 [-0.15 -0.076]	-0.24 [-0.29 -0.19]	-0.41 [-0.54 -0.28]
1-2	-0.11 [-0.15 -0.076]		-0.13 [-0.17 -0.081]	-0.30 [-0.42 -0.17]
3-4	-0.24 [-0.29 -0.19]	-0.13 [-0.17 -0.081]		-0.17 [-0.30 -0.042]
5 or more	-0.41 [-0.54 -0.28]	-0.30 [-0.42 -0.17]	-0.17 [-0.30 -0.042]	

The effect sizes are fairly sizeable given the crude test employed here (estimated reliability 0.65). The effect size for the actual fertility (0 vs. 1+) is d = -0.39. In terms of correlations, the Pearson correlations are -.08 and -.16 (for desired and realized). However, due to the non-normal nature of the data, these correlations are biased downwards. The latent correlations (biserial; (Uebersax, 2015)) are -.09 and -.22 (computed using psych package's *mixedCor()* function; (Revelle, 2020)). Even if we subset to subjects aged 35 or more (n = 8,321), the correlations do not change much: -.07 and -.22. The latent correlation between desired and actual fertility was fairly weak as in prior studies: Pearson r = .15, latent r = .22, and latent r among those aged 35 or more .28.

Finally, we sought to examine whether the differences were due to obvious demographic confounders, such as age, race, and sex. To examine this, we fit 3 ordinal logistic regression models to each outcome with these predictors, as well as the interaction of sex and intelligence. The models were fit using the rms package's *lrm()* function (Harrell,

2019). Table 2 shows the results for desired fertility. The appendix contains the results for actual fertility, which was of less interest here.

Table 2. Regression model results for desired fertility. Base groups are Whites for race, and men for sex. Non-linearity was modelled using natural splines. Values in parentheses are standard errors and p values.

Predictor / Model	Basic	Controls	With interaction
Intelligence	-0.1478 (0.0146; <0.0001)	-0.1392 (0.0153, <0.0001)	-0.141 (0.0174, <0.0001)
race=Mixed		0.2608 (0.0552, <0.0001)	-0.4255 (0.7751, 0.583)
race=Asian		0.3863 (0.0814, <0.0001)	0.2608 (0.0552, <0.0001)
race=Hispanic / Latin		0.4481 (0.0852, <0.0001)	0.3863 (0.0814, <0.0001)
race=Black		0.4817 (0.0873, <0.0001)	0.448 (0.0852, <0.0001)
race=Other		0.1669 (0.1078, 0.1218)	0.4818 (0.0873, <0.0001)
race=Indian		0.0844 (0.1677, 0.6149)	0.1665 (0.1078, 0.1225)
race=Middle Eastern		0.5533 (0.3025, 0.0674)	0.0841 (0.1677, 0.6158)
race=Native American		0.3164 (0.3223, 0.3264)	0.5523 (0.3025, 0.0679)
race=Pacific Islander		0.6169 (0.4374, 0.1584)	0.3153 (0.3224, 0.3281)
sex=Woman		-0.4243 (0.775, 0.5841)	0.6162 (0.4374, 0.1589)
sex * intelligence			0.0075 (0.0359, 0.8353)
Age		(nonlinear)	(nonlinear)
sex * age		(nonlinear)	(nonlinear)
Pseudo-R2	0.007	0.034	0.034
N	16730	15859	15859

Since the model summary is difficult to intuitively understand when an ordinal outcome, nonlinear terms, and interactions are used, we plotted the predicted values from the model using the mean/modal

values for the non-varying variables (marginal effects). Figure 4 shows
the results.

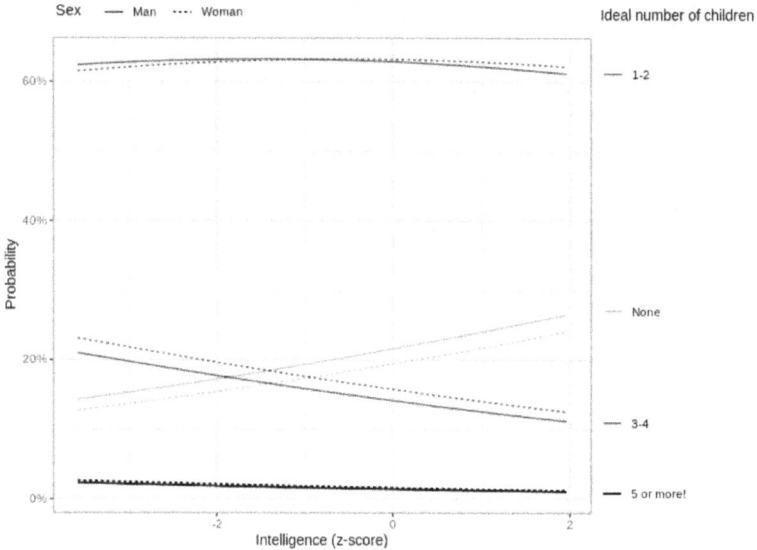

Figure 4. Model predicted ideal number of children by predictor values.

Here we can see that it is mainly the difference between the "3-4" and
"None" group that changes with intelligence. There is no substantial
change predicted for the "1-2" group. Of interest also is the distribution of the ideal number of children by race, controlling for the measured covariates. Figure 5 shows this.

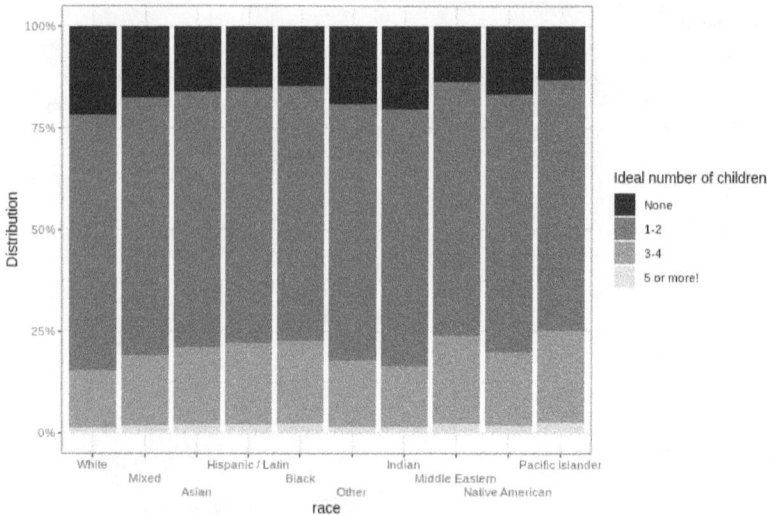

Figure 5. Model predicted ideal number of children
by race holding covariates constant.

The largest differences appear to be due to differences in the size of the "None" group, which is largest for Whites and Indians, and smallest for Middle Easterners and Pacific Islanders (but very sample size for that group). There are concomitant differences in the "3-4" groups.

Discussion

All of the associations with intelligence would be considerably stronger if we had a higher quality measure of intelligence. Estimated reliability was only .65, though this is likely an underestimate of the test-rest reliability. Nevertheless, we can cautiously assert that intelligence is negatively associated with desiring children in the OKCupid sample. Unlike the NLSY-based study, we find that this relationship exists and we find that it is much stronger than that unearthed by Kanazawa (2014) employing a British study.

In making sense of our results, it is worth noting that this does not appear to be the first time in history that intelligence has been negatively associated with having or wanting children. By the 2nd century BC, Greek writers were noting that upper-class men did not desire to have children and tended not to have many of them. By the time of Christ, Roman commentators were observing that upper-class males and females both did not desire children and, relative to members of lower classes, did not have many of them (Dutton & Woodley of Menie, 2018). And there are further parallels. Currently, there are assorted anti-natalist social movements such as 'Birth Strike' (Hunt, 12th March 2019) who aver that we should reject procreation in order to save the planet from the terrible damage done to it by humanity. In the first century AD, many Gnostic movements averred that the world was the Devil's province and that you should focus on achieving supreme knowledge, while certainly avoiding bringing children into this Satanic world (see Gottfried, 2004). Both of these periods in history were marked by 'individualizing moral foundations.' Graham et al. (2009) have argued that humans differ on approximately 5 sets of moral foundations, reflecting the fact that we are group animals but we also desire to attain status within the group. There are the 'Binding Foundations' of in-group loyalty, obedience to authority and concern for sanctity/disgust and there are the individualizing foundations of 'equality' and 'harm avoidance'. Individuals who lack power will covertly play for status by signalling these foundations (Benenson, 2013). Graham et al. (2009) further show that we roughly divide between 'conservatives' and 'liberals', though there is much nuance in between. Overall, conservatives are about the same on all five foundations, whereas liberals are very high on the individualizing foundations but are very low on the binding foundations. The result is asymmetric empathy between conservatives and liberals. This permits liberals to hijack the culture and push it in an ever-more individualistic direction, where people play for status by signalling ever more individualistic values.

In a situation of runaway individualism, this could evolve into bettering the last individualist by saying that you so committed to harm avoidance, in this evil world, that you won't have children. For the reasons already discussed, we would expect those who were intelligent to more strongly embrace and then compete for status within the dominant set of values, helping to explain, in part, the negative relationship between intelligence and fertility. The difference between the American and British data from the same cohort may reflect the fact that America, possibly for partly genetic reasons based on its having been partly founded by Puritans, is more religious and thus more group-oriented (Graham et al., 2009) than is Britain (see Dutton, 2014), meaning it took longer in the US for runaway individualism to get to the point of anti-natalist attitudes. It should be noted, in this regard, that the heritability of fundamentalism has been found to be close to 0.7 (Bradshaw & Ellison, 2008). Under harsh Darwinian conditions, this runaway individualism would be halted by the fact that such a group would be low in group-orientation and it has been demonstrated using computer-modelling that groups that are the highest in positive and negative ethnocentrism — that is binding values — tend to dominate and displace other groups (e.g. Hammond & Axelrod, 2006). However, in a period of weakened selection pressure, such as our low child mortality world or the Roman Warm Period with its concomitant urbanization and relatively high levels of development and of living standards, then this runaway individualism could take place (see Dutton, 2021; Sarraf et al., 2019) and it is even more extreme in our civilization than in Roman civilization.

A second, and related, possibility, proposed by Dutton and van der Linden (2017), is that intelligence is associated with being less 'instinctive' and more environmentally sensitive. They argue that this is because solving-problems involves rising above, and suppressing, instinctive reactions in order to be able to calmly reason. They maintain that it follows that you would be better able to accomplish this if you were attracted to non-instinctive possibilities, as these may be where new knowledge and a more subtle understanding of reality — and so the solving of your problem — lie. They argue that this may explain why intelligence appears to be associated with various non-instinctive, or evolutionarily novel, preferences, such as being nocturnal and even with atheism. Congruous with an intelligence-sensitivity nexus, some studies have found that people with high IQ are more environmentally plastic. For example, in a sample from 11,000 twin pairs: 'individuals with high IQ show high environmental influence on IQ into adolescence (resembling younger children), whereas individuals with low IQ show high heritability of IQ in adolescence (resembling adults), a pattern consistent with an extended sensitive period for intellectual development in more-intelligent individuals' (Brant et al., 2013). This, in turn, would mean that, in order to develop adaptively, intelligent people would be more reliant on being placed, by their group, on an evolutionarily adaptive road map of life and, in an evolutionary mismatch, they would be more likely to suffer from dysphoria due to their environmentally sensitive nature. In that we are evolved to be pack animals, a highly individualistic society would be an example of a dysphoria-inducing evolutionary mismatch.

In this regard it has been shown that there is a relationship between Machiavellianism and liberal values, possibly because, as discussed, liberal values are individualistic (Ok et al., 2020). Anti-natalism, like extreme liberalism more generally, has been found to be associated with Machiavellianism and also with suffering from depression. Indeed, depression mediates (causes) the relationship between anti-natalism and Machiavellianism (Schönegger, 2021). So it may be that, in a pronounced evolutionary mismatch, intelligent people — being more environmentally sensitive — are more likely to become depressed and thus to not want children. This would be a fascinating possibility for future research. One problem with this explanation is that Northern European countries (which are generally rated as the most individualistic) currently have higher fertility than Southern and Eastern European countries (ESHRE Capri Workshop Group, 2010; Davis & Williamson, 2009). A possible explanation for this anomaly may be that not only have these countries lost their religiousness in recent decades — leading to an evolutionary mismatch — but they are relatively poor and cannot fund a lavish welfare system. Welfare-recipient females are the engine of fertility — only families where both parents are on welfare have above replacement fertility, specifically those requiring social-worker and police interventions — and these females have been shown to increase their fertility in response to increased welfare payments. In addition, the fertility of many northern European countries is substantially driven by immigrants (Perkins, 2016).

It is also noteworthy that we do not find any sex differences in the relationship between fertility intentions and intelligence. This is despite the fact that, as we have discussed, dysgenic fertility on intelligence is higher among females than among males. There are a number of possible explanations for this. It may be that the pressures on intelligent females to delay child-bearing, such as through lengthy education and pursuing a career, mean that many end up, without truly wishing to, trading fertility for education and careers. This would be congruous with evidence that intelligence correlates with absorbing and convincing yourself, through effortful control, of the veracity of the dominant ideology, in order to attain the relevant social benefits, as already discussed (Woodley of Menie & Dunkel, 2015). It has been found that females are more socially conformist than males (Eagly & Chrvala, 1986) and, manifestly, their fertility period is more limited. A related explanation is that proposed by Apostolou (2014) who has argued that females are strongly adapted to patriarchy (male control of females, especially of their sexuality), as those who were not were historically selected out, unable to find a partner. Accordingly, females are adapted, to a greater extent than males, to a situation in which choices are made for them, usually by their parents, and particularly by their fathers. Left to their own devices, they are, accordingly, more likely to make choices that are more maladaptive. In this regard, it has been found that societal individualism is correlated with gender equality (Davis & Williamson, 2009).

Supplementary Materials

The data are available in the supplementary materials of the original study (Kirkegaard & Bjerrekær, 2016). The full code and other materials are available at https://osf.io/tw7cf/. The R notebook can also be found at https://rpubs.com/EmilOWK/716454.

References

Al-Shahomee, A. A. & Lynn, R. (2018). Intelligence and Family Size in Libya. *Mankind Quarterly*, 59: 2.

Apostolou, M. (2014). *Sexual Selection Under Parental Choice: The Evolution of Human Mating Behaviour*. Hove: Psychology Press.

Barclay, K. & Kolk, M. (2020). The Influence of Health in Early Adulthood on Male Fertility. *Population and Development Review, 46:* 757-785.

Benenson, J.F. (2013). The development of human female competition: allies and adversaries. *Philosophical Transactions of the Royal Society B,* 368: 2013007920130079

Bjerkedal, T., Kristensen, P., Skjeret, G.A. & Brevik, J.I. (2007). Intelligence test scores and birth order among young Norwegian men (conscripts) analyzed within and between families. *Intelligence, 35:* 503-514.

Bradshaw, M. & C. Ellison. (2008). Do genetic factors influence religious life? Findings from a behavior genetic analysis of twin siblings. *Journal for the Scientific Study of Religion,* 47: 529-544.

Brant, A., Munakata, Y., Boomsma, D. et al. (2013). The nature and nurture of high IQ: an extended sensitive period for intellectual development. *Psychological Science, 24:* 1487-1495.

Clark, G. (2007). *A Farewell to Alms: A Brief Economic History of the World.* Princeton, NJ: Princeton University Press.

Davis, L. & Williamson, C. (2009). Does individualism promote gender equality? *World Development,* 123: 10467.

Dutton, E. (2014). *Religion and Intelligence: An Evolutionary Analysis.* London: Ulster Institute for Social Research.

Dutton, E. (2021). *Witches, Feminism, and the Fall of the West.* Whitefish, MT: Washington Summit.

Dutton, E. & Woodley of Menie, M. A. (2018). *At Our Wits' End: Why We're Becoming Less Intelligent and What It Means for the Future.* Exeter: Imprint Academic.

Dutton, E. & Van der Linden, D. (2017). Why is Intelligence Negatively Associated with Religiousness? *Evolutionary Psychological Science,* 3: 392-403.

Eagly, A. & Chrvala, C. (1986). Sex Differences in Conformity: Status and Gender Role Interpretations. *Psychology of Women Quarterly,* 10: 203-220.

ESHRE Capri Workshop Group. (2010). Europe the continent with the lowest fertility. *Human Reproduction Update,* 16: 590-602.

Galton, F. (1869). *Hereditary Genius: Its Laws and Consequences.* London: Macmillan and Company.

Gottfried, P. (2004). *Multiculturalism and the Politics of Guilt: Towards a Secular Theocracy.* Columbia, MO: University of Missouri Press.

Graham, J., Haidt, J. & Nosek, B. (2009). Liberals and Conservatives Rely on Different Sets of Moral Foundations. *Personality Processes and Individual Differences,* 96: 1029-1046.

Hammond, R. & Axelrod, R. (2006). The Evolution of Ethnocentric Behavior. *Journal of Conflict Resolution,* 50: 1-11.

Harrell, F. E. (2019). *rms: Regression Modeling Strategies* (5.1-3.1) [Computer software]. https://CRAN.R-project.org/package=rms

Hunt, E. (12th March 2019). Birth strikers: meet the women who refuse to have children until climate change ends. *The Guardian, https://www.theguardian. com/lifeandstyle/2019/mar/12/birthstrikers-meet-the-women-who-refuse-to-have-children-until-climate-change-ends*

Hur, Y.-M. (2003). Assortative Mating for Personality Traits, Educational Level, Religious Affiliation, Height, Weight, and Body Mass Index in Parents of a Korean Twin Sample. *Twin Research and Human Genetics, 6: 467-470.*

Jensen, A. R. (2002). Galton's Legacy to Research on Intelligence. *Journal of Biosocial Science,* 34: 145-172.

Kanazawa, S. (2014). Intelligence and Childlessness. *Social Science Research,* 48: 157-170.

Kirkegaard, E. O. W. (2018). Self-reported criminal and anti-social behavior on a dating site: The importance of cognitive ability. *Open Differential Psychology,* 1(1). https://openpsych.net/paper/55

Kirkegaard, E. O. W. (2021). Are there Complex Assortative Mating Patterns for Humans? Analysis of 340 Spanish Couples. *Mankind Quarterly,* 61: 578-598.

Kirkegaard, E. O. W. & Bjerrekær, J. D. (2016). The OKCupid dataset: A very large public dataset of dating site users. *Open Differential Psychology.* https://openpsych.net/paper/46

Kirkegaard, E. O. W. & Lasker, J. (2020). Intelligence and Religiosity among Dating Site Users. *Psych*, 2: 25-33.

Kolk, M. & Barclay, K. (2019). Cognitive ability and fertility among Swedish men born 1951–1967: Evidence from military conscription registers. *Proceedings of the Royal Society B: Biological Sciences, 286*(1902), 20190359. https://doi.org/10.1098/rspb.2019.0359

Kolk, M., & Barclay, K. (2021). Do income and marriage mediate the relationship between cognitive ability and fertility? Data from Swedish taxation and conscriptions registers for men born 1951–1967. *Intelligence, 84*: 101514.

Luo, S. (2017). Assortative mating and couple similarity: Patterns, mechanisms, and consequences. *Social and Personality Psychology Compass, 11*(8), e12337. https://doi.org/10.1111/spc3.12337

Lynn, R. (2011). *Dysgenics: Genetic Deterioration in Modern Populations.* London: Ulster Institute for Social Research.

Meisenberg, G. & Kaul, A. (2010). Effects of Sex, Race, Ethnicity and Marital Status on the Relationship between Intelligence and Fertility. *Mankind Quarterly, 50*: 151-187.

Meisenberg, G., Lawless, E., Lambert, E., & Newton, A. (2006). The Social Ecology of Intelligence on a Caribbean Island. *Mankind Quarterly, 46*: 395–433.

Nam, T. (2017). Who is dating and gaming online? Categorizing, profiling, and predicting online daters and gamers. *Computers in Human Behavior, 73*: 152-160.

Nyborg, H. (2012). The decay of Western civilization: Double relaxed Darwinian Selection. *Personality and Individual Differences, 53*: 118-125.

Ok, E., Qian, Y, Strejcek, B. & Aquino, K. (2020). Signaling Virtuous Victimhood as Indicators of Dark Triad Personalities. *Journal of Personality and Social Psychology,* https://doi.org/10.1037/pspp0000329

Perkins, A. (2016). *The Welfare Trait: How State Benefits Affect Personality.* Basingstoke: Palgrave Macmillan.

Reeve, C. L., Heeney, M. D., & Woodley of Menie, M. A. (2018). A systematic review of the state of literature relating parental general cognitive ability and number of offspring. *Personality and Individual Differences, 134*, 107–118. https://doi.org/10.1016/j.paid.2018.05.036

Revelle, W. (2020). *psych: Procedures for Psychological, Psychometric, and Personality Research* (1.9.12.31) [Computer software]. https://CRAN.R-project.org/package=psych

Sarraf, M. Woodley of Menie, M.A. & Feltham, C. (2019). *Modernity and Cultural Decline: A Biobehavioral Perspective.* Basingstoke: Palgrave Macmillan.

Schönegger, P. (2021). What's up with anti-natalists? An observational study on the relationship between dark triad personality traits and anti-natalist views. *Philosophical Psychology*, doi: 10.1080/09515089.2021.1946026

Uebersax, J. S. (2015). *Introduction to the Tetrachoric and Polychoric Correlation Coefficients*. http://john-uebersax.com/stat/tetra.htm

Woodley of Menie, M.A. & Dunkel, C. (2015). Beyond the Cultural Mediation Hypothesis: A reply to Dutton (2013). *Intelligence*, 49: 186-191.

Appendix

Model results for realized fertility.

Table S1. Regression model results for realized fertility. Base groups are Whites for race, and men for sex. Nonlinearity was modelled using natural splines. Values in parentheses are standard errors and p values.

Predictor / Model	Basic	Controls	With interaction
Intelligence	-0.3551 (0.0170, <0.0001)	-0.3589 (0.0193, <0.0001)	-0.3484 (0.0219, <0.0001)
race=Mixed		-0.0335 (0.0707, 0.6353)	-0.0328 (0.0707, 0.6423)
race=Asian		-1.1707 (0.1538, <0.0001)	-1.1714 (0.1539, <0.0001)
race=Hispanic / Latin		-0.0273 (0.1139, 0.8106)	-0.0268 (0.1139, 0.8140)
race=Black		0.2118 (0.1093, 0.0526)	0.2123 (0.1093, 0.0521)
race=Other		-0.0709 (0.1343, 0.5977)	-0.0684 (0.1343, 0.6103)
race=Indian		-1.1109 (0.3402, 0.0011)	-1.1102 (0.3401, 0.0011)
race=Middle Eastern		-0.8829 (0.4524, 0.0510)	-0.8778 (0.4523, 0.0523)
race=Native American		-0.5326 (0.4320, 0.2176)	-0.5250 (0.4319, 0.2241)
race=Pacific Islander		-0.8568 (0.6192, 0.1664)	-0.8502 (0.6189, 0.1695)
sex=Woman		3.4758 (1.8247, 0.0568)	3.4401 (1.8259, 0.0596)
sex * intelligence			-0.0462 (0.0457, 0.3124)
Age		(nonlinear)	(nonlinear)
sex * age		(nonlinear)	(nonlinear)
Pseudo-R2	0.038	0.245	0.245
N	17554	16637	16637

CHAPTER 8

SEX HORMONES AND GENERAL TRAIT COVARIANCE

LARS LARSEN

Abstract

THIS CHAPTER PROVIDES a brief introduction to how Helmuth Nyborg got interested in sex hormones in the first place and why they are relevant for psychologists. It outlines his model for sex hormone-related general traits in body, brain and behavior (the GTC Model), and it reports results from a study testing the General Trait Model on a large population of middle-aged American men. Finally, it discusses other relevant biochemical factors in human traits and addresses future research in the light of Nyborg's so-called Physicology program.

Introduction

No forces set to work by the genes are more powerful or more crucial than the hormones. They affect almost every function of the brain, not the least its conscious thoughts. The fact that the mind can be captured by its hormones is one of mankind's oldest stories, and one of the newest.

— McEwen & Schmeck, 1994

As this chapter is part of a Festschrift for Helmuth Nyborg at 85, I would like to start with a few words about him, both as a scientist and as a person, before I go on about sex hormones and traits.

A wise woman (perhaps Ellen Parr or Dorothy Parker) once said that the best cure for boredom is curiosity, but that there is no cure for curiosity.

If the above mentioned quote is true, and I think it is, Helmuth Nyborg could never have been bored in his entire scientific career, and he is certainly never boring to those who know him and, as I, have had the great fortune to work with him. He is, still at 85, too busy being curious about human nature to be bored. Besides being curious, he is also courageous, unconventional and scientifically ambitious beyond the borders of his original discipline, Psychology. His many expeditions outside his home university, Aarhus University, is a testament to this trait. Nyborg has been a visiting researcher at a number of very different world-leading research institutions, such as the Institute for Behavioral Genetics at Colorado University (USA), the Max-Planck-Institute of Behavioral Physiology in Seewiesen (Germany), the Department of Experimental Psychology, University of Oxford (England), the Kinsey Institute for Sex, Gender, and Reproduction, Indiana University (USA). the Department of Child Health and Development, University of London (England), the Harold and Margaret Milliken Hatch Laboratory of Neuroendocrinology, Rockefeller University (USA), the University of Washington, Seattle (USA), the Niels Bohr Institute, Copenhagen University (Denmark), the Santa Fe Institute, New Mexico (USA) and the University of California at Berkeley (USA).

On a more personal note, I would like to add that Helmuth is also a humorous, kind and generous man. If it were not for this wonderful combination of traits, both professional and personal, I would probably never have become a scientist myself. It is an honor to have been his student and currently his colleague and friend. As I am sure that Helmuth will find all of this a bit sentimental, I should probably get down to the task at hand.

Though Helmuth has covered a large number of scientific topics in his career, such as visuospatial perception, behavioral genetics, molecular biology of behavior, intelligence, personality and currently cognitive epidemiology, an interest in the biological and natural scientific basis of individual and group differences in traits has always been running through all this.

In my opinion, one of the most fascinating of these many topics is psychoneuroendocrinology. Particularly sex hormones play an important interactive role in shaping individual differences in bodily, psychological and behavioral traits. Individual differences in sex hormone levels are to a certain extent determined genetically and can affect both traits and the environment as it is being adjusted by man to fit his needs. On the other hand, the environment can also affect hormone levels, e.g. through stress, and hormones have the ability to turn genes on and off (McEwen, 2007). As noted by one of the world's most eminent endocrinologists, the late Bruce S. McEwen, sex hormones link nature and nurture (McEwen, 2007). Figure 1 illustrates the transactional nature of this intricate interplay.

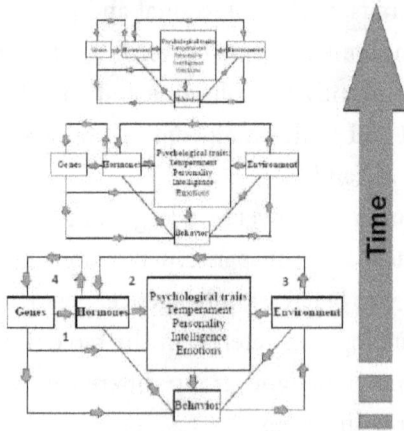

1. Genes to Hormones: At 8 weeks embryos with the single sex gene Y develop testicles. About fourteen weeks after conception, the male fetus begins to pour out adult amounts of testosterone. 2. Hormones to Traits: Hormones affect development of body and brain. 3. Environment to Hormones: Prolonged stress increases cortisol and depresses testosterone. 4. Hormones to Genes: Hormones can turn genes on and off.

Source: Adapted after Larsen, 2003, p.13.

Figure 1. Transactions between Sex Hormones, Genes, Traits and Context.

Early work led Helmuth Nyborg to study sex hormones

Early in his career, Nyborg became interested in studying the perception of the physically upright, guided by visual and tactile stimuli. He conducted a series of experiments in which visuo-spatio-proprioceptive (sense of balance) cues were brought into conflicts (Nyborg, 2021). These studies culminated in 1977 with a doctoral thesis about the so-called rod-and-frame test and the field dependence dimension. The thesis illustrated some of the ways in which humans typically solve experimentally created perceptual conflicts with reference to visuo-spatial and proprioceptive information (Nyborg, 1977). The thesis documented great individual variability and gender differences, and Nyborg wondered whether these differences were largely heritable in nature.

Several years, later Nyborg was contacted by Chief Physician and Head of the Cytogenetic Institute at the Psychiatric Hospital in Risskov, Johannes Nielsen. Given Nyborg's interests in visuo-spatial abilities and their heritability, Nielsen wanted to know if Nyborg would be interested in joining a research team studying girls who showed very poor mathematical ability, were visuo-spatially disoriented, and lacked some X chromosome material (Nyborg, 2021). Nyborg jumped at the chance and accepted the offer, but to the surprise of both Nielsen and Nyborg, the resulting studies did not reveal any clear links between specific chromosome anomalies and the well-defined cognitive deficits in these women with Turner's syndrome (Nyborg & Nielsen, 1977).

Psychoneuroendocrinology and the Vietnam Experience Study database

The studies mentioned above left Nyborg with a feeling that something had been left out of the analyses. Some years later, while working at Oxford University, it struck him that besides the sex chromosome anomalies, girls and women with Turner's syndrome also suffer from abnormally low levels of sex hormones, for which some of them were treated (Nyborg, 2021). This situation had not been in focus in connection with understanding the reason for their cognitive deficit. He therefore decided to investigate the possible effects of hormones on cognition. This newfound interest generated some very interesting work, culminating in the 1994 book *Hormones, Sex, and Society: The Science of Physiology*, which introduced not only a comprehensive account of a model of general trait covariance, the GTC Model, but also a daring new molecular theoretical framework named *Physicology* (Nyborg, 1994a).

In 1986, Nyborg founded the International Research Center for Psychoneuroendocrinology at the Department of Psychology at Aarhus University (Nyborg, 2021). Among other important research initiatives, he managed to get access to a large database from the so-called Vietnam Experience Study (VES) (Center for Disease Control, 1989). It came originally on 5 large magnetic EBCD tape wheels while Nyborg worked at Rockefeller University in New York. As the IT department encountered difficulties in reading the SAS libraries, Nyborg took the wheels with him to Denmark, where local experts transferred them to ordinary PC files. However, it then appeared that data of the thousands of variables were organized under a combination of letters and numbers, whereas the variable specifications were printed out separately on paper. It took Nyborg about three boring months to manually combine just the most important data in the VES study with their specifications for PC analyses, but today the data are being prepared for easy public access. The original purpose of this large scale and very comprehensive VES study was to determine possible health problems related to the herbicide *Agent Orange* during military service in Vietnam. The study thus compared veterans who served in Vietnam with veterans serving elsewhere at the same time on a long list of physical and psychological parameters. Weight, height, and testosterone levels were among the multiple physical measures. Among psychological measures were cognitive performance (e.g. the Armed Forces Qualification Test, AFQT, and WAIS subtests), personality (MMPI II) and psychopathology (Diagnostic Interview Schedule, DIS).

The original VES study did not find significant differences between those who served in Vietnam (N=2,490) and those who served elsewhere (N=1,972), and the two subgroups were comparable in terms of socioeconomic characteristics, age, enlistment status (volunteers and enlisted) and confinement time while in the army (Larsen, 2003). Hence it was feasible to collapse the two subgroups and end up with a sample of more than 4,000 middle-aged men representative of the general American male with data on testosterone levels, other physical measures and psychological test results. This was a unique opportunity to test the sex-hormone-related predictions of the GTC Model, which was one of the goals of the PhD project I began in 1995 as Nyborg's first PhD-student. After a brief introduction to the GTC-Model, I will next outline some of the main findings from that work (Larsen, 1999, 2003).

The General Trait Covariance Model: Basic Principles and Hormotyping

The main assumption of the GTC model is the principle of covariance, which Nyborg defined as follows:

"Sex hormones coordinate the timetables for the concerted appearance and disappearance of sex-related body-brain-behavior traits" (Nyborg, 1994a, p.107).

The covariance principle refers to the fact that sex hormones play an important role in the coordinated development and expression of sex-related traits. According to Nyborg (1994a), this principle is based on the fact that sex hormones act simultaneously and in an ordered, sequential cascade of processes on various tissues that can be widely separated in space and in such a way that the expression of sex-related body, brain and behavioral characteristics are harmonized.

A second important principle in the development of traits and abilities is the optimum range principle. According to this principle, sex hormones are often biologically most efficient with respect to the expression of a given trait when kept within a limited range of concentration (Nyborg, 1994a). The optimum range principle can be illustrated by the following example. Women with Turner's syndrome have typically extremely low levels of plasma estradiol, so they need controlled substitution therapy in order to develop properly. Most of these women do very poorly on tests requiring visuo-spatial ability. Nyborg and Nielsen (1981) demonstrated that it was possible to normalize the development of visuo-spatial abilities in Turner girls with one year of estradiol treatment (or with androgens). A later study (Nyborg et al., 1984) indicated that growth hormone had little effect on the cognitive abilities of Turner girls, whereas estradiol seemed to accelerate the development of specific cognitive abilities, so that after one year the subjects were on par with sister girls, acting as a control group. Two years of treatment with androgens brought them on par with control boys, but the ensuing one-year treatment with estradiol seemed to inhibit the previous superior spatial performance of the androgen-treated group. Assuming that the androgen treatment brought the Turner girls within the optimum range for full expression of spatial abilities, the principle predicts that further administration of estradiol would make the girls overshoot the optimum range, resulting in inhibition of the abilities.

Nyborg (1994a) hypothesizes that an entire covariant pattern of traits of body, personality and intelligence follows the optimum range principle. This implies that it should be possible to predict whole patterns of person characteristics rather than just simple correlations between a couple or more variables. The patterns can be translated into specific predictions about covariant traits related to the sex hormones estradiol and testosterone, respectively.

Hormotyping

Hormotyping takes advantage of the fact that males can be classified in accordance with their plasma androgen concentrations (testosterone) and females in accordance with their plasma estrogen concentrations (estradiol) and accordingly to their degree of sexual differentiation. The male hormotypes are rather logically called androtypes and the female counterparts are called estrotypes. As the following data to be reported is comprised of males only, I will focus on the androtypes.

Males are androtyped into one of five groups with androtype 1 (A1) representing males with very low androgen and a low degree of sexual differentiation and androtype 5 (A5) representing males with very high androgen and a high degree of sexual differentiation. Androtype 3 (A3) represents the average male individual.

About fourteen weeks after conception, the male fetus begins to pour out adult amounts of testosterone in a burst-like manner. Around birth, testosterone increases again, to drop after about two to

six months postnatally. It is believed that fetal and perinatal testosterone and its metabolites pre-masculinize the body and the brain of
the fetus (Nyborg, 1994a). Puberty is characterized by a steeply rising
testosterone level and this is the time when adult androtyping can be
made. However, there are important differences in hormonal development. Some males experience a relatively small and late testosterone
surge in puberty (A1s), whereas other males show a considerable and
early rise (A5s). Nyborg suggests that the A5s tend to decline more in
plasma concentration over the adult years than do the A1s, so that in
old age A5s may actually end up with as low, or lower, testosterone
levels than the A1s. This is important to remember, especially when
conducting longitudinal studies over very long periods of time, e.g.
lifespan studies.

Both male and female hormotypes follow the optimum range
principle and the optimal development for both biological genders
and are expected at the top of the range which corresponds to the
lowest hormotypes, A1 and E1 (see figure 2). In many ways, A1-males
and E1-females often resemble each other more than e.g. A1-males
and A5-males, as they have a more optimal balance between androgen
and estrogen (both males and females produce androgen and estrogen) and are the least sexually differentiated individuals. This opens a
whole new perspective on biological sex differences as they must now
be studied as something that does not only exist between the sexes,
but also within them.

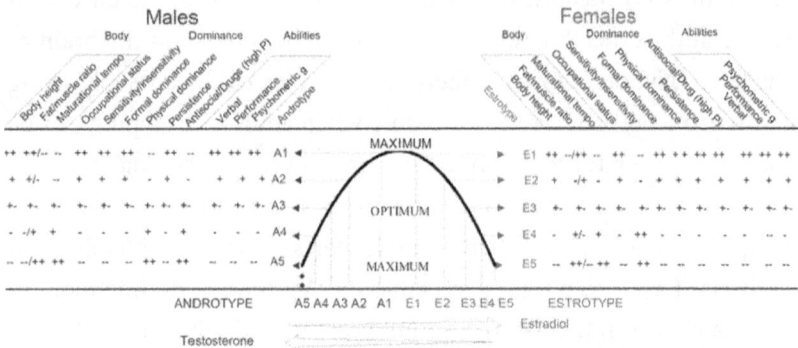

Figure 2. The GTC Model.
Source: Nyborg, 2013, p.268.

Male testosterone level can vary as a function of diurnal rhythm, season, age and experience (eg. drug use, defeat — see Larsen, 2003, chapter 7 for a brief account). Therefore, it becomes central to the validity and reliability of the GTC Model that hormone levels are relatively stable over longer periods of time despite the mentioned variations. Especially when testosterone levels are used in cross sectional studies, relying on a single measuring point in time, as is the case in the Vietnam Experience Study. Fortunately, several studies have demonstrated that testosterone levels are in fact relatively stable (see Larsen, 2003, chapter 8 for a brief account). Vermeulen and Verdonck (1992) have demonstrated this neatly, measuring a group of men over a period of 50 weeks. Eight samples of testosterone were collected during this period., and the correlation between the first samples and the mean testosterone levels over the whole period turned out to be .85 (see. Figure 3).

Male androgen levels are thus reasonably stable, and a single plasma testosterone sample is quite representative of the long-term testosterone level in human males.

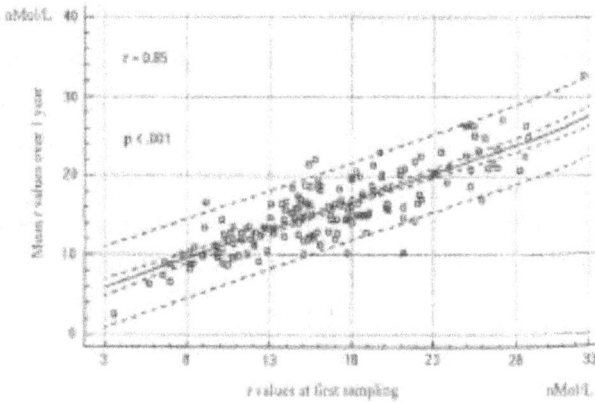

Figure 3. Linear correlation between *t* at first sample and mean annual *t*. Source: Vermeulen & Verdonck, 1992, p. 940.

Even though androtypes are fairly stable, changes occur over the course of life, and it is possible, even likely, that some individuals may move from a higher to a lower androtype as testosterone decreases with age in absolute terms, although not necessarily in relative terms.

Testing the GTC Model

When testing the GTC model on 4,251 middle-aged males from the Vietnam Experience Study (Larsen, 1999, 2003) in a cross sectional design, I used a narrow version of the model to predict that individuals high on testosterone will contrast individuals low on testosterone by being shorter, weighing less and having a lower BMI. They are further expected to demonstrate a high physical energy level, a masculine sexual identity, relatively lower cognitive ability, less education and to score higher on measures of mental instability, sociability and psychopathological tendencies, (Nyborg, Albeck & Larsen, 1997).

Based on the GTC model, the following specific hypotheses were made: height, weight and BMI were expected to be negatively related to testosterone, as were scores on MMPI-II Femininity scale (sexual differentiation), Spearman's *g* and amount of years spent on formal education. On the other hand, Eysenckian P, E and N personality traits and variables related to physical energy level, such as MMPII Hypomania, reflecting hyperactivity in thought and behavior, were expected to be positively related to high testosterone and so was MMPI II Psychopathic deviate, as the GTC model predicts elevated levels of aggression and antisocial tendencies in high testosterone males.

Subjects were categorized into 5 groups based on their testosterone level (androtypes), ranging from very low t (A1, mean 400 ng/dl) to very high t (A5, mean 993 ng/dl) and medium t (A3, mean 654 ng/dl).

BMI was calculated as weight in kilograms divided by height multiplied by itself (BMI=kg/m2)).

Gentry, Wakefield & Friedman (1985) and Nyborg (1994b) have shown that, by a suitable selection of items from MMPI, satisfactory measures of Eysenck's three personality dimensions (P, E and N) can be obtained. Eysenckian personality dimensions were extracted from MMPI II data as described by Nyborg (1994b). A general intelligence factor *g* was distilled from a large number of highly diverse cognitive variables (including scores from the Armed Forces Qualification Test and both verbal and performance subtests from Wechsler's Adult Intelligence Scale) by first principal component analysis.

Multivariate Analysis of Variance (MANOVA) was used to test the overall main effect model, as well as specific predictions. The five androtypes were entered as a grouping variable. The correlation ratios (the ratios of explained to total variations) were calculated in order to express relative power, or size, of the effects.

The MANOVA main effect was highly significant (Wilk's Lambda .87, Rao R (44,16) 14,2, p < 001). This is in accordance with the GTC Model and indicates that plasma testosterone may be used to predict the traits in question. Univariate results for each dependent variable (see table 1) show a significant effect for weight, BMI, P, E and N, MMPI II Hypomania, MMPI II Psychopathic deviate, Educational length and general intelligence. Results for height and MMPI II

Femininity Scale were not significant. Effect sizes were small, indicating that testosterone accounts for between 1 to 10 percent of the variation of the specific traits investigated. Effect sizes may have been weakened by the subjects being middle-aged men. Testosterone drops as a function of age, which could mean that I did not see the full effects of very high levels of testosterone. Kelsey and colleagues (2014) have shown that total testosterone peaks at 15.4 nmol/L, ranging from 7.2–31.1, at an average age of 19 years, and then drops in the average case to 13.0, ranging from 6.6 to 25.3 nmol/L by age 40 years. This is an almost 16% mean drop and an almost 19% drop in maximum testosterone levels from 19 years to 40 years of age. As the mean age of subjects in my analyses was around 38 years, this could have lowered effect sizes.

Body measures

Weight and Body Mass Index were significantly related to testosterone. Individuals with high testosterone concentrations (A5s) were on average 10 kilograms lighter than individuals with low testosterone concentrations and scored significantly lower on the BMI than their low testosterone counterparts (A1s). With respect to body measures, it had previously been found that weight and mass are good predictors of testosterone levels (Mantzoros and Georgiadis, 1995). Hence, it was to be expected that testosterone would also be a good predictor of body weight and mass. Studies of boys and girls during puberty demonstrate the remarkable effects of androgens on the developing human body. Boys show a larger growth spurt at puberty than girls and they continue to grow for quite a number of years after puberty under the influence of anabolic steroids (Nyborg, 1994a). However, the relationship between plasma hormone concentration and bone growth is curvilinear. Intermediate concentrations promote bone growth, where very large doses inhibit it. This means that boys on average turn out higher than girls, but that very high testosterone boys turn out lower than low testosterone males (according to the optimum range principle). Contrary to the hypothesis, height did not conform to the GTC predictions, as no significant testosterone-related differences in height were found. Though results were insignificant, height was, as predicted, negatively correlated with testosterone, but the relationship was weak. One possible explanation for the insignificant results could be that height is influenced by peripubertal testosterone levels rather than adult testosterone levels.

Psychological measures

With respect to Eysenckian personality dimensions, A5 subjects scored significantly higher than A1s on all three dimensions. In other words, they tend to be extraverted, mentally unstable and prone to psychopathology. In agreement with the elevated scores on Psychoticism, and the GTC prediction that A5 subjects have high energy level (not measured directly in the present analysis), they scored significantly higher than A1s on the MMPI II Hypomania scale and on MMPI II Psychopathic deviance, perhaps not surprisingly as Psychoticism, to some extent, covers the same pattern of traits. The latter results are in line with previous both observational (e.g. Dabbs, Jurkovic & Frady, 1991) and experimental (e.g. Dreher, Dunne, Pazderska, Frodl & O'Doherty, 2016) studies of the relationship between antisocial tendencies and testosterone.

Surprisingly, the MMPI Masculinity/Femininity Scale showed no testosterone-related differences. The reason for this result may be that most operationalizations of sexual identity, including the one used in MMPI II, are of questionable reliability and validity (Hoyenga & Hoyenga, 1979). The MMPI II M/F scale was removed in the following versions of MMPI as it turned out to measure a proneness to worry and general aesthetic interests rather than a feminine sexual identity (Graham, 1987). Moreover, there is quite a substantial amount of research suggesting that gender-specific behavior and testosterone are indeed related (Hoyenga & Hoyenga, 1993).

As hypothesized, A5 subjects scored significantly lower on general intelligence (approximately one fourth of a standard deviation). The relationship between intelligence and testosterone has previously been found in several studies (Grouchie & Kimura, 1990, Kirkpatrick, Campbell, Wharry & MacDonald, 1994, Netley, 1992, Tan, 1990, Tan, 1993). The relationship between testosterone and educational length is probably mediated by intelligence. Most likely, the amount of time spent on formal education is primarily controlled by whether or not a person has the intellectual potential for doing well in school (Herrnstein & Murray, 1994). Additionally, high levels of testosterone are related to high levels of energy and a tendency towards an unstable, extraverted and antisocial personality, which may very likely have affected the ability of high testosterone individuals to conform to a traditional educational environment.

The main result of the analysis outlined above was that even a single measure of plasma testosterone was sufficient to predict major aspects of the covariant pattern of traits outlined in the General Trait Model. As the effect sizes were small, a large sample is, most likely, required to pick up these covariant patterns, at least when predictions are based solely on a single hormone sample.

Coincidence, cause and effect

It must be noted that the results reported were correlational and that correlation is, as we very well know, not causation. That a single trait could covary with testosterone by chance is possible (for some of the traits, the statistical uncertainty is close to 5%), but that an entire predicted covariant pattern of traits should conform to a single measure of testosterone by coincidence is unlikely.

Structural equation analyses, applied on the VES data in a later study, support the assumption that testosterone has a causal effect on the covariant pattern of the GTC Model (Reuter, Netter, Hennig, Mohiyeddini & Nyborg, 2003).

Further, we know that testosterone varies as a function of age and though the subjects in the VES are all middle-aged males, there is some age variation (from the early thirties to the mid-forties). This makes it possible to investigate whether GTC predicted traits change in concert with changes in testosterone. If so, that would support GTC model assumptions about the causal role of sex hormones.

As can be seen in figure 4., this is exactly what I found. It is illustrated with the example of MMPI II Psychopathic Deviate Scale score (Larsen, 2003). The Psychopathic score nicely follows the decline of testosterone. Of course, it cannot be ruled out that some underlining common factor causes them both to change.

The only way to make sure that testosterone does actually cause the drop in the psychopathy score is to manipulate the testosterone levels experimentally to see if psychopathy follows. For obvious ethical reasons this is not possible. However, we do have a number of real-life scenarios were male testosterone levels have been raised deliberately for different reasons. Infertile males, for instance, have been treated with androgen-raising hormones (Gonadotropin hormone releasing factor) in order to improve their fertility. Hormonal treatment had the desired effect on fertility, but unfortunately also caused higher levels of aggression and domestic violence (Morris et al.,1984). Similar reactions have been found in bodybuilders who self-administer large amounts of steroid hormones, resulting in so-called "(Ste)roid rage" (National Institute of Drug Abuse, 2018). A recent study (Hauger et al., 2021) confirmed the link between anabolic androgenic steroid abuse, aggression and violence in a weightlifting population. Consistent with previous studies (Beaver et al., 2008, Pope and Katz, 1994, Kouri, Lukas, Pope & Oliva, 1995, Yates et al., 1992, Yesalis and Bahrke, 1995), high levels of aggression and violence were clearly more common among users than among non-exposed weightlifters. Dependents users of anabolic steroids reported significantly more problems with behavioral regulation and higher levels of antisocial personality traits (Hauger et al., 2021).

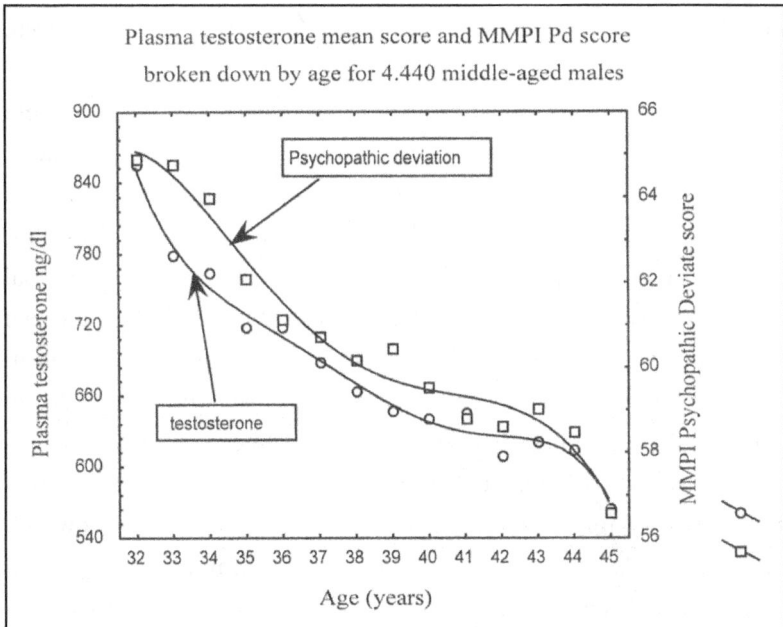

Figure 4. Plasma testosterone and Psychopathic deviance diminishing with age. Source: Larsen, 2003, p.128.

Other biochemical candidates

As effect sizes turned out to be relatively small in the test of the GTC Model, we obviously need to consider alternative, and perhaps complementary, biological candidates when we try to predict human traits.

A wide variety of biochemical agents, such as dopamine, serotonin, norepinephrine (Comings, 2000) glutamate, endorphins (Coyle & Konopaske, 2012), and glucocorticoids (Piazza and Le Moal, 1997), just to mention a few of the most promising candidates, have been linked to some of the various traits relevant to the GTC model, such as psychopathological tendencies, personality and intelligence.

Among other hormones, especially the adrenal hormone cortisol seems to be an interesting candidate. Glucocorticoids, cortisol in humans and corticosterone in rodents, is the final step of the activation of the hypothalamo-pituitary-adrenal (HPA) axis (McEwen, 2012).

These hormones have large effects in the periphery, where they modify metabolism and the activity of the immune system. Glucocorticoids also act at the level of the central nervous system and increased plasma glucocorticoid levels increase dopamine release, but the effect is state dependent (Piazza et al., 1996). Piazza and Le Moal (1997) have reviewed studies indicating that glucocorticoids are one of the substrates of reward. These adrenal hormones are secreted in response to rewarding stimuli, such as food, sex and drugs. Piazza and Le Moal propose that the rewarding effect of glucocorticoids play the role of counteracting the adverse effects of external aggression, allowing for better coping in threatening situations. However, glucocorticoids can also play a role in determining reward-related pathologies. A substantial increase in the functional activity of these adrenal hormones seems able to determine a state of predisposition to develop risk behaviors ranging from high-sensation seeking to drug abuse. Such pathological tendencies resemble the ones predicted and observed in high testosterone males. As the VES database actually has measures of cortisol levels, it was possible to repeat the analysis of the GTC model while controlling for cortisol difference. When doing so, I found minor variations in cortisol (ng/dl) for the five androtypes (A1: 18.02, A2: 18.12, A3: 18.24, A4: 17.90 and A5: 18.70), but despite these minor variations in cortisol levels, no significant changes occurred when I repeated the original analysis and introduced cortisol level as a covariant variable in a MANCOVA design (Larsen, 2003, p.100).

Dopamine seems to be another promising candidate. Psychotic tendencies, as measured by the Eysenckian personalty factor Psychoticism, has been linked to excessive dopamine functioning (Eysenck, 1997). Further, it has been hypothesized that schizophrenia is a result of a relative overstimulation of the dopaminergic system. Inhibition of the dopaminergic process has therefore turned out to be an efficient means of treatment (Li, Snyder & Vanover, 2016). Another hypothesis involves a possible disruption of the balance between dopamine and glutamate systems, as deficiencies or blockade of the glutaminergic systems bears functional similarities to over-stimulation of the dopaminergic systems (McCutcheon, Krystal & Howes, 2020).

Dopamine has also been associated with extraversion. It has been speculated that extraverts are characterized by increased dopaminergic activity. However, results of studies of this relationship are equivocal, but in view of the regulatory role played by dopaminergic activity in sensory input and response output (Le Moal & Simon, 1991), variation in dopaminergic activity may prove to be an important determinant in extraversion (Stelmack, 1997).

Also, central nervous system serotonin and concentration of endorphins in the cerebrospinal fluid have been associated with schizophrenia (Coyle & Konopaske, 2012).

Regarding mood disorders, the monoamine hypothesis has been dominating. It states that depression is caused by functional deficiency in catecholamines, particularly norepinephrine, whereas mania is caused by a functional excess of catecholamines at critical synapses in the brain. The amines dopamine and serotonin have also been linked to depression and mania. In healthy subjects, the personality dimension neuroticism and particularly its constituent trait, vulnerability, has been found positively associated with frontolimbic serotonin 2A binding (Frøkjær et al., 2008). The findings point to a neurobiological link between personality risk factors for affective disorder and the serotonergic transmitter system and identify the serotonin 2A receptor as a biomarker for vulnerability to affective disorder

Serotonin has been associated with intelligence. A study of CFS 5-HIAA turnover, which indirectly measures serotonin activity by measuring how quickly its metabolite is formed, concluded that autistic subjects may have decreased central serotonin activity (Cohen, Caparulo, Shawitz & Bowers, 1977) and autistic children are characterized by lower intelligence. Cook and colleagues (1990) concluded that whole blood serotonin and plasma norepinephrine were inversely correlated with verbal IQ in a sample of autistic children and their first-degree relatives.

Regarding aggression and antisocial tendencies, serotonin is also of interest. Brain serotonin levels are increased in times of stress and high arousal. This increase may act as a homeostatic mechanism, controlling activity and preventing long periods of hyperactivity in limbic system neurons (Hoyenga & Hoyenga, 1993). Besides, serotonin levels are found to be low in the brains of impulsively aggressive individuals (Virkkunen & Linnoilea, 1990). What is more, drugs that increase brain levels of serotonin tend to inhibit aggression (Eichelman, 1987).

It is possible that major parts of the covariant pattern of traits predicted by the narrow version of the GTC (high P, high E, high N and high levels of hypomania and psychopathy and low general intelligence) could also be related especially to a combination of overstimulation of the dopaminergic system and low levels of serotonin. It is therefore advisable to include other biochemical agents, especially dopamine and serotonin, into account in future studies, either considered as possible confounding factors or perhaps even as part of an expanded General Trait Covariance Model, operating with a covariant pattern of biochemical agents that predicts covariant patterns of traits.

When Molecules Move in Complex Systems: Beyond the GTC Model

An even more radical solution, proposed by Nyborg himself (1994a, 1998, 2007), would be to explain human traits and behavior on a purely molecular level and thereby dissolve psychology, and other scientific disciplines for that matter, into mere physics. Then we would avoid operating with distinctions between body, mind and behavior. In the science of Physicology, an all bottom analysis of non-hierarchical, non-linear, dynamic cause and effect in molecules is suggested to explain human nature in a causally coherent model in terms of intra-, inter- and extrasystemic molecular interaction. In other words:

when something happens, molecules move. According to Nyborg, "physiology is a general research program for the evolutionary and ontogenetic analyses of all complex systems in constant exchange with each other and with other environmental factors. Carbon-based systems, like humans… are the prime target, but other complex organic or non-organic systems are equally open for physicological analysis" (Nyborg, 1998, p.5).

Physiology is based on two theoretical assumptions. First, molecules show differential stereotaxic affinity (differences in "mutual attraction") and second, behavior reflects changes in the distribution of energy. All organisms ("living" molecular structures) compete for available energy and the ones who have the most efficient energy flow transformation will prevail. Return on energy (ROE), as Yun and colleagues have coined it, is defined as a ratio of the amount of energy acquired and assimilated by a system per amount of energy consumed to generate that gain (Yun, Lee, Doux & Conley, 2006). Just as is the case with the optimum range of sex hormones, there is an optimum range for energy use in all living organisms. Organisms that can attain energy with the least effort and spend the least energy when performing tasks relevant for survival or reproduction will be the most efficient. In terms of individual variations, in what we presently refer to as psychological performance in humans, one would therefore expect individuals with superior cognitive functions to have more energy-efficient brains. In accordance with this assumption, the neural efficiency hypothesis of intelligence suggests a more efficient use of the cortex in brighter as compared to less bright individuals. PET studies have revealed that highly intelligent individuals need significantly lower brain metabolism to solve certain cognitive tasks than do less intelligent individuals (Neubauer & Fink, 2009). Their brains are simply more energy-efficient.

When resources get sparse, high efficiency is required for survival. This provides us with an interesting opportunity to study the energy efficiency argument. When radiation from the sun reaches the earth, it does not strike all areas of the planet at the same angle. It strikes directly near the equator, but more obliquely near the poles. Global variations in solar flux (concentrated sunlight being radiated within a specified area) creates higher or lower needs for efficient energy consumption. Hence, we should expect people living in natural surroundings with less sunlight (energy) to have evolved more energy-efficient brains and therefore also higher levels of cognitive ability. Nyborg is currently investigating this hypothesis and we will have to await the outcome to see exactly how close the relationship between natural solar energy and cognitive ability turns out to be.

With respect to non-hierarchical, non-linear, dynamic cause and effect, Physicology resembles so-called Dynamic System Theory, DST (Smith & Thelen, E., 1993), although DST does not specify level of analysis. DST has proven relevant when describing "the behavior" of complex, non-linear systems within a wide range of scientific disciplines, such as physics, chemistry and neuroscience (Smith & Thelen, E., 1993). The principles of dynamic complex systems are in fact being used to guide everyday psychotherapeutic work in a so-called feedback driven Dynamic System Approach (Schiepek, Eckert, Aas, Wallot & Wallot, 2015, Tschacher and Haken, 2019). Theoretically, this should be possible on every descriptive level, including the molecular. I imagine that Nyborg would probably express it something like this: psychotherapy is an example of molecular engineering that entails transference of energy from one organism, the therapist, to another, the client, whereby an intended rearrangement of the molecules of the client occurs.

As of yet, it is an open question whether it will be practically possible, and feasible, to conduct complex systems analyses at a molecular, or even lower energy flux, level. However, the idea of describing all aspects of human nature on the same basic level and averting the many different "higher" descriptive levels, as well as the classical Body-Mind Dichotomy, is intriguing.

In 1996, Hans J. Eysenck wrote a special review of Nyborgs book *Hormones, Sex and Society* (1994).

About the Physiology program, Eysenck wrote:

"...Nyborg's advocacy of just one single cause at the molecular level may turn out to be correct, in due course. But at the moment I doubt if we know anything like enough to make an informed choice. We should certainly push reductionist determinism to the limits of experimental expertise, but we are a long way from reducing all of human behaviour (including cognitions, emotions, motivation, etc.) to simple combinations of hormones, neurotransmitters, limbic systems, neurological structures, etc. Research into the connections between these and behaviour and mental states is vitally important, and most welcome for the high quality of Nyborg's own contribution, but it does not and cannot settle the philosophical problem."

Now, 25 years later, we definitely know a lot more, and Nyborg's Physiology program has received additional empirical support, but the jury is still out on whether or not it is possible to deal with all aspects of the complex dynamics of human behavior on a purely molecular or energetic level. Only time will tell.

References

Beaver, K. M., Vaughn, M. G., Delisi, M., & Wright, J. P. (2008). Anabolic-androgenic steroid use and involvement in violent behavior in a nationally representative sample of young adult males in the United States. *American Journal of Public Health, 98*(12), 2185–2187. https://doi.org/10.2105/AJPH.2008.137018.

Centers for Disease Control (1989). Health Status of Vietnam veterans. Atlanta, Georgia.

Cohen, D. J., Caparulo, B. K., Shaywitz, B. A., & Bowers, M. B., Jr (1977). Dopamine and serotonin metabolism in neuropsychiatrically disturbed children. CSF homovanillic acid and 5-hydroxyindoleacetic acid. *Archives of General Psychiatry, 34*(5), 545–550. https://doi.org/10.1001/archpsyc.1977.01770170055004.

Comings, D. E., Gade-Andavolu, R., Gonzalez, N., Wu, S., Muhleman, D., Blake, H., Mann, M. B., Dietz, G., Saucier, G., & MacMurray, J. P. (2000). A multivariate analysis of 59 candidate genes in personality traits: the temperament and character inventory. *Clinical Genetics, 58*(5), 375–385. https://doi.org/10.1034/j.1399-0004.2000.580508.x.

Cook, E. H., Jr, Leventhal, B. L., Heller, W., Metz, J., Wainwright, M., & Freedman, D. X. (1990). Autistic children and their first-degree relatives: relationships between serotonin and norepinephrine levels and intelligence. *The Journal of Meuropsychiatry and Clinical Neurosciences, 2*(3), 268–274. https://doi.org/10.1176/jnp.2.3.268.

Coyle, J. T. & Konopaske, G. (2012). The Neurochemistry of Schizophrenia. In Brady, S. T., Siegel, G. J., Wayne Albers, R. & Price, D. L. (eds.), *Basic Neurochemistry: Principles of Molecular, Cellular, and Medical Neurobiology (8th Edition)*. Academic Press, Elsevier.

Dabbs, J. M., Jurkovic, G. J., & Frady, R. L. (1991). Salivary testosterone and cortisol among late adolescent male offenders. *Journal of Abnormal Child Psychology, 19*(4), 469–478. https://doi.org/10.1007/BF00919089.

Dreher, J-C., Dunne, S., Pazderska, A., Frodl, T., Nolan, J. J, & O'Doherty, J. P. (2016). Testosterone causes both prosocial and antisocial status-enhancing behaviors in human males. *PNAS, 113*(41), 11633-11638. https://doi.org/10.1073/pnas.1608085113.

Eichelman, B. (1987). Neurochemical bases of aggressive behavior. *Psychiatric Annals, 17*(6), 371–374. https://doi.org/10.3928/0048-5713-19870601-07.

Eysenck, H. J. (1996). Special Review. Hormones, sex and society: The science of physiology: Helmuth Nyborg. Westport, CT.: Praeger (1994). Hardback. pp. 1–207. *Personality and Individual Differences, 21*(4), 631-632. https://doi.org/10.1016/0191-8869(96)84411-4.

Eysenck, S. B. G. (1997). Psychoticism as a dimension of personality. In Nyborg, H. (ed.), *The Scientific Study of Human Nature — Tribute to Hans J. Eysenck at Eighty* (pp. 109-121). New York: Elsevier Science Ltd.

Frokjaer, V. G., Mortensen, E. L., Nielsen, F. Å., Haugbol, S., Pinborg, L. H., Adams, K. H., . . . Knudsen, G. M. (2008). Frontolimbic serotonin 2A receptor binding in healthy subjects is associated with personality risk factors for affective disorder. *Biological Psychiatry, 63*(6), 569-576. http://dx.doi.org/10.1016/j.biopsych.2007.07.009.

Gentry, T. A., Wakefield, J. A., & Friedman, A. F. (1985). MMPI Scales for measuring Eysenck's personality factors. *Journal of Personality Assessment, 49*(2), 146–149. https://doi.org/10.1207/s15327752jpa4902_7.

Graham, J. R. (1987). *The MMPI — A Practical Guide (2nd Edition)*. New York: Oxford University Press.

Grouchie, C. & Kimura, D. (1990). The relationship between testosterone levels and cognitive ability patterns. *Psychoneuroendocrinology, 16,* 323-334. https://doi. org/10.1016/0306-4530(91)90018-O.

Hauger, L. E., Havnes, I. A., Jørstad, M. L., & Bjørnebekk, A. (2021). Anabolic androgenic steroids, antisocial personality traits, aggression and violence. *Drug and Alcohol Dependence, 221*(8). doi: http://dx.doi.org/10.1016/j. drugalcdep.2021.108604.

Herrnstein, R. J., & Murray, C. A. (1996). *The Bell Curve: Intelligence and Class Structure in American Life.* New York: Simon & Schuster.

Hoyenga, K. B. & Hoyenga, K. T. (1979). *The Question of Sex Differences: Psychological, Cultural and Biological Issues.* Boston: Little, Brown and Company.

Hoyenga, K. B. & Hoyenga, K. T. (1993). *Gender-Related Differences — Origins and Outcomes.* Massachusetts: Allen and Bacon.

Kelsey, T. W., Li, L. Q., Mitchell, R. T., Whelan, A., Anderson, R. A., & Wallace, W. H. (2014). A validated age-related normative model for male total testosterone shows increasing variance but no decline after age 40 years. *PLoS One, 9*(10). doi: http://dx.doi.org/10.1371/journal.pone.0109346.

Kirkpatrick, S. W., Campbell, P. S., Wharry, R. E., & MacDonald, P. M. (1994). Performance on the Wechsler Intelligence Scale for Children as Related to Salivary Testosterone in Children with Learning Disabilities: A Poststudy Analysis. *Perceptual and Motor Skills, 79*(1), 577-578E. https://doi.org/10.2466/ pms.1994.79.1.577.

Kouri, E. M., Lukas, S. E., Pope, H. G., Jr, & Oliva, P. S. (1995). Increased aggressive responding in male volunteers following the administration of gradually increasing doses of testosterone cypionate. *Drug and Alcohol Dependence, 40*(1), 73–79. https://doi.org/10.1016/0376-8716(95)01192-7.

Larsen, L. (1999). *Testosterone as a Factor in Psychological and Behavioral Traits.* PhD-dissertation. Department of Psychology, Aarhus University.

Larsen, L. (2003). Testosterone as a factor in psychological and behavioral traits. *Psykologisk ph.d. skriftserie, 2*(1). (173 pp).

Le Moal, M., & Simon, H. (1991). Mesocorticolimbic dopaminergic network: functional and regulatory roles. *Physiological Reviews, 71*(1), 155-234. https://doi. org/10.1152/physrev.1991.71.1.155.

Li, P., Snyder, G. L., & Vanover, K. E. (2016). Dopamine Targeting Drugs for the Treatment of Schizophrenia: Past, Present and Future. *Current Topics in Medicinal Chemistry, 16*(29), 3385-3403. https://doi.org/10.2174/15680266166661 60608084834.

Mantzoros, C. S., & Georgiadis, E. I. (1995). Body mass and physical activity are important predictors of serum androgen concentrations in young healthy men. *Epidemiology (Cambridge, Mass.)*, *6*(4), 432-435. https://doi.org/10.1097/00001648-199507000-00020.

McCutcheon, R. A., Krystal, J. H., & Howes, O. D. (2020). Dopamine and glutamate in schizophrenia: biology, symptoms and treatment. *World Psychiatry*, *19*(1), 15-33. https://doi.org/10.1002/wps.20693.

McEwen, B. S., & Schmeck, H. M., Jr. (1994). *The Hostage Brain*. Rockefeller University Press.

McEwen, B. S. (2007). In Einstein G. (ed.), *Steroid hormones and the brain: Linking "nature" and "nurture"* Boston Review, Cambridge, MA. Retrieved from https://www.proquest.com/books/steroid-hormones-brain-linking-nature-nurture/docview/621884050/se-2?accountid=14468.

McEwen, B. (2012). Endocrine Effects on the Brain and their Relationship to Behavior. In Brady, S. T., Siegel, G. J., Wayne Albers, R. & Price, D. L. (eds.), *Basic Neurochemistry: Principles of Molecular, Cellular, and Medical Neurobiology (8th Edition)*. Academic Press, Elsevier.

Mantzoros, C. & Georgiadis, E. (1995). Physical activity and body mass are important predictors of serum androgen concentrations in young healthy men. *Epidemiology*, *6*, 432-402. DOI: 10.1097/00001648-199507000-00020.

Morris, D. V., Adeniyi-Jones, R., Wheeler, M., Sonksen, P., & Jacobs, H. S. (1984). The treatment of hypogonadotrophic hypogonadism in men by the pulsatile infusion of luteinising hormone-releasing hormone. *Clinical Endocrinology*, *21*(2), 189-200. https://doi.org/10.1111/j.1365-2265.1984.tb03459.x.

NIDA (2018). *Anabolic Steroids DrugFacts*. Retrieved from https://www.drugabuse.gov/publications/drugfacts/anabolic-steroids on November 25, 2021.

Netley, C. (1992). Time of pubertal onset, testosterone levels and intelligence in 47 XXY males. *Clinical Genetics*, *42*, 31-34. doi: 10.1111/j.1399-0004.1992.tb03132.x.

Neubauer, A. C., & Fink, A. (2009). Intelligence and neural efficiency: Measures of brain activation versus measures of functional connectivity in the brain. *Intelligence*, *37*(2), 223-229. DOI: 10.1016/j.intell.2008.10.008.

Nyborg, H., (1977). *The rod-and-frame test and the field dependence dimension: Some methodological, conceptual, and developmental considerations*. Copenhagen: Dansk Psykologisk Forlag (186 pp).

Nyborg, H. (1984) Performance and intelligence in hormonally different groups. In G. J. de Vries, J. P. C. de Bruin, H. B. M. Uylings & M. A. Corner (eds.) *Sex Differences in the Brain: The Relation between Structure and Function*. Progress in Brain Research, 61. Amsterdam: Elsevier Biomedical Press, p. 491-508.

Nyborg, H. (1994a). *Hormones, Sex, and Society: The Science of Physicology.* Westport, CT: Greenwood Publishing Group.

Nyborg, H. (1994b). *Extracting Eysenck's personality dimensions from clinical MMPI 1 and II data.* Unpublished manuscript.

Nyborg, H. (1998). Molecular man in a molecular world: Applied physicology. *Psyche & Logos, 18,* 457-474.

Nyborg, H. (2007). Intelligence, hormones, sex, brain size and biochemistry: It all needs to have equal causal standing before integration is possible. *Behavioral and Brain Sciences, 30,* 164-165. DOI:10.1017/S0140525X07001264.

Nyborg, H. (2013). Migratory selection for inversely related covariant T-, and IQ-Nexus traits: Testing the IQ/T-Geo-Climatic-Origin theory by the General Trait Covariance model. *Personality and Individual Differences, 55*(3), 267-272. DOI: https://doi.org/10.1016/j.paid.2012.06.006.

Nyborg, H. (2021). *Sex- and other hormones.* www.helmuthnyborg.dk. Retrieved on November 13th.

Nyborg, H., Albeck, H., & Larsen, L. (1997). *Covariant development of drug abuse, body, intelligence, personality and psychopathology as a function of testosterone: A life-time prevalence study of 4,429 androtyped males.* Abstract from College on Problem of Drug Dependence: Fifty-Eighth Annual Scientific Meeting, San Juan, Puerto Rico.

Nyborg, H. & Nielsen, J. (1977) Sex chromosome abnormalities and cognitive performance. III. Field dependence, frame dependence, and failing development of perceptual stability in girls with Turner's syndrome. *Journal of Psychology, 96,* 205-211. DOI: 10.1080/00223980.1977.9915903.

Nyborg, H. & Nielsen, J. (1981) Sex hormone treatment and spatial ability in women with Turner's syndrome. In W. Schmid & J. Nielsen (Eds.) *Human Behavior and Genetics.* Amsterdam: Elsevier/North-Holland Biomedical Press, p. 167-182.

Piazza, P. V., Deroche V., Deminiere, J. M., Maccari, S., Le Moal, M. & Simon, H. (1993). Corticosterone in the range of stress-induced levels possesses reinforcing properties: implications for sensation-seeking behaviors. *Proc Natl Acad Sci USA 90:* 11738–11742. doi: 10.1073/pnas.90.24.11738.

Piazza, P. V., Le Moal, M. (1997). Glucocorticoids as a biological substrate of reward: physiological and pathophysiological implications. *Brain Research Review, 25,* 359–372. https://doi.org/10.1016/S0165-0173(97)00025-8.

Pope, H. G. & Katz, D. L. (1994). Psychiatric and Medical Effects of Anabolic-Androgenic Steroid Use: A Controlled Study of 160 Athletes. *Archives of General Psychiatry, 51*(5), 375-382. doi:10.1001/archpsyc.1994.03950050035004.

Reuter, M., Netter, P., Hennig, J., Mohiyeddini, C., & Nyborg H. (2003). Test of Nyborg's General Trait Covariance (GTC) model for hormonally guided development by means of structural equation modelling. *European Journal of Personality, 17,* 221-235. https://doi.org/10.1002/per.475.

Schiepek, G., Eckert, H., Aas, B., Wallot, S. & Wallot, A. (2015). *Integrative Psychotherapy. A Feedback-Driven Dynamic Systems Approach.* Boston, MA: Hogrefe International Publishing.

Smith, L. B., & Thelen, E. (Eds.). (1993). *A DynamicSsystems Spproach to Sevelopment: Applications.* The MIT Press.

Stelmack, R. M. (1997). The psychophysics and psychophysiology of extraversion and arousal. In Nyborg, H. (Ed.), *The Scientific Study of Human Nature — Tribute to Hans J. Eysenck at Eighty* (pp. 388-403). New York: Elsevier Science Ltd.

Tan, Ü. (1990). Testosterone and nonverbal intelligence in right-handed men and women. International *Journal of Neuroscience, 54*(3-4), 277-282. https://doi.org/10.3109/00207459008986644.

Tan, (1993). Relationship among non-verbal intelligence, hand speed and serum testosterone level in left-handed male subjects. *International Journal of Neuroscience, 71,* 21-28. https://doi.org/10.3109/00207459309000588.

Tschacher, W., & Haken, H. (2019). *The Process of Psychotherapy Causation and Chance.* Springer International Publishing. https://doi.org/10.1007/978-3-030-12748-0.

Vermeulen, A., & Verdonck, G. (1992). Representativeness of a single point plasma testosterone level for the long-term hormonal milieu in men. *The Journal of Clinical Endocrinology and Metabolism, 74*(4), 939–942. https://doi.org/10.1210/jcem.74.4.1548361.

Virkkunen, M., & Linnoila, M. (1993). Brain serotonin, type II alcoholism and impulsive violence. *Journal of Studies on Alcohol. Supplement, 11,* 163-169. https://doi.org/10.15288/jsas.1993.s11.163.

Yates, W. R., Perry, P. & Murray, S. (1992). Aggression and hostility in anabolic steroid users. *Biological Psychiatry, 31*(12), 1232-1234. https://doi.org/10.1016/0006-3223(92)90344-Y.

Yesalis, C. E., & Bahrke, M. S. (1995). Anabolic-androgenic steroids. Current issues. *Sports Medicine (Auckland, N.Z.), 19*(5), 326-340. https://doi.org/10.2165/00007256-199519050-00003.

Yun, A. J., Lee, P. Y., Doux, J. D. & Conley, B. R. (2006). A general theory of evolution based on energy efficiency: its implications for diseases. *Medical Hypotheses, 66*(3), 664-670. https://doi.org/10.1016/j.mehy.2005.07.002.

CHAPTER 9

THE NEW ESTATE OF
SEX DIFFERENCES

GUY MADISON, PROFESSOR OF
PSYCHOLOGY AT UMEÅ UNIVERSITY

EXACTLY 50 YEARS AGO a small book was published in Denmark, concluding that "[w]e "know that the genes influence [behaviour] — but we do not know how, and only little about to what extent... We also know little, as yet, about the complex interaction between the genotype and environment of the individual...there is reason to expect explosive developments [in this area] in coming years...[and this will give a] significant contribution to understanding the background of human behaviour"[1] (Nyborg, 1972, 125). Prophetic as this turned out to be, it set off the jagged and sometimes bumpy

---

1   My translation of excerpts from "Vi står kortere sagt i den situation, at vi ved, at generne virker - men vi ved ikke hvordan, og vi kender kun lidt til i hvilken udstrækning de virker. Vi ved heller ikke meget endnu om den komplicerede interaktion mellem genotype og miljø hos den enkelte: netop her ligger psykogenetikkens kerneproblem. Løses det tilfredsstilende, vil et væsentligt bidrag til forståelse af baggrunden for human adfærd være givet. Og der er grund til at antage, at de nærmest kommende år vil vise eksplosiv udvikling indenfor det nyetablerede fag 'Psykogenetik', en udvikling der ikke indebærer en positivistisk genopvækkelse, men et supplement til et mangelfuldt beskrivelsesgrundlag for human adfærd."

career trajectory of an original and independent thinker, true to his cause and to his colours.

Understanding human behaviour is no joke. Our prehistoric survival depended on eliciting support during our development and avoiding getting expelled or killed. To these ends, we derive patterns from those close to us, and apply them to predicting the behaviour of strangers. It stands to reason that the more information we have at hand, the better predictions we can make. Thus, taking the understanding of human behaviour seriously means following the data, wherever they take us; even if they take us somewhere emotionally unpalatable. Another virtue is to bring research to bear on real-life problems, as most taxpayers would attest. Conversely, that means identifying relevant social issues, in the case of behavioural science, and addressing them impartially.

Throughout his career, Helmuth Nyborg has doggedly followed these two paths, at the cost of, ironically, getting him expelled from his university (see Lynn, in this volume, for a detailed description of these events, as well as Nyborg and Vig [2016]). It turns out that they led to questions and results that were too unpleasant to endure for some people. Genetic influences on psychological traits remains an unpopular notion in many camps, even with the massive empirical support it now enjoys, 50 years later (e.g., Bouchard & McGue, 2018; Polderman et al., 2015). And so does research on sex differences, the focus of the present chapter.

I will first briefly summarise Helmuth's work on sex differences, then discuss the most important contributions and how they relate to current research, and finally reflect upon his impact on the scientific community.

Some of this work relates to the rod-and-frame test, which was the focus of Helmuth's PhD thesis. He there devised a new scoring method that took different sources of the deviation error into account (Nyborg, 1977). This is the angular difference between the adjusted rod and the vertical plane, and is assumed to reflect "field dependence", in the sense of relying on the initial tilt of the rod and the tilt of the frame that surrounds the rod. Being "field independent" means accurately adjusting the rod to a vertical position, presumably relying on gravity acting through the vestibular and somatosensory systems.

Helmuth then studied groups of individuals with a range of different genetic deviations, with an eye to unravelling associations between particular genetic deviations and psychological traits, such as aggressiveness, assertiveness, cognitive abilities, and interests in people vs. things. A main conclusion was that little or no systematic associations were found between these traits and the genetic deviations per se but with the hormonal levels induced by them (Nyborg, 1984). The Turner syndrome constitutes partly or completely missing an X-chromosome, leading to lower oestrogen levels. Applying the new scoring method to girls with Turner syndrome showed that their poor performance compared to the control group was due to inconsistent responses rather than a bias induced by the tilt of the rod or frame (Nyborg, 1977, 74-89). Typically developing females tend to have lower spatial ability than males, and Turner syndrome females perform even worse on the rod-and-frame test. Assuming that this was a result of their lower oestrogen levels, Nyborg and Nielsen (1981) found that treatment with oestrogen replacement improved spatial ability to the level of their typically developed sisters. The nature of the differences between these groups was analysed in further detail (Nyborg, 1990).

The observations from both males and females with non-typical hormone levels were combined with a comprehensive review of the previous literature, leading to a formalisation of the idea that the development and adult levels of a range of psychological traits are influenced by oestrogens, specifically oestradiol (E2) (Nyborg, 1983). For example, maximal spatial and cognitive ability were proposed to rely on optimal levels of oestradiol, which leads to a complex set of sex-specific relations with both oestradiol and testosterone (Nyborg, 1983, 125-127). One prediction is that a male advantage in spatial ability should appear in puberty in typically developing children. This was indeed the case for 16-year olds, but not for 8, 10, 12 or 14- olds, on the rod-and-frame test (Nyborg, 1988a). Another prediction was that most females overshoot the optimum level of oestradiol in the brain for full expression of spatial ability, whereas most males under- shoot. It was argued that this explains why spatial ability is highest in androgynous males and in late maturing, androgynous females (first mentioned in Nyborg, 1988b).

These sets of ideas were further developed into the General Trait Covariance-Androgen/Oestrogen (GTC) model for development (see Lynn, and Larsen, this volume). Here, I will focus on its implications for sex differences. Recent versions feature ten "hormotypes" based on the level of testosterone in males and the level of oestradiol in females (Nyborg, 1994a; Nyborg, 1994b). Thus, females are classified as estro- types E1 through E5, where 1 is low, 3 is average, and 5 high levels of oestradiol, and males are likewise classified as androtypes A1 through A5. According to this model, average levels of androgen/oestrogen lead to average levels of general intelligence (Spearman's g), while optimum expression of g follows from intermediate plasma hormone levels in each sex, i.e. lower than average for females and higher than average for males. High hormone levels lead to reinforced secondary sexual differentiation of body and personality traits and different gene switching (Nyborg, 1997b). As mathematical ability implies both high intelligence and high spatial ability, the GTC model was suggested to make predictions about the hormonal, corporal, and psychologi- cal properties of mathematically eminent persons, as a result of their sexual development (Nyborg, 1988b).

A central point of the model is that "...hormonally guided body and brain development is better considered a continuous than as a categorical phenomenon" (Nyborg, 2003b, 216). This reminds us, of course, of the public debate about "gender fluidity" and the need for three or more "genders". People vary in their expression of femininity and masculinity, both physically and behaviourally, and there is in- deed a very small proportion whose sex may be difficult to categorize with their clothes on or even off. The "gender" approach attempts to account for this variation by rejecting the reality of biological sex, replacing it with a hypothetical continuous dimension of feminine-masculine performance. The GTC model is a much more sophisticated tool for explaining this variation, which does not in any way contradict the underlying biological facts. As mathematical ability implies both high intelligence and spatial ability, as already noted, the GTC model was suggested to make predictions about the hormonal, physical, and psychological properties of mathematically eminent persons, as a result of their sexual development (Nyborg, 1988b).

Recognizing the "massive male preponderance in high-level chess competition, musical composition, theoretical physics, economy and in the numerous other areas of demonstrated high-level male dominance" (Nyborg, 2003b, 215), Helmuth proposed the Very High End Male g Hypothesis. It simply acknowledges that if males have a small lead in g, the proportion of men to women will nevertheless be substantially higher at the highest levels of g. Indeed, "the importance of the observed sex difference in g is not to be found in the group mean. No sensible prediction can be made for any individual male or female by referring to a mean average difference of just 0.37 SD. However, a brief consultation of the characteristics of Gaussian distribution theory teaches us that even a moderate mean advantage in g will have a considerable effect on the male/female ratio of individuals with high or very high g" (Nyborg, 2003b, 212). How this modest mean difference combined with higher male variance would lead to startling male/female ratios for IQs higher than 1.5 SD above the mean is exemplified graphically (p. 214).

Quality criteria for assessing studies of sex differences in intelligence was another important contribution of this chapter, which was part of a book in honour of Arthur Jensen (Nyborg, 2003c). I find these criteria most relevant, because determining sex differences in intelligence entails particular problems: there are many specific cognitive abilities, and they are more or less representative of the construct or definition of intelligence one wants to address, and more or less easy for males and females. This means that the selection of test items can affect the sex difference, and this problem must be minimised by clearly defining which aspect of intelligence to examine. Another problem is that the difference is small, so one needs large statistical power to detect it. A third problem is that there is a range of potential confounding factors that may act through sex-selection or sex-instrument interactions, and this is particularly severe in the face of the small group difference. To deal with this, Helmuth proposed the following five principles: (1) a truly representative sample, (2) a proper operational definition of intelligence, (3) a multitude of tests that differ as much as possible in content, (4) aggregating item or subtest scores in an analytically appropriate and motivated fashion, well beyond simple summing, and (5) controlling for potential confounders.

Evaluating ten studies, Helmuth found that only two fulfilled these criteria — his own study that would be published two years later (Nyborg, 2005) and Colom et al. (2002). It is an interesting twist that, contrary to these authors' own conclusions, he found a highly significant male lead when applying a statistical test to the effect (Nyborg, 2003b, 208). Meticulously following his own criteria, Helmuth thus found a male advantage in *g*, applying hierarchical factors analysis with the Schmid–Leiman transformation to 20 sub-tests in a small but highly representative sample (Nyborg, 2005), and later replicated it in a larger sample (Nyborg, 2015). The magnitude of the difference was consistent with measured head circumference, used as a proxy for brain volume. Recent studies confirm the mediating effect of brain size on *g* (Ritchie et al., 2018; Cox, Ritchie, Fawns-Ritchie, Tucker-Drob, & Deary, 2019) and more specifically on sex differences in *g* (van der Linden, Dunkel, & Madison, 2017).

In my estimation, Helmuth's major contributions to the study of sex differences are fourfold. First, he took on the stupendous task to integrate biology and behaviour, as it were, under the rubric of physicology, using sexual differentiation as a model. His stated goal was to do away with the classical but counterproductive mentalistic and superorganismic ideas about human nature and society and to replace them with "the study of physicochemical processes behind body, brain, behaviour, and society" (Nyborg, 1994a, xx). Specifically, "[p]hysicology addresses the same phenomena as traditional behavioral sciences, but it substitutes all psychic, social, cultural, and superorganismic explanations with analyses of the underlying physico-chemical processes" (ibid.). This is a quite ambitious and bold endeavour, parts of which are meritoriously described by Larsen (this volume). The book goes into great depths of detail and suggests a gargantuan effort, as reflected by, for example, a 25-page bibliography with more than 400 references. It is my impression that this approach remains underused. To my knowledge, few of the predictions that can be derived from the General Trait Covariance model or the physicology research program more generally have yet been tested. Using data from male military veterans, Nyborg and Jensen (Nyborg & Jensen, 2000) found a depression of g only for extremely low and high t levels, rather than the expected curvilinear relationship. Relationships between body mass index, education, income, and two intelligence sub-scores from the WAIS was partly consistent with the model (Reuter, Netter, Hennig, Mohiyeddini, & Nyborg, 2003). None of these relate directly to sex differences, however.

Second, Helmuth has revitalised the association between intelligence and brain size, and the kittle but theoretically crucial connection between the sex difference in brain size and the sex difference in intelligence (Nyborg, 1994a; Nyborg, 1994b; Nyborg, 2003b; Nyborg, 2005; Nyborg, 2015; Nyborg, 2017). Thus, brain imaging studies have found that hemispheric asymmetry is stronger in males (Hirnstein, Hugdahl, & Hausmann, 2019), that g is correlated with total brain volume, structural patterns of these correlations, and that these correlations are invariant across the sexes (Cox et al., 2019). Also, males had higher white matter fractional anisotropy, greater variance across structural measures, and stronger connectivity in sensorimotor cortices, while females had higher raw cortical thickness, white matter tract complexity, and stronger connectivity in the default mode network (Ritchie et al., 2018), and the sex difference in g is actually mediated by individual differences in brain volume (van der Linden et al., 2017). Even more detailed functional connectivity analyses have found that intelligence of males and females is related to different brain structures, consistent with sex differences in spatial and verbal ability (Jiang et al., 2021).

Third, Helmuth has adamantly connected his and others' research on sex differences to real-life outcomes and their social consequences. A central goal for scientific inquiry is, after all, to solve real problems. This is surely an ideal, in particular when taxpayers' money is used. Inequality can be a serious problem, as it creates tension and resentment, in particular if its causes are interpreted as wrongful. We have seen a strong trend to increasingly attribute sex differences in outcomes to discrimination and other external causes since the Suffragette era, accelerating considerably in recent decades. This is counterintuitive in light of the concurrently increasing knowledge about biologically based sex differences. In addition to g, as reviewed above, substantial sex differences are found in cognitive tilt, consistent with differences in outcomes (Wai, Hodges, & Makel, 2018; Dekhtyar, Weber, Helgertz, & Herlitz, 2018; Coyle, 2020).This is also true for, e.g., interests (Lippa, 2010a), personality (Verweij, Mosing, Ullén, & Madison, 2016; Kaiser, Del Giudice, & Booth, 2019; Del Giudice, Booth, & Irwing, 2012), and occupational preferences (Lippa, 2010b). Both trait (Lippa, Collaer, & Peters, 2010; Asperholm, 2020) and outcome differences tend to increase with the level of gender equality and freedom of choice in society (Falk & Hermle, 2018; Stoet & Geary, 2020), which is known as the sexual paradox (Pinker, 2009), seeming to occur because females strongly follow their innate preferences — such as pursuing "caring" professions and family-career balance — in a situation where they have maximum freedom. The biological influence is supported by the fact that environmental causes predict the opposite relationship.

Variations over these points have repeatedly been made (Nyborg, 1988b; Nyborg, 2003b; Nyborg, 2003d; Nyborg, 2013b; Nyborg, 1972; Nyborg, 2005; Nyborg, 2015; Nyborg, 2017; Nyborg & Kirkegaard, 2021).

This has inspired meta-scientific inquiries as to methods and the scientific quality of disciplines, such as "gender studies", which exclusively consider environmental causes, such as "social structures", and ignore biological causes (Eagly & Riger, 2014; Eagly, 2018; Söderlund & Madison, 2015; Söderlund & Madison, 2017; Madison & Söderlund, 2018). Ironically, feminist activists tend to be more masculine than other women, both biologically, in terms of a lower 2nd-to-4th digit ratio, and behaviourally, in terms of so-called directiveness (Madison, Wallert, Aasa, & Woodley, 2014). This suggests that their representativeness to speak for the interests of typical women is questionable.

The goal to achieve more equal sex proportions in domains that are heavily dominated by one sex, such as nurses and veterinarians versus construction workers and computer programmers, may be laudable. For example, the social milieu tends to be less pleasant in single-sex workplaces. However, opposing biologically influenced tendencies may harm both sexes, and make both men and women less fulfilled. For example, 56% of both men and women indicated that they preferred to share the chores equally with their partner, consistent with the current norm, while their enjoyment of a wide array of activities revealed a consistent traditional sex-specific pattern regarding e.g. child care, cooking, cleaning, gardening, and decoration (Bleske-Rechek & Gunseor, 2021). Importantly, men did not enjoy a single child care task more than did women. Applying sex quotas, openly or covertly, logically entails a range of destructive consequences (Madison, 2017), and is typically motivated by transferring power and influence, rather than the alleged improved competence and productivity (Madison, 2019). It has also been found to actually increase the sex difference in competence amongst academic professors (Madison & Fahlman, 2020) and to decrease productivity (Yu & Madison, 2021).

Fourth, and perhaps most importantly, Helmuth stands out as an example for other academics. He has followed the data, maintained relevant and urgent research questions, and sought what is true and not what is expedient. Following the narrow path of genuine science has unfortunately brought his work into conflict with the current fashion regarding what is socially desirable. Similar experiences are being reported by more and more academics (e.g., Browne, 2018; Delhez, 2019; Del Giudice, 2021; Duarte et al., 2014; Eagly, 2018; Kaufman, 2019; Schmitt, 2017). The intellectual climate has certainly deteriorated across the five decades of Helmuth's academic career.

Still, Helmuth has persisted unfailingly, even in the face of acrimony, social exclusion, and outright threats to his work and livelihood. For example, "sex differences could, if substantiated, provide an objective explanation of the long history of male dominance in areas requiring raw intellectual power [such as] politics, warfare, chess, musical composition, mathematics, science, business, and other areas requiring intellectual brilliance. It could facilitate our understanding of why so few women get Nobel Prizes and ... it is paradoxical that many experts still support the idea of zero adult sex differences in intelligence, and tend to rather support any other explanation, such as learned helplessness, glass ceilings, and old boys networks" (Nyborg, 2017, 77). Whether mainly a function of intelligence, systematizing, or striving for social status, Nobel Prizes as well as scientific productivity were found to be associated with country-level androgen indices (Dutton, van der Linden, & Madison, 2020; van der Linden, Dutton, & Madison, 2020) (see also Furnham, this volume).

Another feat is to repeatedly raise awareness of scientific denial and dishonesty (e.g., Nyborg, 1997a; Nyborg, 2003d; Nyborg, 2003a; Nyborg, 2011; Nyborg, 2012; Nyborg, 2013a; Nyborg, 2017; Nyborg & Kirkegaard, 2021). Let me end by paraphrasing an op-ed in *Politiken*, a major Danish newspaper: "Traditional researchers allow themselves to be 'astounded', year after year, that women and men tend to prefer different educational and occupational paths, similar to those we have

followed for as long as we know. This follows from their conviction
that the distributions in interests and abilities within each sex are
exactly the same in both sexes. Shedding their ideological blinders
could have spared decades of futile rooting for socio-economic and
male chauvinist causes, at great economic and human cost, allowing an evolutionary biological explanation to resolve these apparent
mysteries."[2] (Nyborg & Kirkegaard, 2021).

In vernacular terms, this sums up both the general scientific findings, how they are thwarted, and how this wastes intellectual and material resources. It reproaches the totalitarian instinct to force people
to become the way that an elite has decided, by means of biased
information, quotas, and by reprimanding and firing dissenters. Odd
as it may seem to cite an op-ed in the context of reviewing a body of
scientific work, it casts a revealing light on the treatment of so-called
"controversial" topics, and on the students of such topics. It is chilling
that this is done with the full power of the state, against the scientific
evidence, but with the support of academic work that promotes the
narrative of "dominant, old, and grumpy misogynistic men who keep
women out of work and research communities". A tragic consequence
of ideological forces that nudge and pry individuals away from their

---

2 Freely paraphrased from: "Alligevel lader køns-, undervisnings-, og erhvervs-
forskere sig 'forbløffe' år efter år over at de dukker op eller stadig er her. De
anvender uanfægtet fortsat ineffektive socialkonstruktivistiske modeller, og
kræver opgør med skøre og hæmmende forestillinger. Hvad er der så galt med
kønsforskernes forståelsesmodel? Jo, de bruger en implicit todelt model: 1) Der
er en vis diversitet i interesser og evner inden for hvert køn og 2) Mænd og
kvinder har præcis samme fordeling af disse interesser og evner. Heraf følger,
at skævheder i uddannelsesoptag og på jobmarkedet skyldes, at 'samfundet
allokerer' mænd og kvinder suboptimalt og det er økonomisk ineffektivt og
således dyrt. - - - Vi må konkludere, at de traditionelle kønsforskeres todelte
lighedsmodel bryder sammen, i det øjeblik en evolutionær biologisk forklaring
opløser alle disse mysterier.
    Det er derfor tiden til at gøre op med feministernes og moderne kønsfor-
skeres udokumenterede 'Glasloft' og 'Rip-Rap-Rup' effekter og deres gentagne
klager over dominante gamle, sure kvindehadende mænd, der holder kvinder
ude af arbejds- og forskningsfællesskaber."

genuine, phenotypical preferences and interests is to arguably make them less fulfilled and probably less productive.

Thus, Helmuth's motion to "balance the more environmentally-oriented psychology by...reassessment of the [genetic] factors that contribute to adequate understanding of human behaviour"[3] (Nyborg, 1972, 10) was well supported and has been well acted upon. The circle is closed.

References

Asperholm, M. (2020). *Investigating and explaining sex differences in episodic memory.* Department of Clinical Neuroscience, Karolinska Institutet.

Bleske-Rechek, A. L. & Gunseor, M. M. (2021). Gendered perspectives on sharing the load: Men's and women's attitudes toward family roles and household and childcare tasks. *Evolutionary Behavioral Sciences.*

Bouchard, T. J. & McGue, M. (2018). Genetic and environmental influences on human psychological differences. *Journal of Neurobiology, 54,* 4-45.

Browne, K. R. (2018). The quixotic quest for "gender equality" in the workplace. *University of Toledo Law Review, 49,* 685-714.

Colom, R., Garcia, L. F., Juan-Espinoza, M., & Abad, F. (2002). Null sex differences in general intelligence: evidence from the WAIS-III. *Spanish Journal of Psychology, 5,* 29-35.

Cox, S. R., Ritchie, S. J., Fawns-Ritchie, C., Tucker-Drob, E. M., & Deary, I. J. (2019). Structural brain imaging correlates of general intelligence in UK Biobank. *Intelligence, 76,* 101376.

Coyle, T. R. (2020). Sex differences in tech tilt: Support for investment theories. *Intelligence, 80,* 101437.

Dekhtyar, S., Weber, D., Helgertz, J., & Herlitz, A. (2018). Sex differences in academic strengths contribute to gender segregation in education and occupation: A longitudinal examination of 167,776 individuals. *Intelligence, 67,* 84-92.

Del Giudice, M. (2021). Ideological bias in the psychology of sex and gender. In C. L.Frisby, W. T. O'Donohue, R. E. Redding, & S. O. Lilienfeld (eds.), *Ideological*

---

3   My translation of excerpts from "Denne arbejdstekst bør da betragtes som et forsøg på at afbalancere den mere miljøprægede psykologi ved at missionere for delvis nyvurdering af hvilke faktorer der er medbetingende for fyldestgørende forklaringer af menneskelig adfærd."

and Political Bias in Psychology: Nature, Scope, and Solutions. New York: Springer.

Del Giudice, M., Booth, T., & Irwing, P. (2012). The distance between Mars and Venus: Measuring global sex differences in personality. *PLoS ONE, 7,* e29265.

Delhez, J. (2019). Evolutionary perspectives on human sex differences and their discontents. *Evolution, Mind and Behaviour, 17,* 48-53.

Duarte, J. L., Crawford, J. T., Stern, C., Haidt, J., Jussim, L., & Tetlock, P. E. (2014). Political diversity will improve social psychological science. *Behavioral and Brain Sciences, 38,* e130.

Dutton, E., van der Linden, D., & Madison, G. (2020). Why do high IQ societies differ in intellectual acheivement? The role of schizophrenia and left-handedness in per capita scientific publications and Nobel Prizes. *Journal of Creative Behavior, 54,* 871-883.

Eagly, A. H. (2018). The shaping of science by ideology: How feminism inspired, led, and constrained scientific understanding of sex and gender. *Journal of Social Issues, 74,* 9-10.

Eagly, A. H. & Riger, S. (2014). Feminism and psychology: critiques of methods and epistemology. *American Psychologist, 69,* 685-702.

Falk, A. & Hermle, J. (2018). Relationship of gender differences in preferences to economic development and gender equality. *Science, 362,* 307.

Hirnstein, M., Hugdahl, K., & Hausmann, M. (2019). Cognitive sex differences and hemispheric asymmetry: A critical review of 40 years of research. *Laterality: Asymmetries of Body, Brain and Cognition, 24,* 204-252.

Jiang, R., Calhoun, V. D., Fan, L., Zuo, N., Jung, R. E., Qi, S. et al. (2021). Gender differences in connectome-based predictions of individualized intelligence quotient and sub-domain scores. *Cerebral Cortex, 30,* 888-900.

Kaiser, T., Del Giudice, M., & Booth, T. (2019). The distance between Mars and Venus: Measuring global sex differences in personality. *Journal of Personality, 88,* 415-429.

Kaufman, S. B. (2019). Taking sex differences in personality seriously. *Scientific American,* November 6, 2019.

Lippa, R. (2010a). Gender differences in personality and interests: When, where, and why? *Social and Personality Psychology Compass, 4,* 1098-1110.

Lippa, R. (2010b). Sex differences in personality traits and gender-related occupational preferences across 53 nations: testing evolutionary and social-environmental theories. *Archives of Sexual Behavior, 39,* 619-636.

Lippa, R., Collaer, M. L., & Peters, M. (2010). Sex differences in mental rotation and line angle judgments are positively associated with gender equality and economic development across 53 nations. *Archives of Sexual Behavior, 39,* 990-997.

Madison, G. (2017). Presumption and prejudice: Quotas may solve some problems, but create many more. *Mankind Quarterly, 58,* 117-138.

Madison, G. (2019). Explicating politicians' arguments for sex quotas in Sweden: Increasing power and influence rather than increasing quality and productivity. *Frontiers in Communication, 4,* 1.

Madison, G. & Fahlman, P. (2020). Sex differences in the number of scientific publications and citations when attaining the rank of professor in Sweden. *Studies in Higher Education.*

Madison, G. & Söderlund, T. (2018). Comparisons of content and scientific quality indicators across populations of peer-reviewed journal articles with more or less gender perspective: Gender studies can do better. *Scientometrics, 115,* 1161-1183.

Madison, G., Wallert, J., Aasa, U., & Woodley, M. A. (2014). Feminist activist women are masculinized in terms of digit-ratio and dominance: A possible explanation for the feminist paradox. *Frontiers in Psychology: Evolutionary Psychology and Neuroscience, 5,* 1011.

Nyborg, H. (1972). *Psykologi og genetik. En introduktion til psykogenetik.* Munksgaard.

Nyborg, H. (1977). *The rod-and-fram test and the field dependence dimension: Some methodological, conceptual, and developmental considerations.* Dansk Psykologisk Forlag, Hellerup, DK.

Nyborg, H. (1983). Spatial ability in men and women: Review and new theory. *Advances in Behaviour Research and Therapy, 5,* 89-140.

Nyborg, H. (1984). Performance and intelligence in hormonally different groups. In G. J. de Vries, J. de Bruin, H. Uylings, & M. Cormer (eds.), *Progress in Brain Research* (pp. 491-508). Amsterdam: Elsevier Biomedical Press.

Nyborg, H. (1988a). Change at puberty in spatioperceptual strategy on the rod-and-frame test. *Perceptual and Motor Skills, 67,* 129-130.

Nyborg, H. (1988b). Mathematics, sex hormones, and brain function. *Behavioral and Brain Sciences, 11,* 206-207.

Nyborg, H. (1990). Sex hormones, brain development and spatio-perceptual strategies in Turner Syndrome. In D. B. Berch & B. G. Bender (eds.), *Sex chromosome abnormalities and human behavior: Psychological Studies* (pp. 100-128). Boulder, CO: Westview Press.

Nyborg, H. (1994a). *Hormones, Sex, and Society: The Science of Physicology.* Westport, CT: Praeger.

Nyborg, H. (1994b). The neuropsychology of sex-related differences in brain and specific abilities: Hormones, developmental dynamics, and new paradigm. In P. A.Vernon (ed.), *The* Neuropsychology of Individual Differences (pp. 59-113). San Diego, CA: Academic Press.

Nyborg, H. (1997a). Molecular man in a molecular world: Applied physiology. *Psyche & Logos, 18,* 457-474.

Nyborg, H. (1997b). Personality, psychology, and the molecular wave: Covariation of genes with hormones, experience, and traits. In J. Bermudez, J. de Raad, A. de Vries, A. Perez-Garcia, & G. van Heck (eds.), *Personality Psychology in Europe* (pp. 159-173). Tilburg University Press.

Nyborg, H. (2003a). General introduction: Arthur Jensen — The man, his friends and this book. In H. Nyborg (ed.), *The Scientific Study of General Intelligence: Tribute to Arthur R. Jensen* (pp. xiii-xxvi). London, UK: Pergamon Press.

Nyborg, H. (2003b). Sex Differences in *g.* In H. Nyborg (ed.), *The Scientific Study of General Intelligence: Tribute to Arthur R. Jensen* (pp. 187-222). London, UK: Pergamon Press.

Nyborg, H. (2003c). *The Scientific Study of General Intelligence: Tribute to Arthur Jensen.* London, UK: Pergamon Press.

Nyborg, H. (2003d). The sociology of psychometric and bio-behavioral sciences: A case study of destructive social reductionism and collective fraud in 20th century academia. In H. Nyborg (ed.), *The scientific study of general intelligence: Tribute to Arthur R. Jensen* (pp. 441-502). London, UK: Pergamon Press.

Nyborg, H. (2005). Sex-related differences in general intelligence g, brain size, and social status. *Personality and Individual Differences, 39,* 497-509.

Nyborg, H. (2011). The greatest collective scientific fraud of the 20th century: The demolition of differential psychology and eugenics. *Mankind Quarterly, 53,* 118-125.

Nyborg, H. (2012). A conversation with Richard Lynn. *Personality and Individual Differences, 53,* 79-84.

Nyborg, H. (2013a). In conversation with J. Philippe Rushton. *Personality and Individual Differences, 55,* 205-211.

Nyborg, H. (2013b). *Race and Sex Differences in Intelligence and Personality: A Tribute to Richard Lynn at 80.* London, UK: Ulster Institute for Social Research.

Nyborg, H. (2015). Sex differences across different racial ability levels: Theories of origin and societal consequences. *Intelligence, 52,* 44-62.

Nyborg, H. (2017). Common paradoxes in the study of sex differences in intelligence. *Mankind Quarterly, 58,* 76-82.

Nyborg, H. & Jensen, A. R. (2000). Testosterone levels as modifiers of psychometric g. *Personality and Individual Differences, 28,* 601-607.

Nyborg, Helmuth and Kirkegaard, Emil O. W. (2021, January 5). Hvorfor nægter lighedsfundamentalister at se i øjnene, at der er forskel på mænd og kvinder — også når det gælder arbejde og karriere? *Politiken.*

Nyborg, H. & Nielsen, J. (1981). Sex hormone treatment and spatial ability in women with Turner's syndrome. In W.Schmid & J. Nielsen (Eds.), *Human Behavior and Genetics* (pp. 167-182). Amsterdam: Elsevier/North-Holland Biomedical Press.

Nyborg, H. & Vig, J. E. (2016). Science suffers when political extremism and state censure take over: Sex and ethnic differences in case.

Ref Type: Unpublished Work

Pinker, S. (2009). *The Sexual Paradox. Men, Women, and the Real Gender Gap.* New York: Scribner.

Polderman, T., Benyamin, B., de Leeuw, C. A., Sullivan, P. F., van Bochoven, A., Visscher, P. M. et al. (2015). Meta-analysis of the heritability of human traits based on fifty years of twin studies. *Nature Genetics, 47,* 702-709.

Reuter, M., Netter, P., Hennig, J., Mohiyeddini, C., & Nyborg, H. (2003). Test of Nyborg's General Trait Covariance (GTC) model for hormonally guided development by means of structural equation modeling. *European Journal of Personality, 17,* 221-235.

Ritchie, S. J., Cox, S. R., Shen, X., Lombardo, M. V., Reus, L., et al. (2018). Sex differences in the adult human brain: Evidence from 5216 UK biobank participants. *Cerebral Cortex, 28,* 2959-2975.

Schmitt, D. P. (2017). The truth about sex differences. *Psychology Today,* November 7.

Söderlund, T. & Madison, G. (2015). Characteristics of gender studies publications: a bibliometric analysis based on a Swedish population database. *Scientometrics, 105,* 1347-1387.

Söderlund, T. & Madison, G. (2017). Objectivity and realms of explanation in academic journal articles concerning sex/gender: a comparison of Gender studies and the other social sciences. *Scientometrics, 112,* 1093-1109.

Stoet, G. & Geary, D. C. (2020). Sex-specific academic ability and attitude patterns in students across developed countries. *Intelligence, 81,* 101453.

van der Linden, D., Dunkel, C. S., & Madison, G. (2017). Sex differences in brain size and general intelligence (g). *Intelligence, 63,* 78-88.

van der Linden, D., Dutton, E., & Madison, G. (2020). National-level indicators of androgens are related to the global distribution of scientific productivity and Nobel Prizes. *Journal of Creative Behavior, 54,* 134-149.

Verweij, K. J. H., Mosing, M. A., Ullén, F., & Madison, G. (2016). Individual differences in personality masculinity-femininity: examining the effects of genes, environment, and prenatal hormone transfer. *Twin Research and Human Genetics, 19,* 87-96.

Wai, J., Hodges, J., & Makel, M. C. (2018). Sex differences in ability tilt in the right tail of cognitive abilities: A 35-year examination. *Intelligence, 67,* 76-83.

Yu, J. J. & Madison, G. (2021). Gender quotas and company financial performance: A systematic review. *Economic Affairs, 41,* 377-390.

CHAPTER 10

THE FUTURE OF INTELLIGENCE IN GERMANY: ASSUMPTIONS, MODELS AND PREDICTIONS

HEINER RINDERMANN

Abstract

BASED ON PAST HISTORICAL development and on assumptions about factors influencing a development of cognitive competence at the societal level, we design a model for the future development of intelligence in the 21" century in Germany. Factors include the FLynn effect, education, migration, the recent refugee waves, different birth rates, and general cultural and environmental changes. The results of various assumptions, including a simple linear model based on the latest developments of the German IQB student achievement study, are compared. Depending on assumptions and models, the average IQ for Germany in 2100 is expected to be between 97 and 77 IQ points, which, starting from an IQ of 99 in 2100, corresponds to a loss of between 3 and 22 IQ points. We assume an IQ of 91 as the most likely value, which corresponds to a loss of 8 IQ points. We compare the results with more recent data from OECD, IQB and further student achievement studies and show that, if their past trends were extended linearly, the projections for the year 2100 would be far more negative (around IQ 78). The future of intelligence in Germany:

Assumptions, Models and Predictions

International Predictions

In the 2018 book *Cognitive Capitalism*, I attempted to predict the development of intelligence in the 21ˢᵗ century for eight different regions around the world (see Figure 1). Only minor changes were predicted for East Asia and Eastern Europe. For the West (Central, Northern and Southern Europe, North America, Australia and New Zealand), however, a decline of four IQ points was estimated. Increases were expected in all other regions of the world, especially for sub-Saharan Africa. Assumed causes are expansion — longer life, more people — and improvement in education and general improvement in living conditions relevant to cognitive abilities, such as health care. In the West, on the other hand, further improvements are hardly possible; here, negative factors come into play: the immigration of people from countries with significantly lower ability levels and the lower number of children among educated and smart people. The highest losses worldwide until the year 2100 were calculated for Central Europe (−7.14 IQ). These results were somewhat more optimistic than the ones of the pioneering study of Helmuth Nyborg (2012) with −9.38 IQ points for the West. Helmuth Nyborg's prediction study in *Personality and Individual Differences* in 2012 garnered much attention and criticism, but in light of further research, his then-controversial findings seem plausible.[1]

---

1   Experts also take a rather critical view of future intelligence development in the West (Rindermann, Becker & Coyle, 2017, Table 3; −4.03 IQ points for the West

Even if we do not like certain predictions, for example concerning climate change, we should not be guided by our wishful thinking (or fears), but try to describe past development, understand its causes and design models for future development. For some, intelligence research is considered controversial, and there is harsh opposition (cf. Nyborg, 2003; Carl & Woodley, 2019; Rindermann, 2022), but we should simply follow the rules of epistemic rationality and scientific thinking, including reflection on the limits of our knowledge, even under difficult conditions (e.g., Pinker, 2021).

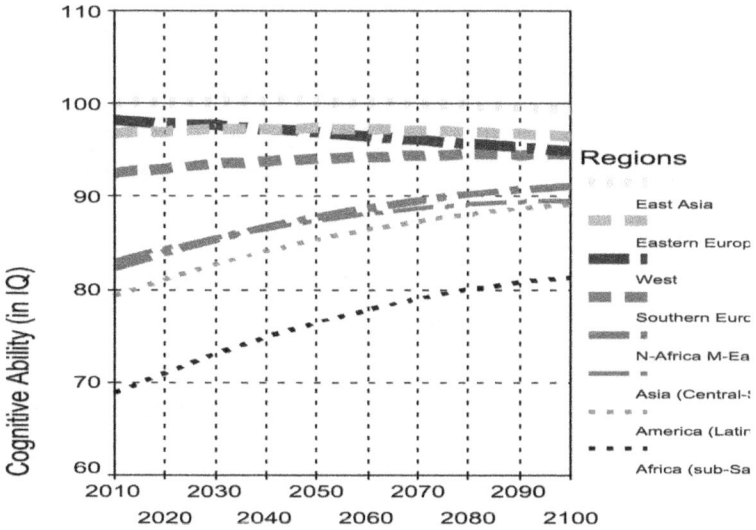

Figure 1. Previous final model predictions of cognitive development in the twenty-first century (from Rindermann, 2018, there Figure 13.13).

Here in this paper on future intelligence we will focus on Germany. We will also use studies conducted only within Germany and supplement the older models with information on more recent demographic changes.

by 2100).

Ability Rise to Date and Possible Factors

In the 20th century, there was a sharp rise in intelligence test scores (Flynn, 2012). First in the West, then in East Asia, finally worldwide. The increases ranged from 2.31 to 2.83 IQ points per decade (Trahan et al., 2014; Pietschnig & Voracek, 2015). For a long time it was disputed whether these are gains in real abilities or only test gains ("IQ inflation"). Some arguments speak for real gains, i.e. for the improvement of thinking abilities:

- In the 20th century, the *average age of chess players* decreased (Howard, 1999). This represents a developmental acceleration in childhood and adolescence.

- *Height* increased in the 20th century, by 1.2cm per decade, equivalent to $d=0.17$ or $dec=2.57$ "IQ".[2] These numbers are very similar to the cognitive gains (Lynn, 1990).

- Mean *brain sizes* also increased, measured by skull sizes equivalent to $d=0.20$ or $dec=3.00$ "IQ" — again very similar to cognitive gains (Lynn, 1990; 4.69g per decade, Miller & Corsellis, 1977).

- The best predictor of intelligence at the individual level and one of the determinants of cognitive development, educational attainment, increased sharply in the 20th century (Meyer et al., 1992).

- *General living conditions* have improved extremely (e.g., Moore & Simon, 2000), from health to cognitive stimulation, which make a real increase in thinking ability very plausible.

- A much higher percentage of people today are *academics*.

- People have to cope with *higher cognitive demands* than before. The average cognitive ability of the population must have increased in the 20th century to cope with these challenges. A concrete example for farmers from Seymour Itzkoff (1994, p. 97):

---

2   "*dec*" represents a development of 10 years, per decade.

"The modern farmer is an abstract symbolic analyst. ... The modern farmer cares for a multitude of specialized machines, consulting manuals for maintenance and repair. Constant reading of weather and climate reports, governmental publications on new seed, fertilizer, anti-bacterial and pest treatments, study of the complex price support programs, as well as decision making about whether or when to take land out of production, feed cattle, or plant other crops, are all part of a modern farmer's job. The farmer has to plan next year's program, of necessity speculating on the commodity futures market in Chicago, prices at the storage bins in the area, as well as negotiate the usual yearly bank loans, now linked to the interest rates set on Wall Street."

Therefore, we can assume with some certainty that there was an actual increase in cognitive abilities at the societal level. But what were the factors? The most important factors are likely to be:

- Improved *nutrition*;
- improved *health care*;
- improved *medical care* for mother and child during pregnancy and childbirth;
- *visual and hearing aids* (e.g., hearing aids, glasses and surgery);
- *generally improved living conditions,* such as less heavy physical labor and fewer natural and artificial environmental toxins;
- *fewer consanguineous marriages* (exogamy, not marriage within kinship groups, thus heterosis; e.g., Jensen, 1983);
- more *quantity and quality of school education,* including kindergarten;
- greater proportion of a cohort attending *school longer*;
- greater proportion of a cohort *attending school regularly*;
- more *higher education* and *further vocational training*;
- *support concepts* for *disadvantaged* (cognitively weak) groups;

- more *conducive educational behavior* of parents, more *educated parents*;
- shift in teaching and testing *from knowing to thinking*;
- *modernization* in general;
- increased *cognitive demands* of working life;
- reduction in the *volume of work*;
- more *leisure time* that can be used for cognitive activity;
- higher *stimulation* and *higher cognitive complexity of everyday life* for all (television, access to computers, newspapers and books, group size, urbanization, travel, smart phones);
- *money* as a means of payment in trade instead of exchange of goods;
- *family changes* (fewer children and siblings, higher age of parents and fewer teen pregnancies);
- *higher intelligence of others* promotes intelligence again (positive feedback loops);
- *learning society* and learning institutions that improve their actions in the long run (e.g., by evaluation and feedback);
- more *test experience*, better test-taking (e.g., guessing where solution is not known).

The latter would not be a change in ability, but only an improvement in the measurement result. However, testing experience can also have an ability-enhancing effect. Like any cognitive exercise, testing may promote thinking.

Increase in Cognitive
Demands (and Income)

Above we had an example from Seymour Itzkoff of the increase in cognitive demands in everyday life. This served as indirect evidence for the "FLynn effect"; people today have to cope with these higher demands. However, these increasing requirements also pose a problem because simple jobs disappear with them. An example given by an employee of mine from Chemnitz:

> "It's crazy how professions still associated as 'simple' have become more cognitively demanding: my neighbor is a garbage driver, who has and must have all of West Saxony in his head as a geo-road-climate-season map or matrix; he must maneuver the garbage truck through mountains and cities in the depths of winter, generally pay attention to colleagues jumping off and on, traffic conditions and passers-by, and prepare and post-process each trip computer-wise. He recently told me about accidents and colleague changes that occur when there are mental and physical problems."[3]

And a second example is of a neighbor active in engine production. When testing new industrial engines in 2011, the information had to be taken from four monitors, but in 2016 from seven monitors. This is an annual increase in complexity of 15%.[4]

While these were real-life examples, there are also statistical analyses. For example, the OECD (2013, p. 49ff., PIAAC study) analyzed the development of the labor market between the years 1998 and 2010 according to the average ability level of professionals. It can be seen here (our Figure 2) that the occupations exercised by people with the highest abilities are increasing (top line) and the occupations of those with rather below-average abilities are decreasing.

---

3   October 2015.

4   19/06/2016.

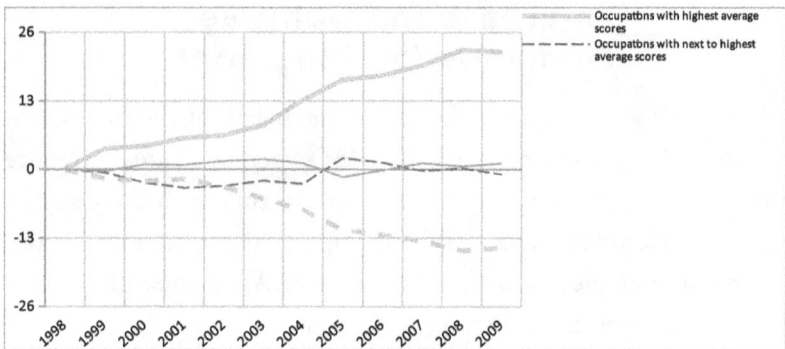

Figure 2. Development of the labor market by ability level of the employed (OECD, 2013, their Figure 1.6).[5]

There are also such reports from the USA. Activities with higher cognitive demands ("non-routine") have been increasing in percentage terms since the 1960s (our Figure 3; Autor & Price, 2013). Individuals who can master these cognitive demands earn more relative to others, and the income gap is widening (Figure 4; Autor, 2014). For the highly educated, real income has almost doubled since 1963; for the others, it has hardly doubled at all.

---

5 Figures of other authors in this paper were reprinted with permission of the authors or publishers.

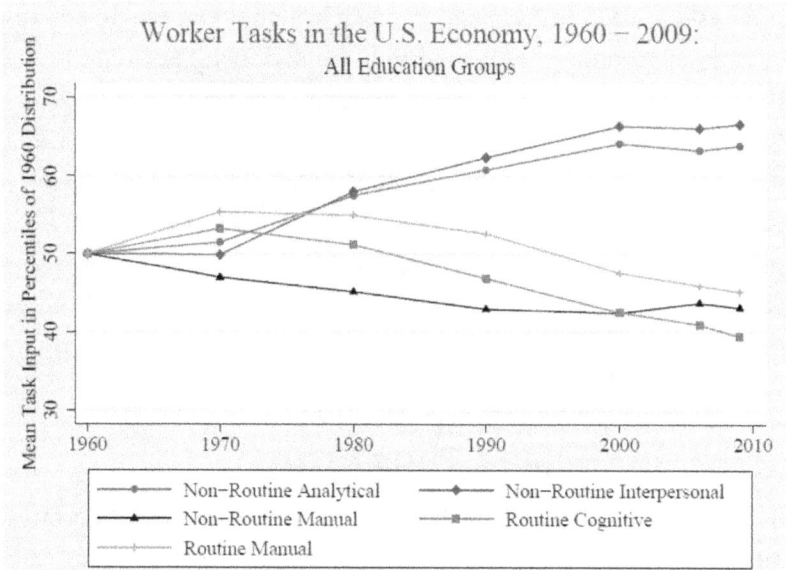

Figure 3. Evolution of occupational activities by level
of demand (Autor & Price, 2013, their Figure 2).

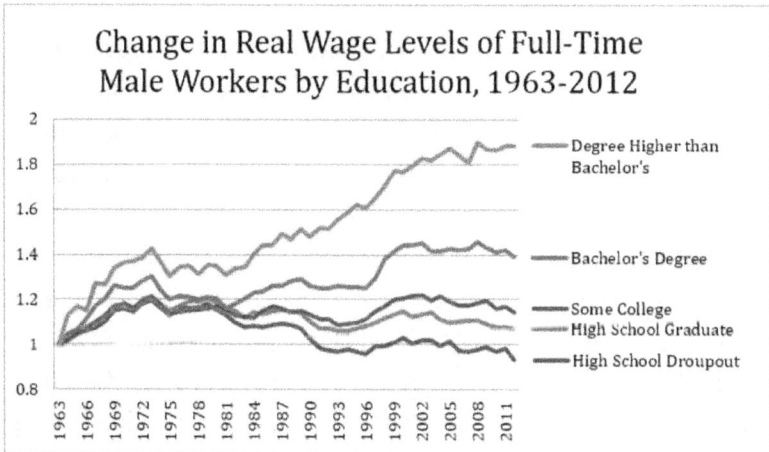

Figure 4. Trends in income in the US by education
(Autor, 2014, his Figure 6a, first version).

This now leads to the concern that people in the future will no longer
be able to cope with the cognitive demands. As early as 1995, Earl

Hunt asked, "Will we be smart enough?" In addition, the differences in income according to qualification are increasing not only in the USA (see Figure 4), but also in Germany. For example, Bönke and Lüthen (2014) compared two generations, those born in 1935 and 1972. During this period, inequality doubled, partly because poorer people (less qualified) were more often unemployed, and partly because higher-income people (better qualified) earned more. In recent decades, there has been no discernible increase in real-life earnings for the lower income groups.

Increase in Cognitive Demands (and Thus Errors)

In the modern age, technical devices and processes are becoming increasingly complex. Compare an SLR camera from the 1980s with one of today, for example. In the case of a Nikon FG (1982), only the exposure meter and the program automatic could break down, in addition to the mechanics. In a pinch, it functioned completely without electronics.

On a Nikon Z7 (2018), on the other hand, there are so many setting options and technical software-related specifications that hardly anyone can overlook them all, including Nikon engineers. For example, on an earlier model, the Nikon D800 (2012), there were problems with the autofocus, more specifically with some autofocus fields on the left side that caused the camera to stop focusing ("back focus"). This made the D800 unusable except for studio photography. Camera and lens problems were also reported by the competition (e.g., Canon).

Problems also exist in the development of software due to the increase in complexity. An example is Adobe Creative Cloud (image editing), according to the photographer Nasim Mansurov:

> "I have grown very frustrated with Adobe's lack of quality control when new software updates are released. ... It feels like the company doesn't care to do much testing before releasing these updates, causing all sorts of problems for end users. We have previously seen Lightroom crash non-stop

after an update. ... I have experienced many crashes of it on both desktop
(PC and Mac-Book Pro) and mobile versions of the software (iPad Pro). ...
I spent hours trying to find a solution to this problem. Read a bunch of
topics on Adobe Forums and tried many different things including clearing
cache — all to no avail. I gave up, downgraded back to the previous version
of Premiere Pro and After Effects. ...
I have experienced similar problems with other software as well, including
Photoshop. ... I could list a lot more issues like this, but I am honestly sick
and tired of dealing with them, to the point where I gave up using most of
Adobe's software."[6]

Compared to technical and software errors in aircraft, these are
all harmless problems. In the Boeing 737 Max, the Maneuvering
Characteristics Augmentation System (MCAS) is said to be malfunc-
tioning and responsible for two plane crashes with almost 350 fatali-
ties.[7] However, there were not only errors on the part of Boeing, but
also on the part of the air traffic control authority. Technology seems
to become too complex for its developers and for the controllers.

Dystopias and Predictions of Negative Future Development

There are a number of dystopias, such as the movies *Mad Max* and
Logan's Run, but none like *Idiocracy* (2006) explicitly addresses the
decline of society due to a decline in intelligence. The film captures
dysgenics with a theoretical introduction: educated people delay
parenthood and eventually have no children at all, while lower-class
families multiply in an uncontrolled way. In the future, nothing works
properly anymore; nobody understands questions; lawyers don't understand anything about defense; the president of the USA is a former
wrestler and porn star; garbage is everywhere; plants are fertilized
with salt water and therefore do not grow, etc.

---

6   09/05/2019, https://photographylife.com/adobe-creative-cloud-issues
7   03/12/2021,   https://en.wikipedia.org/wiki/Maneuvering_Characteristics_
     Augmentation_System

This all sounds highly exaggerated, but there is an example of such a historical process: the development of science and art in antiquity. In the Roman imperial period, much that the Greeks had developed was no longer understood (e.g., Oesterdiekhoff, 2013, pp. 292ff.). For art, one example is the *Arch of Constantine* in Rome from 315:

> "For the decoration of the three-arched victory monument, the Roman sculptors partly took reliefs from older buildings. Obviously, at the beginning of the 4th century they were not up to such a big task and were no longer at the height of art, even that of copying." (Fischer, 1986, p. 230; translation by HR)

Much research has postulated a decline in intelligence for decades:

- According to Retherford and Sewell (1989), there is a negative correlation between intelligence and the number of children in the USA, especially among women. An increase of 30 IQ points reduces the number of children by 0.17 for men and almost twice as much by 0.32 for women. Consequently, −0.2857 IQ points would be lost in 10 years, and −0.1178 IQ points genotypically.

- Similarly, according to Loehlin (1997), in the early 1990s women with a low level of education (<high school graduate; estimated IQ 80) had on average 2.69 children, with an average level of education (high school graduate; estimated IQ 100) 2.07 children, with a slightly above-average level of education (some college and associate degree; estimated IQ 105) 2.12 or 1.93 children, with an above-average level of education (Bachelors degree; estimated IQ 110) 1.31 children and with the highest level of education (graduate or professional degree; estimated IQ 120) 1.31 children. Without taking into account the differences in generation length, this results in a loss of −0.795 IQ per generation. If the generation is set to 28 years, there is a loss of −0.2839 IQ points per decade. If we do not assume a regression to the mean and consider that African

Americans have more children according to Loehlin data, the result is a loss of −0.6541 IQ per decade.

- Likewise for the U.S., but for the cohort 1940 to 1949, Lynn and Van Court (2004) found a correlation between intelligence and number of children of $r=-.17$. More intelligent people have fewer children. The dysgenic decline per decade (generation of 28 years) is −0.3214 IQ.

- Lynn and Harvey (2008) expect a global decline of −1.3 IQ (genotypic) from 2000 to 2050.

- For the West, Helmuth Nyborg (2012, his Table 2) expects until 2072 a decline of −9.38 IQ points by 2072; only because of fertility −4.28 IQ, per decade −0.69 IQ points.[8]

- According to Sophie von Stumm, Batty, and Deary (2011), in Scotland and for birth year 1950, individuals who have children in their lifetime have lower intelligence in their own 11th year of life, men −1.84 IQ points, women −2.54 IQ points; average −2.19 IQ points.

- Gerhard Meisenberg (2010) found particularly strong negative effects in the USA in the area of giftedness. In general, intelligence and the number of children were negatively correlated ($r=-.122$) in the large-scale study NLSY79 (National Longitudinal Survey of Youth 1979). This resulted in a loss of −0.29 IQ points per decade. For the highly gifted:

"The proportion of highly gifted people with an IQ higher than 130 will decline by 11.5% in one generation and by 37.7% in one century." (p. 228) Gerhard Meisenberg also assumes institutional effects (cf. the film *Idiocracy*):

---

8   We were more optimistic in our own forecast for the West (by −2 IQ by 2070) because we assumed continuous environmental improvements (Rindermann, 2018, p. 447, there Figure 13.14).

"Small reductions in the average intelligence of educational administrators will result in an increased probability that educational reforms will reduce rather than enhance students' intelligence, and thereby lead to even lower intelligence in the next generation of educational administrators and even greater deterioration of the educational system." (Meisenberg, 2010, p. 228)

- Negative patterns are also found in non-Western countries, such as China (Wang, Fuerst & Ren, 2016): intelligence and number of children are negatively correlated ($r=-.10$), even more so education and number of children ($r=-.36$), especially for women (men $r=-.30$, women $r=-.42$). Depending on the formula used, the loss per decade is -0.31 to -0.66 IQ.

- Woodley (2015) pointed out another factor: First, more intelligent people have fewer children, resulting in $dec=-0.39$ IQ points in a decade on average in a meta-analysis of 10 studies from the US and UK. On top of that, however, there is an increase in mutation load due to higher age of fathers and milder selection resulting in $dec=-0.84$, in total $dec=-1.23$, immigration effects are $dec=-0.28$, in total $dec=-1.51$ IQ points.

Finally, my own analysis:

- In Germany, the education of mothers and the number of children are negatively correlated ($r=-.13$).[9] Converted, this results in a loss of $dec=-0.30$ IQ.

But the strength of the "FLynn effect", i.e. environmental improvements, had in the past far outweighed plausible negative effects. An exception is the study by Woodley, te Nijenhuis, and Murphy (2013), who found a decline in measurable information processing speed from 1889 to 2004 using reaction time measurements. Other studies

---

9   Cohorts 1959 to 1963 and 1964 to 1968, women aged 40 to 49, means of three measures of education; Statistisches Bundesamt (2010).

move in a similar direction, such as less frequent use of difficult words or poorer discrimination of colors (Dutton & Woodley, 2018).

Genetic analyses also show (at least partial) dysgenic trends: according to Kong et al. (2017), a polygenic score associated with education (and thus intelligence) would decline in Iceland over the generations from 1910 to 1990: "The decline of POLYFULL [polygenic score] would lead to a decline of $0.038 \times (30/3.74) = 0.30$ IQ points per decade. This would be a very substantial effect if the trend persists for centuries." In 100 years, the loss would thus be between $d=0.10$ and 0.25, or 1.50 to 3.75 IQ points.

Brain Drain

Relatively poorer, less free and less safe countries suffer from "brain drain", i.e., an exodus of highly qualified workers or a flight of the intelligentsia. This was and is especially true for Eastern Europe, India, China, Latin America, the Arab-Muslim and African regions. Examples:

- The founder of WhatsApp, *Jan Koum* (*1976 in Kiev, Jewish background), is from Ukraine who emigrated to the USA.

- The former head of Deutsche Bank, *Anshu Jain* (1963 in Jaipur, a Jain), is from India.

- The Nobel Prize winner in physics *Daniel C. Tsui* (*1939 in China) emigrated to the USA.

- *Ricardo Hausmann* (*1956), a Venezuelan economist and former minister, is now a professor at Harvard.

- The businessman and scientist *Nassim Nicholas Taleb* (*1960) comes from a Christian family in Lebanon and now works in the USA. Similarly, *Gad Saad* (*1964, a Jew), who is now a professor of psychology in Canada.

- The former president of the TU (University of Technology) Chemnitz, *Arnold van Zyl* (*1959), comes from South Africa.

According to Benno Ndulu (2004), significant parts of the intelligentsia would leave Africa. 88% of African immigrants in the U.S. have a university degree; more African scientists and engineers work in the U.S. than in Africa; 60% of all doctors trained in Ghana are said to have left the country; 45% of all doctors trained by the University of the Witwatersrand have left South Africa in the last 35 years. For every well-educated person who emigrated, about 10 more jobs were lost.

Also according to a recent study (UNDP, 2019), the more educated relative to African natives would migrate from Africa. Relative to natives in destination countries, however, they are less educated and intelligent (see explanatory Figure 5). This migration-ability paradox leads to a double loss of ability in migration: in the country of origin, because the more intelligent emigrate, in the destination country, because the less intelligent immigrate. The figure shows only one example with an IQ difference between countries of 15 points. If migration from Africa to Europe takes place with an IQ difference of 30 points on average, then it is almost impossible that the target region benefits from such immigration. There are simply too few people in Africa with an intelligence above 100!

99.87%	+3d		130	+2d
97.73%	+2d	tiny resource	115	+1d
84.13%	+1d	small resource	100	0d
50.00%	+0d	large resource	85	-1d
15.87%	-1d		70	-2d
2.28%	-2d		55	-3d

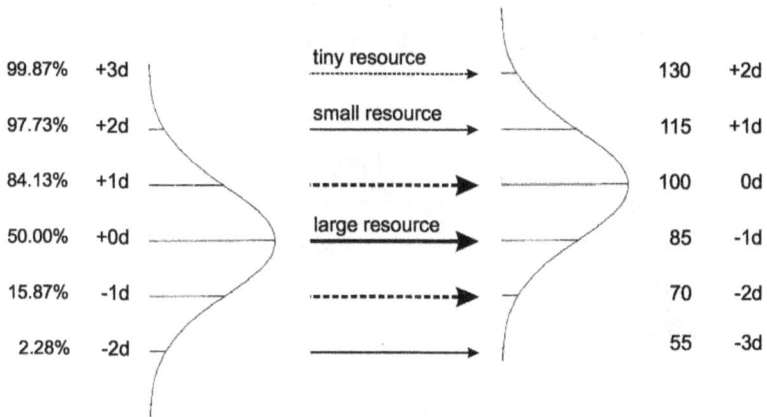

Figure 5. Migration-ability-paradox exemplified for two countries with a
d=1 (15 IQ) gap (similar to United States and Mexico, France and Tunisia,
UK and Trinidad, Germany and Turkey; Rindermann, 2018, p. 422)

On the other hand, if cognitive elites from China migrate to the U.S. or the absolute top from India migrates to Europe, then this has a boosting effect for the destination country. According to Robert Weissberg (2010), by attracting cognitive elites from other parts of the world, formerly from Germany and Eastern Europe, now from India and East Asia, the U.S. would succeed in keeping its universities and economy at the top. In physics, natural sciences, computer science and engineering, around 50% of the doctoral graduates would be of foreign origin (p. 139).

Previous Prediction Models with a Focus on Germany

There are no prediction models from other scientists for the ability development in the 21st century in different countries. There are predictions about the effects for single countries, but these models did not take into account the (mostly) positive environmental effects that are still occurring simultaneously. More often, there are predictions for economic growth, for example by Hanushek et al. (2013, p. 61), but only for the U.S. and under hypothetical assumptions concerning ability development: What if the U.S. would reach the ability level of Singapore? In my earlier models, the assumptions were (see Rindermann, 2018, chapter 13.2):

There are further environmental improvements relevant to cognitive development, but these are nearly exhausted in the First World, but not in the Third World, where there is still greater potential for development.

Achievable target levels through environmental improvements are different and limited in principle, such as not IQ 120 for Germany.

Asymmetric number of children and generation length. Adults with lower education and intelligence have more children and at younger ages.

Migration has positive or negative effects depending on the country of origin and destination; for the Arab Emirates, for example, positive effects (expats), but for Western Europe negative effects (migrants from North Africa, the Near and Middle East and sub-Saharan Africa).

Table 1. Cognitive ability predictions (models 2018 and 2011 compared for 97 countries)

	2018 model for 2100			2011 model for 2100		
	CA corrected 2010	Cognitive ability 2100	IQ gain decade ('10-100)	CA corrected 2010	Cognitive ability 2100	IQ gain decade ('10-100)
Africa (sub-Sahara)	71.10	85	1.58	78.07	78	0.01
Nigeria	74.72	82	0.83	85.48	83	-0.28
N-Africa M-East	83.11	92	0.99	81.30	83	0.24
Egypt	83.72	87	0.36	82.72	82	-0.11
America (North, Engl)	99.45	97	-0.26	100.45	99	-0.20
USA	98.33	96	-0.28	98.99	97	-0.19
America (Latin, C-S)	83.76	93	1.06	80.55	83	0.29
Mexico	85.87	94	0.86	85.12	83	-0.24

	2018 model for 2100			2011 model for 2100		
	CA corrected 2010	Cognitive ability 2100	IQ gain decade ('10-100)	CA corrected 2010	Cognitive ability 2100	IQ gain decade ('10-100)
Asia (Central-South)	81.40	92	1.14	80.73	84	0.33
India	77.60	89	1.26	87.70	87	-0.13
East Asia	101.17	100	-0.12	102.81	101	-0.23
China	100.77	101	0.04	104.11	102	-0.28
Southeast Asia, Pacific	85.90	91	0.62	86.40	87	0.03
Philippines	80.38	88	0.87	75.59	81	0.65
Australia-NZ (English)	99.06	99	-0.01	101.13	100	-0.14
New Zealand	99.17	99	-0.06	100.50	99	-0.14
Western Europe	98.83	94	-0.50	100.48	98	-0.24
United Kingdom	99.60	96	-0.44	100.00	99	-0.15
Scandinavia	98.89	96	-0.32	99.56	98	-0.20
Norway	97.91	97	-0.05	96.89	97	-0.02
Central Europe	98.85	92	-0.79	100.24	97	-0.31
Germany	98.82	93	-0.61	99.82	97	-0.29
Eastnorth Europe	97.08	97	-0.05	98.78	97	-0.18
Russia	97.26	96	-0.15	98.23	96	-0.20
Southwest Europe	96.06	95	-0.16	95.24	93	-0.30
Italy	97.52	94	-0.38	97.00	93	-0.44
Southeast Europe	91.00	95	0.41	91.17	90	-0.15
Greece	94.98	91	-0.44	94.64	91	-0.35
Average	90.18	94	0.41	90.43	90	-0.03

Notes: *N*=97 countries with student achievement data, models from Rindermann (2018) and Rindermann & Thompson (2011). Source: Table 13.8 in Rindermann (2018).

According to these models, the highest cognitive gains are expected for Africa, Central Asia, Latin America, and the Arab-Muslim region. The West, Europe, North America and Australia-New Zealand will lose, with Central Europe losing the most. For the German-speaking region, the losses could be around –8 IQ points.

The 2011 forecast results were somewhat more skeptical for developing countries and more optimistic for Western countries. However, the correlations between the older and more recent decade changes are $r=.73$ ($N=97$ countries) and between the two forecasts for the year 2100 are $r=.61$ ($N=97$). Thus, they are quite similar.

While some readers might think this is negativist speculation, the OECD (2016, p. 86) has somewhat covertly published not so different results. The OECD researchers had compared trends in PISA before and after demographic change was taken into account. For Germany, for example, the difference in the three-year trend is 2.58 SASQ (equivalent to 0.387 IQ points). Without demographic change, which is mainly due to immigration, the trend would be 0.387 IQ points better within these three years. Converted to 10 years, it would be –8.59 SASQ or –1.29 IQ points. From 2010 to 2100, the interval chosen in Table 1, it would result in a decline in intelligence of –11.59 IQ points. *Dramatic!* Our estimate of a migration loss for Germany of –7.32 IQ points (buffered somewhat by positive trends in other areas; Rindermann, 2018, Table 13.4 there) was comparatively optimistic!

The correlation between OECD demographic trends (immigration, based on PISA results from 2000 to 2015) and own immigration trends (Rindermann, 2018) is $r=.61$ across 66 countries. The two 10-year effects are $decOECD=-0.29$ and $decMigr=-0.21$ IQ points. This high similarity exists despite the fact that the OECD value is based only on a past 15-year interval, and my estimate, however, includes assumptions about the future, e.g., about some reduction in the ability gap. The high agreement confirms to a certain degree the quality of my approach.

Further support comes from the "adult PISA", the PIAAC study. Here, 25- to 34-year-olds were compared with 55- to 65-year-olds. When the ability difference is corrected for mental aging (slowing down with age; "unadjusted minus adjusted"), the best historical trend over the past 30 years is seen in Singapore (and then Korea) and the worst in Germany (and then other European countries and the

U.S.). The correlation of this PIAAC trend across countries with the PISA trend is r=.66 and with our demographic trend is r=.38. That is, the past 30-year trend in adult ability is related to the trend in student outcomes in PISA and my forecast for 2010 to 2100.

An even greater loss would result if the results of the intra-German IQB study from 2017 were used (Stanat et al., 2017, pp. 159, 176). Here, the abilities of fourth graders in 2011 and 2016 were compared. The loss here was –16.33 SASQ, which corresponds to a 10-year effect of dec=–4.90 IQ points. Linearly extrapolated to a 90-year period, this would correspond to a loss of –44.10 IQ points, resulting in an IQ of 56 IQ points in 2100. That would be *Idiocracy*. Of course, this forecast is qualitatively sub-optimal. At some point, one would try to counteract it. Besides, there are other IQB studies with more favorable results (see our Table 3).

The German education economist Ludger Wößmann (2021) used available German student assessment data in a much more systematic way and found a reversal of the FLynn effect. For this purpose, he analyzed student achievement studies from 2000 to 2019, namely those of PISA, TIMSS, PIRLS and IQB, these among 15-year-old students or students in the 4th or 9th grade.[10] Bringing these data all together, Wößmann found an increase in abilities from 2000 to 2010/11 and a decrease since then (see Figure 6). From 2000 to 2010/11, the results increased by d=0.23; since then they decreased by d=–0.14. Converted to a decade, this corresponds to a loss of d=–0.1647 or dec=–2.47 IQ

---

10 *PISA*: Programme for International Student Assessment, since 2000 every three years, measures reading literacy, mathematics and sciences of 15-year-old students in secondary school. *TIMSS*: Trends in International Mathematics and Science Study, since 1995, measures curriculum-related competence in mathematics and science for fourth, eighth/ninth, and twelfth graders. *PIRLS*: Progress in International Reading Literacy Study, since 2001, every five years measures reading literacy of students in grade 4 in primary school. *IQB*: Institut zur Qualitätsentwicklung im Bildungswesen, student assessment studies, 2009, 2011, 2012, 2015, 2016 etc., measure curriculum-related reading in German, orthography, foreign languages, mathematics and sciences of students in grade 4 and 9 in primary and secondary school.

points; for a linear forecast from 2019 to 2100, a decrease of $d=-1.3341$ or -20.01 IQ points would lead to an IQ level of 79 in 2100 in Germany.

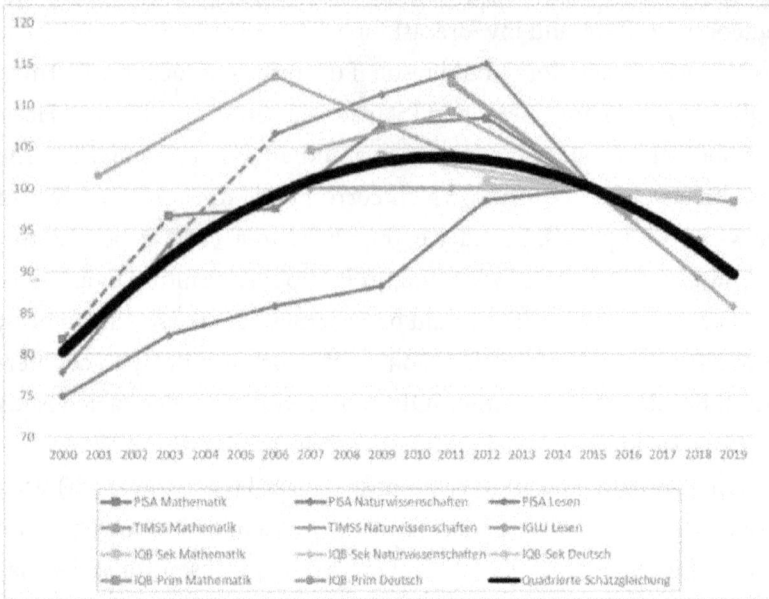

Figure 6. Increase and decrease in ability development of German pupils in student assessment studies, colored lines stand for individual dimensions and studies, the thick bold for the total value (Wößmann, 2021, p. 3).

A similar reversal of the FLynn-effect was found in Austria by Pietschnig and Gittler (2015). They used tests of spatial intelligence and found a peak around the year 1997 (see Figure 7).

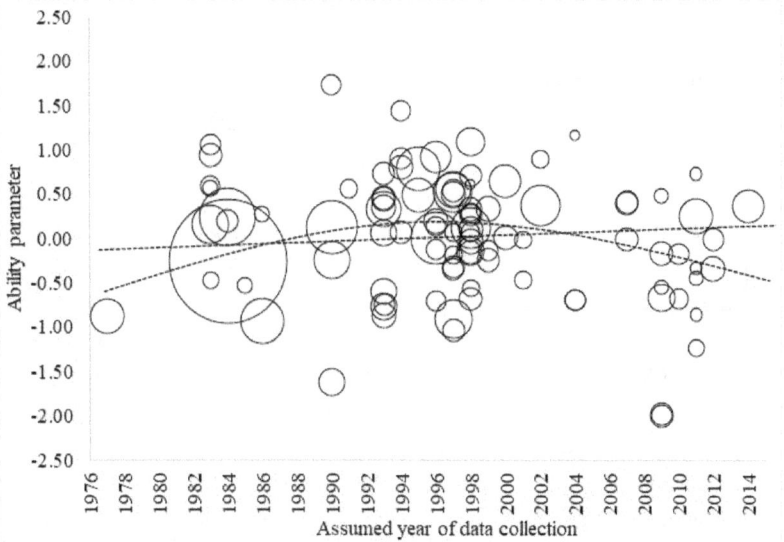

Figure 7. Intelligence development as measured by spatial perception between 1976 and 2015 in Austria (Pietschnig & Gittler, 2015, their figure 2a, redrawn by us based on data presented in their Table 1): uphill until 1997, downhill since then.

Demographic Change (Immigration)

The demographic phenomenon mentioned above in the context of the OECD study can also be well exemplified by data from the USA. In a US student achievement study, NAEP[11], which measures reading ability and mathematics, the results in all ethnic groups increased over the years. But as the percentages of the relatively better achieving ethnic group (Whites) decrease and of the relatively weaker achieving increase (Hispanics)[12], the overall trend has remained sideways since the 1970s. Thus, projections show little increase — but at least no decline either (Rindermann & Pichelmann, 2015).

---

11   National Assessment of Educational Progress (e. g., Rampey, Dion & Donahue, 2009). Also see: 28/04/09, www.nytimes.com/2009/04/29/education/29scores.html.

12   1971: 87% of 17-year-olds white, 12% minorities; 2008 59% white, 41% minorities.

The fear of a similar development for Germany was expressed in 2011 by the German "PISA pope" Jürgen Baumert: there would be gains in PISA, presumably due to teaching and school reforms, but these would be "undone" again by socio-structural change.[13] And in 2017, the journalist Martin Spiewak wrote:

> "One person had already predicted the trend reversal years ago: Jürgen Baumert, PISA-pope of the first hour, warned in 2011 in a study with the meaningful title *Origin and Education* that the population development threatens to undermine the educational progress in schools. Baumert didn't need any prophet-like abilities to make his prediction; he projected the demographic makeup of newborns onto later schoolchildren. 'The younger cohorts of students are getting smaller. At the same time, the proportion of immigrants who come from socially weaker backgrounds is rising', the school researcher said in the *ZEIT* interview. More educational poverty in families, fewer children who speak German at home — this will almost inevitably have an impact on the average learning level in elementary schools. Is it now coming as predicted?"[14]

Similarly, student achievement researcher and leader of the German IBQ studies Petra Stanat:

> "What is often cited as an explanation is the change in the composition of the student body. There is indeed some truth in that. The proportion of migrants has increased, as has the proportion of students with special needs who are taught at general schools. This means that teachers now have to deal with an extremely heterogeneous student body. This is a challenge. It's extremely challenging to teach in a way that children with different cognitive and linguistic backgrounds and different cultural backgrounds benefit equally."[15]

---

13   20.04.11, www.zeit.de/2011/17/C-Interview-Baumert

14   13/10/2017,   www.zeit.de/gesellschaft/schule/2017-10/grundschulen-schueler-iqb-bildungstrend-leistungen-vergleich, translation by HR.

15   13/10/2017,   www.spiegel.de/lebenundlernen/schule/iqb-bildungsstudie-die-kinder-haben-keine-schuld-a-1172835.html, translation by HR.

Short and sweet, die *Zeit*, a German national weekly newspaper with long articles for the educated and rather left-liberal audience. stated:

> "Migration and inclusion are probably the main causes of poorer performance in elementary school. And not the neglect of the reading primer."[16]

To the extent that migration and inclusion continue, or that students with an immigrant background from educationally disadvantaged families and students with special needs increase in percentage terms, the trend will not look good in the 21st century. But the effects are not simple. Positive and negative effects work at the same time, also for migrants:

- In Western countries, migrants *improve* from first to second generation (Kirkegaard & Fedorov, 2021; Nijenhuis et al., 2004). For Germany and according to Stanat et al. (2017, supplementary materials, p. 52), the first generation has an average of 423 SASQ points in German and mathematics, but the second generation has 463 SASQ points. The value is still far below the value of natives of 513, but the gap to natives decreases from 89.5 SASQ to 50 SASQ or from 13.43 IQ to 7.50 IQ. However, it is unclear here: Perhaps the two migrant groups differ in origin, for example, are some Arabs and others Polish? And if there is an increase due to integration, does a further increase take place afterwards, from the second to the third generation, or has a plateau already been reached with the second generation?

- In a mirror-inverted trend, *the educational background of immigrants decreased* by −1.20 years from 2011 to 2016 (Stanat et al., 2017, supplementary materials, pp. 44–45). According to Ritchie and Tucker-Drob (2018), the intelligence gain per school year is +3.39 IQ points. −1.20 years less schooling thus means −4.07 IQ

---

16   19/09/2018,   www.zeit.de/gesellschaft/schule/2018-09/schreiben-nach-gehoer-rechtschreibung-lernmethoden-grundschule-lehrer-zeitmangel, translation by HR.

points loss for parents. If one calculates that for all immigrant groups combined and extrapolates to 10 years, the result is a −4.05 IQ points loss among immigrant families.

In addition, according to the OECD (2016, p. 252, their Figure I.7.7), Germany has the world's weakest performing immigrant pupils after Denmark — by contrast, Qatar, the Emirates, Macao and Singapore have the best.

Moreover, there is usually a measurement problem: almost always, for example in IQB 2012 (Pant et al., 2013), the values calculated from native percent and migrant percent as well as total means and native means for the resulting migrant mean do not match the values actually reported for migrants. The difference is very large, amounting to 50 SASQ (475 vs. 426 SASQ) or 7.50 IQ points. This means that there must be a group with an unknown migration (or native) background and with very weak results. Presumably, the difference between natives and migrants is still clearly underestimated.

The decline in the educational level of migrant parents could increase in the 21st century, because immigration is to be expected precisely from areas with until now low levels of education and intelligence, from Africa, according to the German historian Rolf Peter Sieferle (2015, p. 23):

"Europe is in an exceptional situation in this respect, which has to do with its geographical location. Other industrial zones in the world are also threatened by immigration, but nowhere does it reach European proportions. Southern America has a population of about 400 million, which means that the number of potential emigrants is about the same as that of the inhabitants of northern America (USA and Canada). In Europe, this number is three times higher (500 million vs. 1500 million). The land border of the U.S. with Mexico is relatively small and can be secured relatively easily, since there is basically only one country from which immigrants can flow into the U.S.. In Europe, this is quite different. It is virtually impossible physically to secure the external borders."[17]

This is not an isolated position: Stephen Smith (2019a, 2019b), professor of African studies at Duke University, came to a similar assessment. And from a historical perspective, becoming even more pessimistic, Rolf Peter Sieferle (2015, p. 27f.):

> "If such a movement were to get under way, we would have before us an evolutionary process of self-destruction of an industrial society: a certain cultural constellation has historically produced the successful complex 'industrialization and modernity', but this complex has developed normative features of humanitarian universalism which make it impossible for it to regulate or prevent the influx of members of foreign cultures. Such a society, which is no longer capable of distinguishing between itself and the forces that dissolve it, lives morally beyond its means. From a normative point of view, it is not 'sustainable' [It has no means of maintaining its norms.] Through relativization, it finally destroys its cultural identity, which was the prerequisite for its efficiency. Thus it puts an end to itself."[18]

Another critical development is that the world's fastest growing religious group is one that is comparatively anti-education, anti-thinking, and has lower educational, academic achievement, and intelligence scores — Muslims (UNDP, 2003). According to the report *Why Muslims are rising fastest* by the Pew Research Center (2015), their share worldwide is expected to rise from 20% in 2010 to 30% in 2050. As seen in 2015 and following, Muslims in particular are immigrating in Europe and especially in Germany. As always, there are interindividual differences, i.e., there are also very intelligent individuals from Muslim backgrounds, but the overall group shows lower levels of ability.

The Pew Research Center (2017) expects, in its report *Europe's growing Muslim population,* an increase in the proportion of Muslims

---

17   Translation by HR.

18   Translation by HR; text in brackets [] added by HR.

in Europe.[19] Especially in Scandinavia, Western Europe, then in Central Europe and Southern Europe, the Muslim population share would increase. Empirically, the increase in Muslims in Europe between 2010 and 2016 is negatively correlated with increases in PISA ($r=-.25$, $N=29$). That is, in countries with more growth in Muslims, school performance scores have developed worse.

The Munich-based economist Niklas Potrafke (2012, p. 191) has pointed out further problematic consequences of an increase in Muslims, especially for other groups in a society:

> "A large Muslim population share, apart from having a direct negative influence on human development and economic performance thus also gives rise to a reinforcing indirect effect working through the political institutions. ... By compromising these democratic institutions, countries with Muslim majorities tend to have relatively low living standards. ... The non-Muslim population living in democracies may confront the end of democracy and also the end of accompanying high incomes if there is sufficient demographic change."[20]

So a large percentage of Muslims in a society has not only a direct negative effect on the quality of life, but an indirect one via an impairment of institutions including for non-Muslim groups.

For the U.S., the American psychologist Byron Roth has attempted to outline cognitive development through mid-century:

> "Population projections and IQ estimates for various groups suggest that the overall IQ of the U. S. population will probably fall from about 98 today to about 95 by mid-century." (Roth, 2014/2010, p. 471)
>
> "The most obvious effect of the demographic changes in the United States will be a decline in relative standards of living for most Americans and this will be felt quite differently for different segments of the country's

---

19   See also already in 2006 the historian Bernard Lewis: "Christians are becoming a minority in Europe. ... Provided current trends of immigration and demographics remain, then Europe will become Islamic." 19/04/2006, www.welt.de/print-welt/article211310/Europa-wird-islamisch.html. Translation by HR.

20   References in footnote omitted.

population. Tensions between groups with divergent economic success will likely be most pronounced in states and regions with large numbers of Hispanics and blacks." (Roth, 2014/2010, p. 474)
"Those demographics suggest that in the future American educational performance will decline, social trust, harmony, and faith in American institutions will decline, as will economic productivity." (Roth, 2014/2010, p. 481)

Byron Roth thus assumes that the reduction in intelligence increases tensions between groups, especially between the less successful and the more successful. In addition to immigration, another effect to be noted is that migrants have more children on average. In 2019, the Federal Statistical Office (Statistische Bundesamt, 2019) spoke of a baby boom among migrant women (p. 22): women born in Germany have an average of 1.5 children, while women born abroad have an average of 2.0 children. Foreign-born women with low education, 41% of foreign-born women, have a particularly high number of children (2.4 children). The figures still underestimate the proportion of children with a migration background, because among women born in Germany there are also many with a migration background, who in turn have relatively more children.

According to the German demographer Herwig Birg (2008), 54% of the population in Germany will have a migration background in 2100 (according to the citizenship law until 31/12/1999). In my own independent estimate (Rindermann, 2018, p. 443, Table 13.6), it would be 52% in 2100 — there is only a deviation of 2% to Birg's prediction! Among children, according to Birg, 65% would have a migration background in 2100.

What does the 2015 wave of immigration (refugees) mean for cognitive ability?

We want to develop the model step by step, taking into account more and more assumptions.

Actual State

In 2015, Germany had a mean cognitive ability level expressed in an international IQ scale of 99.20 IQ points for approximately 80 million inhabitants.

Immigration 2015

About one million migrants entered the country in 2015 — about 850,000 official refugees, plus other family migrants in 2015 plus non-registered persons. All numbers are estimates. 75% of these came from Arab or Muslim countries (e.g., Syria, Afghanistan) with a mean ability level of IQ 83.28 and 25% from sub-Saharan Africa with an IQ of 69.19 (Rindermann, 2018, p. 433, Table 13.3). (We do without relatively few refugee migrants from other regions here.) The calculation is as follows: (80 million x IQ 99.20 + 0.75 million x IQ 83.28 + 0.25 million x IQ 69.19) / 81 million = 98.96 IQ.

The loss for the total population is –0.24 IQ points, which is not much. The decrease is negligible, certainly it could be compensated by environmental improvements. But the immigrants have a different *age structure*. They are quite young, one would have to compare them to the part of society of the same age. This young group reflects the intelligence of the future.

In the Young Generation

Let us assume that the one million immigrants correspond to the 25 million younger Germans. The calculation looks like this: (25 million x IQ 99.20 + 0.75 million x IQ 83.28 + 0.25 million x IQ 69.19) / 26 million = 98.45 IQ. In this generation, we then have a loss of –0.75 IQ points.

Catching Up

We know from economic studies that differences between immigrant groups in their incomes level off somewhat over time, but we also see from the U.S. example that income patterns remain very stable across generations: 1880–1910 r=.92, 1880–1940 r=.83, 1910–1940 r=.93, for 19 countries of origin (self-calculated based on Ward, 2020, p. 84, his Table 1). Both Nijenhuis and Stanat spoke of a narrowing of cognitive gaps between the first and second generations (see above). So let's assume that immigrants catch up somewhat over time, an increase of +5 IQ. Calculation: (25 million x IQ 99.20 + 0.75 million x IQ 88.28 + 0.25 million x IQ 74.19) / 26 million = 98.64 IQ. This would correspond to a loss in this generation of –0.56 IQ points.

Family Reunification and Children

Let us add the assumption that later there is a family reunification and the migrants have children over the decades. One migrant becomes three, a spouse (usually a wife from the country of origin) and a child, a very conservative assumption. Calculation: (25 million x IQ 99.20 + 2.25 million x IQ 88.28 + 0.75 million x IQ 74.19)/28=97.65 IQ. The loss in this generation is then around –1.55 IQ points.

Further Immigration

It can also be assumed that more immigrants will come in the future, even if not so many per year, assuming a sixfold increase over the decades. 24% of the future generation will then come from the Arab, Muslim and African regions, which is still rather conservative (cf. above Birg, Lewis, Pew, Sieferle, Smith). Calculation: (25 million x IQ 99.20 + 4.50 million x IQ 88.28 + 1.50 million x IQ 74.19) / 31 million = 96.40 IQ. The loss in this generation is –2.80 IQ points.

Further Catch-Up

Let us assume a further IQ alignment of the migrants, especially in the case of the relatively most downward deviating: (25 million x IQ 99.20 + 4.50 million x IQ 90.00 + 1.50 million x IQ 84.00) / 31 million = 97.13 IQ. The loss in this generation is –2.07 IQ points.

In 2100 (or before), half of the population has a migration background. Let's assume, like the other authors mentioned above, that just under half of the population (45%) of the future generation will be from Arab, Muslim and African backgrounds: (0.55 x IQ 99.20 + 0.3375 x IQ 90.00 + 0.1125 x IQ 84.00) / 1=94.39 IQ[21] This corresponds to a loss in this generation of –4.82 IQ points.

Institutional Deterioration

If we also consider that the conditions in institutions relevant for cognitive development (e.g., in kindergarten, school and university) will deteriorate in the future due to a strong increase in educationally and intellectually challenged groups, we arrive at a total loss of about –5 IQ points.

Table 2. Prediction of the change in cognitive abilities in Germany due to the influx of refugees (migrants) in 2015 and the following

	IQ-value	Lost
(1) Germany beginning 2015	99.20	0
(2) Germany end 2015	98.96	–0.24
(3) Young Germany end 2015	98.45	–0.75
(4) Young Germany end 2015, immigrants catch up	98.64	–0.56
(5) Young Germany end 2050, catch up, family reunification and children	97.65	–1.55
(6) Young Germany end 2050, catch up, family reunification, children, further immigration	96.40	–2.80
(7) Young Germany end 2050, catch up, family reunification, children, further immigration, further catch up	97.13	–2.07
(8) Young Germany end 2100/2050, catch up, 45% migrants	94.39	–4.82
(9) Young Germany end 2100/2050, catch up, 45% migrants, institutional deterioration	94.20	–5.00

Notes: Based on migration assumptions only (excluding environmental improvement, excluding asymmetric fertility within natives).

Table 2 shows an overview of the results of the various assumptions. We must remain aware that forecasts always depend on the respective assumptions, even if only on the assumption of a continuation of the actual state. The assumptions must be justified and — if new information contradicting these assumptions comes from reality — corrected.

---

21 The number 0.55 corresponds to 55%.

As far as the influx of migrants from Muslim countries is concerned, for example, there are discernible differences between various models. Thilo Sarrazin (2016, p. 214), for example, assumes a multiplier of 5 of a refugee within 20 years. He calculated various models: without further waves of refugees, but with family reunification and children, there would be 6 million "refugees" in Germany in 2050; but with an annual new refugee influx of 200,000, there would then be 32.6 million in Germany in 2050; with an annual new refugee influx of 0.5 million in 2050, even 70 million! The more migrants there are in Germany, the smaller the support effect of the German environment will presumably be. Sarrazin (2016, p. 302):

> "However, the necessary cultural acclimatization to the host society becomes all the more difficult the higher the number of immigrants with low cognitive competence, the lower the proportion of Germans in the total population and the more the natural cohesion of culturally similar immigrant groups favors tendencies toward segregation."[22]

Or the German mathematician Axel Latka in a long and complex model calculation, greatly abbreviated by me[23]:

> "In 2014, around 4.3 million Muslims lived in Germany. That corresponded to about 5% of the population. Now the birth rates of non-Muslims are no longer sufficient to keep the population constant. Within one generation (about 30 years), the number of non-Muslims would decline by a third without immigration. ...
> For a projection of Muslim immigration to Germany until the end of 2024, we assume that about 200,000 non-European migrants will enter Germany annually. This is roughly equivalent to the current monthly immigration, extrapolated to one year. We assume that 80% of the immigrants are Muslims and come from countries to which removal does not take place.

---

22 Translation by HR.

23 Axel Latka, Bevölkerungsentwicklung in Deutschland [Population development in Germany], 6/04/2017, www.tichyseinblick.de/gastbeitrag/bevoelkerungsentwicklung-in-deutschland.

These migrants will therefore remain in Germany permanently. ... The average birth rate per woman is 2.5 children. ...

The proportion of the Muslim population would be around 10 percent of the total population in 2025. There can be no talk of Islamization yet. ...

For our scenario, we assume that a political and social caesura will take place in 2040. On the one hand, immigration is restricted to family reunification and the immigration of well-qualified workers. On the other hand, an exodus of able-bodied and wealthy citizens to more attractive countries begins. In our scenario, we assume the reduction of the population growth of the Muslim population to 250,000 persons per year until 2045 and to 100,000 persons per year from 2046. We assume the birth rate of Muslims at 2 children per woman. For the period up to 2045, we still include births that are a consequence of increased immigration in the 2030s. The non-Muslim population would shrink by 1.3% annually due to the constant low birth rate of 1.4 children per woman and by 0.5% annually due to migration losses.

In the year 2100, our scenario results in a Muslim population majority in Germany."

Depending on the assumptions (e.g., average birth rate per woman and its decline among immigrants), different outcomes result. However, all known models assume an increase in the proportion of the population who have a background that is compared to the native population poorly educated and low in intelligence.

New Prediction Models for Germany

In Table 3 we present the different prediction models and their results. In the first two rows, we have entered the results of old models, that of 2011 and 2018 (see Table 1). Several assumptions were incorporated here:

Further, but almost exhausted, environmental improvements in Germany.

The target cognitive level theoretically achievable for Germany (maximum value IQ 105; Rindermann, 2018, Table 13.2, p. 431).

Asymmetric number of children and generation length (less educated and intelligent persons have more children and at younger ages).

Further migration and limited alignment (Rindermann, 2018, chapters 12 and 13).

The 2018 model did not yet include the most recent waves of migration in 2015 and subsequent years. This is taken into account now in models 3 (younger German population, migrants catching up somewhat, family reunification and higher numbers of children than natives) and 4 (more migrants coming from countries with lower ability levels, these catching up somewhat in their abilities).

Table 3. Prediction of the development of cognitive abilities in Germany until the year 2100.

	IQ 2010	IQ 2100	Change in IQ
(1) Model 2011 (Rindermann & Thompson, 2011)	99.82	97.22	–2.60
(2) Model 2018 (Rindermann, 2018, p. 449)	98.82	93.35	–5.47
(3) Model 2018 plus refugee wave 2015 (Model 5)	98.82	91.80	–7.02
(4) Model 2018 plus refugee wave 2015 plus further immigration and catch up (model 7 from Table 2 above)	98.82	91.28	–7.54
(5) IQB-development 2009 to 2018, continued linearly by HR Independent calculation by a research assistant	99.00 99.00	76.95 79.39	–22.05 –19.61
(6) Student achievement development 2010/11 to 2019 (Wößmann, 2021), continued linearly by HR from 2019 on	(99.00)	78.99	–20.01

Notes: HR: Heiner Rindermann.

Models 5 and 6 are completely new: For model 5, developments in the same subjects (e.g., mathematics) and grade levels (e.g., grade 9) were calculated in the IQB studies (also see Wößmann, 2021):

- In grade 9 reading, listening, and spelling between 2009 and 2015 (converted to a decade in school performance points *dec*=–6.67 SASQ).

- In grade 4 reading, listening, and mathematics between 2011 and 2016 (language *dec*=-23.00 SASQ, math *dec*=-34.00 SASQ).

- In grade 9 mathematics between 2012 and 2018 (*dec*=-1.67 SASQ).

These results were averaged and converted to the IQ metric, from a standard deviation of 100 to a standard deviation of 15, resulting in *dec*=-16.33 SASQ or *dec*=-2.45 IQ in ten years. This number was converted to 90 years, for the development from 2010 to 2100. The initial value is IQ 99 in 2010. For Model 6, we adopted the trend in student achievement studies calculated by Wößmann (2021) for 2010/11 through 2019 and linearly extrapolated the trend through 2100.

The results for the IQB and student achievement studies are dramatic. Linear extrapolation would put Germany in the year 2100 at an IQ level of 78 points, roughly where Syria or Sudan are today. All three linear predictions came to a similar result (IQ 77 to 79). A great advantage of simple linear extrapolation is that accusations of political bias, as they are often made against intelligence research by interested (left-wing) parties ("racism", "classism", etc.), do not apply here. There is no causal model, no consideration of environmental or genetic effects, no influence of group-related assumptions, nothing, only the idea of a continuation. Of course, it could be criticized which period of the past was chosen for the forecast of the future. If, for example, the last century had been chosen instead of the last decade, the forecast would be positive. One would have to justify that one considers the development of the last decade as informative for the future and not the development of the last century. Such a justification is missing here.

Let us return to contentual assumptions and justifications. Presumably, the result will not be quite so dramatic in the end:

- We assume that among less intelligent groups the FLynn effect, i.e., gains from environmental improvements in nutrition, education, and through modernization, will continue to work.

- The lower the level, the less harmful bad environment becomes, because people are already close to the lower limit. For example, someone who is dieting can lose more weight as an overweight person than a thin person.

- We expect a change in policy regarding immigration. At some point, the negative consequences will become so obvious that a correction will be inevitable (cf. above the considerations of the mathematician Axel Latka).

However, the change could come so late that negative institutional effects (cf. Meisenberg, 2010, above) become so strong—for example through dysfunctional teachers, civil servants and classmates and consequently poor teaching, through inadequate crime control, poor administration and police, irrational voting decisions and bad role models—that too far a step downward has been taken and society, institutions and the population find themselves in a downward spiral. In any case, the linear extrapolation of the IQB and student assessment studies (Wößmann) trends shows that my own previous models are not dramatically negative, but if anything too positive!

If we average all seven calculations in Table 3, we arrive at a mean value of IQ 87.00. If we first average the last three projections (simple linear projection of past development) and then calculate the mean value, the final result is IQ 90.41. However, the last three numbers reflect only a hypothetical-linear and too simple model. We think that the more complex model 7 (line (4)) is the most valid, a model that takes into account both positive and negative working factors and political as well as institutional changes. Thus, our final estimate for Germany in 2100 is an IQ of 91, which corresponds to a decline of 8 IQ points.

This does not look good. Only a god can save us. A miracle pill. Genetic interventions. Positive birth policies. All such far-reaching measures will also have undesirable side effects. They would be controversial in any case.

Perhaps the result may seem a bit gloomy to some readers. Or implausible, not conceivable. A similar paper for Denmark by Helmuth Nyborg in 2012 caused an academic outcry. But if one simply extrapolates the development of the last decade, in the example of Germany, one arrives at even higher losses than predicted by Nyborg: Helmuth Nyborg predicted an IQ of about 90 for the year 2100, a linear extrapolation would lead to an IQ of about 78 in Germany in 2100.

That the development in recent times has been negative for Germany (or the German-speaking countries) is a consensus of the most diverse researchers, from psychology, educational economics and student assessment research, from Germany and Austria, from left to right into the middle. No matter which source or method one uses, the forecasts are gloomy. And surprisingly, no one seems to mind, as education economist Ludger Wößmann noted a few months ago:

> "What stirs me up is that the ministers of education accept this relegation and, after every education study, sell a partial aspect as good news. According to the motto: it's not all that bad."[24]

I am curious to see how people will react in the year 2100 when they read this paper.

References

Autor, D. H. (2014). Skills, education, and the rise of earnings inequality among the "other 99 percent". *Science, 344*, 843–851.

Autor, D. H. & Price, B. (2013). *The Changing Task Composition of the US Labor Market: An Update of Autor, Levy, and Murnane (2003)*. Cambridge: MIT. Retrieved from https://economics.mit.edu/files/9758

Birg, H. (2008). *Population projections and forecasts for Germany*. Presentation at the workshop "Demographic Change in Europe", 1–2 April 2008, American Academy, Berlin.

24　06.10.2021,　www.zeit.de/2021/41/bildung-deutschland-pisa-studie-bildungspolitik-ludger-woessmann-forschung; translation by HR.

Bönke, T. & Lüthen, H. (2014). Lebenseinkommen von Arbeitnehmern in Deutschland: Ungleichheit verdoppelt sich zwischen den Geburtsjahrgängen 1935 und 1972. [Lifetime income of employees in Germany: Inequality doubles between the 1935 and 1972 birth cohorts.] *DIW Wochenbericht, 49,* 1271–1277.

Carl, N. & Woodley of Menie, M. A. (2019). A scientometric analysis of controversies in the field of intelligence research. *Intelligence, 77,* 101397.

Dutton, E. & Woodley of Menie, M. A. (2018). *At our wits' end: Why we're becoming less intelligent and what it means for the future.* Exeter: Imprint Academic.

Fischer, H.-J. (1986). *Rom: Zweieinhalb Jahrtausende Kunst und Kultur in der Ewigen Stadt.* [Rome: Two and a half millennia of art and culture in the Eternal City.] Köln: DuMont.

Flynn, J. R. (2012). *Are we getting smarter? Rising IQ in the twenty-first century.* Cambridge: Cambridge University Press.

Hanushek, E. A., Peterson, P. E. & Woessmann, L. (2013). *Endangering Prosperity.* Washington: Brookings.

Howard, R. W. (1999). Preliminary real-world evidence that average intelligence really is rising. *Intelligence, 27,* 235–250.

Hunt, E. (1995). *Will Ee Be Smart Enough? A Cognitive Analysis of the Coming Workforce.* New York: Russell Sage Foundation.

Itzkoff, S. W. (1994). *The Decline of Intelligence in America. A Strategy for National Renewal.* Westport: Praeger.

Jensen, A. R. (1983). Effects of inbreeding on mental-ability factors. *Personality and Individual Differences, 4,* 71–87.

Kirkegaard, E. O. W. & Fedorov, J. (2021). Country of origin IQ and Muslim percentage predict grade point average in school among 116 immigrant groups in Denmark. *Mankind Quarterly, 61*(3), 599–625.

Kong, A., Frigge, M. L., Thorleifsson, G., Stefansson, H., Young, A. I., Zink, F., … Stefansson, K. (2017). Selection against variants in the genome associated with educational attainment. *Proceedings of the National Academy of Sciences, 114,* E727–E732.

Loehlin, J. C. (1997). Dysgenesis and IQ. What evidence is relevant? *American Psychologist, 52,* 1236–1239.

Lynn, R. (1990). The role of nutrition in secular increases in intelligence. *Personality and Individual Differences, 11,* 273–285.

Lynn, R. & Harvey, J. (2008). The decline of the world's IQ. *Intelligence, 36,* 112–120.

Lynn, R. & Van Court, M. (2004). New evidence of dysgenic fertility for intelligence in the United States. *Intelligence, 32,* 193–201.

Meisenberg, G. (2010). The reproduction of intelligence. *Intelligence*, *38*, 220–230.

Meyer, J. W., Ramirez, F. O. & Soysal, Y. N. (1992). World expansion of mass education, 1870–1980. *Sociology of Education*, *65*, 128–149.

Miller, A. K. H. & Corsellis, J. A. N. (1977). Evidence for a secular increase in human brain weight during the past century. *Annals of Human Biology*, *4*, 253–257.

Moore, S. & Simon, J. L. (2000). *It's Getting Better All the Time*. Washington: Cato.

Ndulu, B. J. (2004). Human capital flight: Stratification, globalization, and the challenges to tertiary education in Africa. *Journal of Higher Education in Africa*, *2*, 57–91.

Nijenhuis, J., de Jong, M.-J., Evers, A. & van der Flier, H. (2004). Are cognitive differences between immigrant and majority groups diminishing? *European Journal of Personality*, *18*, 405–434.

Nyborg, H. (2003). The sociology of psychometric and bio-behavioral sciences: A case study of destructive social reductionism and collective fraud in 20ᵗʰ century academia. In H. Nyborg (Ed.), *The Scientific Study of General Intelligence. Tribute to Arthur R. Jensen* (pp. 441–502). Oxford: Pergamon.

Nyborg, H. (2012). The decay of Western civilization: Double relaxed Darwinian selection. *Personality and Individual Differences*, *53*, 118–125.

OECD (2013). *OECD Skills Outlook 2013. First Results from the Survey of Adult Skills (PIAAC)*. Paris: OECD.

OECD (2016). *PISA 2015 Results (Volume I): Excellence and Equity in Education*. Paris: OECD.

Oesterdiekhoff, G. W. (2013). *Die Entwicklung der Menschheit von der Kindheitsphase zur Erwachsenenreife*. [The development of humanity from the childhood phase to adult maturity.] Berlin: Springer.

Pant, H. A., Stanat, P., Schroeders, U., Alexander Roppelt, Siegle, T. & Pöhlmann, C. (2013). *IQB-Ländervergleich 2012*. [IQB state comparison 2012.] Münster: Waxmann.

Pew Research Center (2015). *The Future of World Religions: Population Growth Projections, 2010–2050. Why Muslims Are Rising Fastest and the Unaffiliated are Shrinking as a Share of the World's Population*. Washington: Pew Research Center.

Pew Research Center (2017). *Europe's Growing Muslim Population*. Washington, D.C.: Pew Research Center.

Pietschnig, J. & Gittler, G. (2015). A reversal of the Flynn effect for spatial perception in German-speaking countries: Evidence from a cross-temporal IRT-based meta-analysis (1977–2014). *Intelligence*, *53*, 145–153.

Pietschnig, J. & Voracek, M. (2015). One century of global IQ gains: A formal meta-analysis of the Flynn effect (1909–2013). *Perspectives on Psychological Science, 10*, 282–306.

Pinker, S. (2021). *Rationality: What It Is, Why It Seems Scarce, Why It Matters*. New York: Viking.

Potrafke, N. (2012). Islam and democracy. *Public Choice, 151*, 185–192.

Rampey, B. D., Dion, G. S. & Donahue, P. L. (2009). *NAEP 2008 Trends in Academic Progress*. Washington: National Center for Education Statistics.

Retherford, R. D. & Sewell, W. H. (1989). How intelligence affects fertility. *Intelligence, 13*, 169–185.

Rindermann, H. (2018). *Cognitive Capitalism: Human Capital and the Wellbeing of Nations*. Cambridge University Press.

Rindermann, H. (2022). The advantages of having a minority viewpoint in politicized psychology: A case study of intelligence. In C. L. Frisby, R. Redding, W. T. O'Donohue & S. O. Lilienfeld (Eds.), *Political Bias in Psychology: Nature, Scope, and Solutions*. Cham: Springer.

Rindermann, H. & Pichelmann, S. (2015). Future cognitive ability: US IQ prediction until 2060 based on NAEP. *PLoS ONE, 10*(10), e0138412.

Rindermann, H. & Thompson, J. (2011). *Intelligence of the future and economic development*. Talk at 10. December 2011 at the 12th Conference of the International Society for Intelligence Research (ISIR) in Limassol, Cyprus.

Rindermann, H., Becker, D. & Coyle, Th. R. (2017). Survey of expert opinion on intelligence: The FLynn effect and the future of intelligence. *Personality and Individual Differences, 106*, 242–247.

Ritchie, S. J. & Tucker-Drob, E. M. (2018). How much does education improve intelligence? A meta-analysis. *Psychological Science, 29*, 1358–1369.

Roth, B. M. (2014/2010). *The Perils of Diversity: Immigration and Human Nature*. Augusta: Washington Summit.

Sarrazin, Th. (2016). *Wunschdenken. Europa, Währung, Bildung, Einwanderung — warum Politik so häufig scheitert*. [Wishful thinking. Europe, currency, education, immigration - why politics fail so often.] München: DVA.

Sieferle, R. P. (2015). Deutschland, Schlaraffenland. Auf dem Weg in die multitribale Gesellschaft. [Germany, land of milk and honey. On the way to a multitribal society.] *Tumult. Vierteljahresschrift für Konsensstörung, 4*, 23–28.

Smith, S. (2019a/2018). *The Scramble for Europe. Young Africa on Its Way to the Old Continent*. Cambridge: Polity.

Smith, S. (2019b). The scramble for Europe. The number of Africans migrating overseas is bound to rise significantly, and most will head for Europe. *The Security Times, February*, p. 29.

Stanat, P., Schipolowski, S., Rjosk, C., Weirich, S. & Haag, N. (Eds.). (2017). *IQB-Bildungstrend 2016*. [IQB-trend in education 2016.] Münster: Waxmann.

Statistisches Bundesamt (2010). *Mikrozensus 2008 — Neue Daten zur Kinderlosigkeit in Deutschland*. Ergänzende Tabellen zur Pressekonferenz. Überarbeitete und erweiterte Version, Stand: Dezember 2010. [Microcensus 2008.] Wiesbaden: Destatis.

Statistisches Bundesamt (Destatis) (2019). *Kinderlosigkeit, Geburten und Familien. Ergebnisse des Mikrozensus 2018*. [Childlessness, births, and families. Results of the Microcensus 2018.] Wiesbaden: Destatis.

Stumm, S. v., Batty, G. D. & Deary, I. J. (2011). Marital status and reproduction: Associations with childhood intelligence and adult social class in the Aberdeen children of the 1950s study. *Intelligence, 39*, 161–167.

Trahan, L. H., Stuebing, K. K., Fletcher, J. M. & Hiscock, M. (2014). The Flynn effect: A meta-analysis. *Psychological Bulletin, 140*, 1332–1360.

UNDP (2003). *Arab Human Development Report 2003. Building a Knowledge Society*. New York: UNDP.

UNDP (2019). *Scaling fences: Voices of Irregular African Migrants to Europe*. New York: UNDP Regional Bureau for Africa.

Wang, M., Fuerst, J. & Ren, J. (2016). Evidence of dysgenic fertility in China. *Intelligence, 57*, 15–24.

Ward, Z. (2020). The not-so-hot melting pot: The persistence of outcomes for descendants of the age of mass migration. *American Economic Journal: Applied Economics, 12*, 73–102.

Weissberg, R. (2010). *Bad Students, Not Bad Schools*. New Brunswick: Transaction.

Woodley of Menie, M. A. (2015). How fragile is our intellect? Estimating losses in general intelligence due to both selection and mutation accumulation. *Personality and Individual Differences, 75*, 80–84.

Woodley, M. A., te Nijenhuis, J. & Murphy, R. (2013). Were the Victorians cleverer than us? The decline in general intelligence estimated from a meta-analysis of the slowing of simple reaction time. *Intelligence, 41*, 843–850.

Wößmann, L. (2021). *Testleistungen deutscher Schüler:innen über die Zeit, Methodik der Darstellung*. [Test performance of German pupils over time, methodology of presentation.] München: IFO. Retrieved from https://drive.google.com/file/d/1ozhDq1tKTPsOR7kR9JFu5ro_hdvZQ3c1/view?usp=sharing.

CHAPTER 11

VERY STRONG BUT IMPERFECT JENSEN EFFECTS FOR RACIAL AND ETHNIC MINORITIES

JAN TE NIJENHUIS

1. Introduction: Helmuth Nyborg

WHEN SOMEONE FINISHES primary school at age 13, he generally is a slow learner. When somebody ends primary school at age 14, it often concerns a very slow learner. In Professor Helmuth Nyborg's case, he finished primary school at age 25 (te Nijenhuis, 2007: Interview with Helmuth Nyborg). Could it be that the term 'very slow learner' is not strong enough to describe this influential intelligence researcher, and do we require an expression containing the words 'box' and 'bricks'? After all, spending one-third of your time outside of the classroom, selling floor wax, and being a ship's stoker are rarely part of the CV of persons of high intelligence. However, his nickname in primary school was already 'Fessor', the Danish abbreviation for 'professor', the equivalent of 'prof', as Danes have the habit of leaving out the first part of a word in some of their abbreviations. Therefore, these anecdotes about the young Helmuth Nyborg are probably best interpreted as showing the behavior of a recalcitrant personality. In this case, a person that goes his own way, that goes where the empirical evidence leads him, and only briefly mourns the loss of a couple of insufficiently open-minded friends along the way.

It is a great pleasure and a great honor to be invited to contribute to this Festschrift in honor of Helmuth Nyborg. Where sometimes social scientists are accused of predicting that the light goes on when you hit the light switch, Nyborg does not shy away from engaging in fundamental scientific discussions. For example, one of the hottest fundamental discussions in social science concerns the causes of the often-large differences in mean IQ scores between racial/ethnic groups, and Nyborg fearlessly dove into that hot debate. In two of Nyborg's classical contributions to the discussion, he tested Jensen's default hypothesis for IQ differences between groups, namely that causes of within-group differences are the same as causes of between-group differences. As large-scale research has shown that general intelligence is the most important cause of differences within a homogeneous group, it is expected that general intelligence is also the most important cause of differences between racial groups. Nyborg contributed to this discussion with two influential papers: one co-authored with Arthur Jensen (Nyborg & Jensen, 2000), where he looked at the causes of mean IQ differences between Blacks and Whites, and one co-authored with Peter Hartmann (Hartmann, Kruuse, & Nyborg, 2007), where he looked at the mean IQ differences between Hispanics and non-Hispanic Whites. Below we will discuss how these two studies and other findings offer strong support for Jensen's default hypothesis and explain the research method used, namely the method of correlated vectors.

2. Jensen Effects, Anti-Jensen Effects, and Neutral Effects

We first introduce a method from fundamental intelligence research, the method of correlated vectors. Secondly, we will show how the outcomes can be organized into three clusters.

2.1 The Method of Correlated Vectors

Thousands of tests have been developed to measure intelligence. For some tests you have to reason, other tests tap your short-term memory, some tests require you to play with numbers, and yet other tests require you to rotate figures in three-dimensional space. These tests all look very different, but when they are given to a large group of people, all the tests correlate positively and substantially. So, a person with a low score on reasoning most likely also has low scores on the other three tests, and a person with a high score on a numerical test most likely also has above-average scores on the other tests. When the correlation matrix of all these tests is analyzed in a factor-analysis, without exception, a strong general factor of intelligence (g) appears, and the tests with high cognitive complexity show strong correlations with this g factor, and the tests with low cognitive complexity show lower correlations with this g factor. These correlations of intelligence tests with the g factor are called g loadings.

Jensen (1998) used intelligence tests' considerable variation in cognitive complexity, and therefore g-loadedness, when he developed the method of correlated vectors (MCV). The basic statistics of MCV are quite simple. Let's say you have an IQ battery with ten subtests, then the ten g loadings of these subtests form your vector of g loadings. The second vector of the same subtests takes its data from another variable, such as the heritabilities of these same subtests, as computed using samples of monozygotic and dizygotic twins. So, the g loadings in the g vector vary from large to small, and the heritabilities in the heritabilities vector vary from large to small, and MCV tests how strongly the vector of g loadings predicts the vector of heritabilities. Suppose there is a very strong correlation between g loadings and heritabilities, then it means that the complexity of the subtests very strongly determines the strength of the heritability coefficient on these subtests.

Jensen (1998) developed the method of correlated vectors to go to the heart of g, to find the variables central to understanding the g factor. Rushton (1998) stated that when variables showed a strong correlation with g loadings, they should be called Jensen effects. Rushton (1998) also stated that when variables did not show Jensen effects, they were also interesting: an absence of Jensen effects helps understand what general intelligence is not. For several decades, many studies used the method of correlated vectors. The outcomes of these studies show a crystal-clear pattern (te Nijenhuis et al., 2019): biological-genetic variables show Jensen effects, environmental, cultural variables show anti-Jensen effects, meaning a strong negative correlation with g loadings, and environmental, biological-non-genetic variables show neutral effects, meaning zero-ish correlations with g loadings. We will discuss these findings in more detail below.

2.2 The Validity of g Loadings

At various places, James Flynn has written that subtests of an intelligence battery differ in cognitive complexity; when independent variables, for instance heritability, reflect the varying degrees of cognitive complexity, Flynn talks about 'the g pattern', or what Rushton called 'Jensen effects'. Flynn's position that g loadings reflect cognitive complexity has been firmly established. Table 1 shows various studies that support the validity of g loadings, including the strength of the Jensen effects and the sample size on which the study was based. An excellent Spanish study (Arend et al., 2003) empirically measured the difficulty of tests and also used three models to describe the cognitive complexity of tests: a spatial model, a linguistic model, and a model that combined the two previous models. These four outcomes were correlated with g loadings of the tests, which yielded four strong correlations. Also, Armstrong et al. (2014) rated the abstractness of IQ subtests and found a strong relationship with g loadings. Finally, Vernon (1989) used simple information processing tests that correlate with traditional IQ tests, looked at the complexity of these information processing tests, and found strong correlations with g loadings.

Some other studies give proof of the validity of g loadings, using data on the relationship with crucial measures for success in life, namely school performance, work training performance, and job performance. Using MCV yielded strong correlations for school performance (Jensen, 1998, p. 280), training performance (Ree & Earles, 1991; Ree & Earles, 1994), and job performance (Jensen, 1998, p. 286). Moreover, measures of learning ability also show strong correlations with cognitive complexity (Jensen, 1998, p. 277). So, the validity of g loadings has been firmly established.

Table 1. Several studies on the validity of g loadings.

Study	Central variable	r	N
Arend, Colom, Botella, Contreras, Rubio, & Santacreu (2003)	empirical difficulty tasks	.52	1,968
	cognitive complexity tasks: spatial model	.63	1,968
	cognitive complexity tasks: linguistic model	.47	1,968
	cognitive complexity tasks: spatial + linguistic model	.54	1,968
Armstrong, te Nijenhuis, et al. (2016)	abstractness of IQ subtests	.61	902
Vernon (1989a)	information processing complexity	.68	102
Jensen (1998, p. 277)	learning ability	.82	448
		.87	431
Jensen (1998, p. 280)	scholastic performance high school juniors	.73	n.r.
	scholastic performance college freshmen	.91	n.r.
Ree & Earles (1991)	training performance	.75	24,000
Ree & Earles (1994)	training performance	.96	78,000
Jensen (1998, p. 286)	job performance	.65	n.r.

Note. n.r. = not reported or could not be obtained.

2.3 Jensen Effects

Variables showing Jensen effects go to the heart of *g*, and Table 2 lists many biological-genetic variables that show Jensen effects in many studies, albeit not all. However, from a meta-analytical perspective, this is not surprising, because when there is a substantial number of studies, there is a risk of outliers and even extreme outliers, especially when there are many small studies in the meta-analytical database (see: Hunter & Schmidt, 1990); the focus should be on the overall value from all the studies. Fourteen studies are on genetic factors, namely heritability, inbreeding, and hybrid vigor, and this collection includes a meta-analysis of Japanese studies. Interestingly, Woodley, Fernandes, and Hopkins (2015) show that Jensen effects can also be found for the heritability of intelligence tests taken by chimpanzees. The overall picture of these studies is a very strong relationship between *g* loadings and heritability.

Seventeen correlations are from twelve studies on the brain, which measure variables such as various brain activities, brain size, including sex differences in brain size, and head size. Interestingly, Crinella and Yu (1995) show that Jensen effects can also be found in brain studies on rats, focusing on the number of brain structures involved in task performance and differences between lesioned and un-lesioned rats. All these brain-related variables have been shown to be clearly heritable (see: Jensen, 1998) or can be expected to be clearly heritable. The overall picture of these studies is a very strong relationship between *g* loadings and brain variables.

Table 2. Various studies on biological-genetic variables showing Jensen effects.

Study	Variable	r	N
Schull & Neel (1965)	inbreeding	.79	865
Block (1968)	heritability	.62	240

Study	Variable	r	N
Tambs, Sundet, & Magnus (1984)	heritability	.55	160
Nagoshi & Johnson (1986)	hybrid vigor	.52	2,096
Pedersen, Plomin, Nesselroade, & McClearn (1992)	heritability	.77	604
Badarudozza & Afzal (1993)	inbreeding	.83	50
Rijsdijk, Vernon, & Boomsma (2002)	heritability	.43	388
te Nijenhuis, Kura, & Hur (2014)	heritability	.42	1,808
Voronin, te Nijenhuis, & Malykh (2016)	heritability	-.45 -.60	402 296
Choi, Cho, & Lee (2015)	heritability	-.11	88
Woodley, te Nijenhuis, & Murphy (2014)	heritability	.47	n.r.
Woodley of Menie & Dunkel (2015)	heritability	.45	687
Woodley, Fernandes, & Hopkins (2015)	heritability chimpanzees	.61	99
	additive genetic variance chimpanzees	.43	99
Lasker, Pesta, Fuerst, & Kirkegaard (2019)	heritability	.37	6634
Schafer (1985)	brain's evoked potential habituation index	.77	52
Eysenck & Barrett (1985)	brain's averaged evoked potential	.95	219
Haier, Siegel, Tang, Abel, & Buchsbaum (1992)	brain's glucose metabolic rate	.79	8
Vernon & Mori (1992), Vernon (1993)	peripheral nerve conduction velocity	.44	85
Jensen (1994)	head size	.64	286
Wickett, Vernon, & Lee (1994)	brain volume	.65	80
Crinella & Yu (1995)	number brain structures involved in task performance (rats)	.91	120
	lesioned/ unlesioned differences (rats)	.75	120
	presence of any brain lesion (rats)	-.45	120

Study	Variable	r	N
Rae et al. (1996)	intercellular brain pH	.63	42
Schoenemann (1997)	brain volume	.51	72
	brain's cortical grey matter	.66	72
Colom, Jung, & Haier (2006)	brain grey matter	.82	23
	brain grey matter	.36	25
Lee et al. (2006)	brain activity	.61	36
van der Linden, Dunkel, & Madison (2017)	brain size	**.84**	**896**
	sex differences in brain size	**.85**	**896**

Note. n.r. = not reported or could not be obtained. Many of the correlations were taken from Jensen (1998), but the authors of the original studies are listed in the Table.

Figures in bold are based upon meta-analyses; [1] these correlations are corrected for statistical artifacts.

2.4 Neutral Effects

Variables showing Jensen effects go to the heart of g, and variables showing neutral effects do not go to the heart of g. Table 3 lists many environmental, biological-non-genetic variables that show a clear neutral effect in many studies, albeit not all. As stated above, the general trend in the data is most important. The number of studies is only four, which is limited, but of the six correlations, there are no less than four representing the outcome of a meta-analysis.

The correlations with g loadings are all small or quite close to zero for iodine deficiency, prenatal cocaine exposure, fetal alcohol syndrome, traumatic brain injury, lead exposure, air pollution, and organic mercury exposure; the only exception is the $r = .42$ for the large-scale study on methylmercury exposure. Flynn, te Nijenhuis, and Metzen (2014) reported five meta-analytical means, which yielded an average value of 0.00; computing the mean of all the values of r in

Table 4 produces a highly similar value. So, the overall picture of these studies is a zero relationship between *g* loadings and environmental, biological-non-genetic variables.

Table 3. Various studies on biological-non-genetic variables showing neutral effects.

Study	Variable	r	N
Flynn, te Nijenhuis & Metzen (2014)	iodine deficiency	.01	196
Flynn, te Nijenhuis & Metzen (2014)	prenatal cocaine exposure	-.23	215
Flynn, te Nijenhuis & Metzen (2014)	fetal alcohol syndrome / fetal alcohol effects	.16	110
Flynn, te Nijenhuis & Metzen (2014)	degree of fetal alcohol syndrome	.12	125
Flynn, te Nijenhuis & Metzen (2014)	traumatic brain injury	-.07	629
Woodley of Menie, te Nijenhuis, Shibaev, Li, & Smit (2018)	lead exposure	.10	1,935
Woodley of Menie, te Nijenhuis, Shibaev, Li, & Smit (2018)	air pollution	-.17	73
Debes, Ludvig, Budtz-Jørgensen, Weihe, & Grandjean (2015)	methylmercury exposure	.42	1022
Woodley of Menie, Sarraf, Peñaherrera-Aguirre, Fernandes, Becker (2018)	organic mercury exposure	-.18	365

Note. Figures in bold are based upon meta-analyses.

2.5 Anti-Jensen Effects

Table 4 lists many environmental, cultural variables that show strong anti-Jensen effects in many studies, albeit not all. Heritability shows Jensen effects and heritability also plays a crucial role in the anti-Jensen effects but in reverse. For instance, Table 4 shows many studies on test-retest effects, even including a large-scale meta-analysis. The strong negative correlation between score gains and *g* loadings means that there are smaller gains on the tests with high *g* loadings, so the tests with strong heritability, and larger gains on the tests with low *g* loadings, so the tests with weak heritability. So, the environmental component is strongest in the tests with low heritability, making it easier to improve your score on them. On the other hand, the scores on the tests with high *g* loadings are most difficult to change, due to their strong genetic component. So, the anti-Jensen effects are also strongly influenced by heritability, but reversely.

Apart from test-retest gains, there are studies on various other environmental, cultural variables, including learning potential training gains, Headstart gains, adoption gains, and the differences in IQ scores between normal and hearing-impaired individuals. Theoretically interesting are Scarr-Rowe effects, meaning lower $h2$ for lower-SES groups, an environmental effect. A large meta-analysis on schooling gains shows a zero-ish correlation and not the theoretically predicted strong negative correlation. However, one could argue that Flynn effect gains are strongly driven by schooling gains (Jensen, 1998) and that Flynn (2008) stated that teachers don't care about the *g*-loadedness of their school courses when they are trying to improve the knowledge and skills of their pupils. Flynn has argued that modern schools teach children to think abstractly, to put on scientific spectacles, and that IQ tests requiring this abstract thinking ability have seen the largest increases, regardless of their *g* loadings. Just as the Flynn effect is largely on the subtests requiring abstract thinking ability, so the schooling gains are most likely also on the school topics requiring abstract thinking ability, which most likely is a limited number of school topics. The result would then be a zero-ish correlation with *g*-loadedness.

Table 4. Various studies on cultural variables showing anti-Jensen effects.

Study	Variable	*r*	*N*
te Nijenhuis, van Vianen, & van der Flier (2007)	test-retest gains	-1.00[1]	26,990
	learning potential training gains	-.39	95
Reeve & Lam (2007)	test-retest gains		
	first testing to second testing	-.80	n.r.
	first testing to third testing	-.81	n.r.
Arendasy & Sommer (2013)	test-retest gains	-.29	358

Study	Variable	r	N
te Nijenhuis, Jongeneel-Grimen, & Kirkegaard (2014)	Headstart gains	-.80[1]	602
te Nijenhuis, Jongeneel-Grimen, & Armstrong (2015)	adoption gains	-1.06[1]	664
Braden (1989)	IQ scores of non-genetic deaf	-.76	325
te Nijenhuis, van der Boor, Choi, Choi & Lee (2019)	schooling gains	.13	60,993
Kirkegaard, Woodley of Menie, Williams, Fuerst, & Meisenberg (2019)	Scarr-Rowe effect	-.35	1369

Note. n.r. = not reported or could not be obtained. Figures in bold are based upon meta-analyses; [1] these correlations are corrected for statistical artifacts.

2.6 The value of MCV

Opinions differ on the value of MCV, with Rushton (1999, p. 837) writing positively on "the discriminating power of the Jensen effect". Flynn (2013, pp. 19-20), however, is quite negative, writing: "... actually, its results cannot really discriminate even in favor of biological versus cultural". Flynn (2013, p.25) wrote further: "... to disentangle cultural and genetic factors ... MCV is useless ...". The nomological net of studies based on MCV shows that Flynn is wrong because MCV can disentangle environmental and genetic factors and successfully separates environmental, cultural factors from environmental, biological non-genetic factors. So, MCV is a valuable tool yielding three clear-cut clusters of outcomes; however, it should be taken into account that one should not rely on the application of MCV to one single dataset, so the use of meta-analysis is required.

3. Racial/Ethnic Differences in IQ Scores and MCV

Jensen (1980, 1998) showed large differences in mean intelligence scores between US Blacks and Whites, and te Nijenhuis, de Jong, Evers, and van der Flier (2004) showed large differences between

Dutch and non-Western immigrants. There are many other instances of racial groups differing in their mean intelligence score (David & Lynn, 2007; Rindermann, Baumeister, Groper, 2014; Rindermann & Thompson, 2016). Generally, Whites are the highest scoring race in these comparison studies, but East Asians and Ashkenazi Jews clearly outscore non-Jewish Whites (Lynn, 2011; Lynn & Vanhanen, 2002).

3.1 Explaining Racial/Ethnic Differences in Intelligence

Jensen (1985) hypothesized that the Black/White differences in mean scores on the subtests of an IQ battery would be large on the subtests with high cognitive complexity (high g loadings) and small on subtests with low cognitive complexity (low g loadings). According to Jensen's default hypothesis, one should not expect a correlation of $r = 1$, as these racial differences are not completely but ⅔ genetically caused (Jensen, 1998). Jensen (1985) showed that US Blacks have lower mean scores on virtually all intelligence tests and that when Blacks are matched with Whites with the same overall IQ score, Whites have better scores than Blacks on tests of spatial rotation, and Blacks have better scores than Whites on tests of short-term memory. Jensen (1998) reviewed a large number of studies and concluded that what James Flynn calls 'the g pattern' is a law-like phenomenon for B/W differences.

MCV has also been applied to other racial/ethnic differences, and in many cases strong Jensen effects were found. For example, the meta-analysis of te Nijenhuis, Willigers, Dragt, and van der Flier (2016) showed strong Jensen effects when comparing the scores of ethnic Dutch and non-Western immigrants. Other meta-analyses showed Jensen effects for Amerindians (te Nijenhuis, van den Hoek, & Armstrong, 2015), Black adults (te Nijenhuis & van den Hoek, 2016), and Hispanics (te Nijenhuis, van den Hoek, & Dragt, 2019). Moreover, there is a cottage industry of test developers stating that the lower mean scores of many minority groups are due to test bias, and their alternative intelligence tests should be used. Te Nijenhuis, van den Hoek, and Willigers (2017) conducted a meta-analysis showing that these alternative tests also yield strong Jensen effects. As an aside, the smaller group differences usually found on these alternative test batteries are clearly due to the inclusion of a larger percentage of tests with lower cognitive complexity compared to classical IQ batteries. Finally, applying the MCV also yields Jensen effects in comparisons between sub-races, for instance, European Jews versus Oriental Jews in Israel and non-Jewish Whites versus Jews in the US (te Nijenhuis, David, Metzen, & Armstrong, 2014).

However, Jensen effects are not ubiquitous when comparing intelligence scores of groups; they were absent when comparing Sámi and Finns (Armstrong, Woodley & Lynn, 2014), Black and White prisoners (Jensen & Faulstich, 1988), and Whites and East Asians (Dalliard, 2013; Kane, 2007). All these studies show an unusual Verbal/Performance profile compared to other group comparisons, which is the cause of the anomalous outcomes (te Nijenhuis, van den Hoek, Metzen, & David, 2017). MCV studies often use the Wechsler batteries, where the generally lower-g Performance subtests usually yield smaller values of d, and the generally higher-g Verbal subtests usually show higher values of d, so that Spearman's hypothesis is strongly confirmed. However, the groups with the anomalous MCV outcomes show smaller ds on Verbal subtests and larger ds on Performance subtests, so there are no Jensen effects (te Nijenhuis et al., 2017, p. 53). Te Nijenhuis et al. (2017) carried out a series of meta-analyses where they bypassed the unusual V/P profile by applying MCV separately to the Verbal subtests and the Performance, yielding Jensen effects in the majority of comparisons, albeit not all.

3.2 Jensen Effects on Other Instruments Measuring Cognition

Te Nijenhuis et al. (2019) describe how Jensen effects are ubiquitous when using instruments other than intelligence tests. First, managerial competencies are the skills, motives, habits, attitudes, and knowledge required to manage people successfully; examples are creative problem solving, written and oral communication skills, teamwork skills, results orientation, and customer focus. These competencies differ in their cognitive complexity, and Black/White differences are larger on the more complex ones and smaller on the less complex ones (Goldstein, Yusko, & Nicolopoulos, 2001).

Secondly, there are popular instruments in selection psychology that are often used to reduce the large Black/White differences found on intelligence tests, namely Assessment Centre (AC) exercises and Situational Judgment Tests (SJTs). SJTs measure an applicant's ability to choose the most appropriate action in workplace situations they will encounter in their new job. ACs consist of job simulations where applicants can show they master the behaviors relevant to the most critical aspects of the job. The cognitive complexity of the tasks making up the SJTs and the ACs can be rated for cognitive complexity, and then the data show clear Jensen effects (Goldstein, Yusko, Braverman, Smith, & Chung, 1998; Whetzel, McDaniel, & Nguyen, 2008).

Thirdly, there are elementary cognitive tasks (ECTs), which are simple laboratory tests where research participants perform very easy tasks and have to make easy decisions. The response times of the test takers are measured, and they are usually shorter than one second. These tasks are very dissimilar to traditional intelligence tests, and they also show clear Jensen effects (Jensen, 1993, 1998).

Fourthly, in selection psychology, the goal is to predict the future job performance of applicants. It is known that the various predictors, such as structured interviews, biodata, Situational Judgment Tests, integrity tests, and tests of occupational interests vary widely in cognitive complexity, as indicated by their correlation with the total score on an IQ battery. Dahlke and Sackett (2017) showed that the instruments with the highest cognitive complexity yielded the largest Black/White differences, meaning they showed strong Jensen effects.

3.3 Nyborg's Contributions to the Discussion

Nyborg contributed two important papers to the discussion on the causes of racial/ethnic differences in intelligence using MCV. First, Jensen applied MCV to many datasets of Black and White children, but analyses of data on adults were rarer. Nyborg and Jensen (2000) used a large sample of American Armed Services veterans, which used many less current intelligence tests. They showed that the findings from children could be generalized to middle-aged veterans. Second, Jensen carried out almost all his MCV studies comparing Blacks and Whites. Based on two large datasets, Hartmann, Kruuse, and Nyborg (2007) were the first to test whether the Jensen effects generalized from Blacks to Hispanics. Both datasets yielded strong Jensen effects.

3.4 Jensen Effects are a Law-like Phenomenon

Jensen (1998) concluded that 'the g pattern' is a law-like phenomenon for Black/White comparisons, and Nyborg and Jensen's (2000) study and te Nijenhuis and van den Hoek's (2016) meta-analysis strengthened that conclusion. Also, Jensen's conclusions can be generalized from Black/White comparisons to many other racial/ethnic comparisons, with the strongest evidence available: a series of meta-analyses. The unweighted average value from all the meta-analyses by te Nijenhuis and co-authors is .6

Jensen (1998, Ch. 10) emphasizes that the correlations resulting from MCV contain a substantial amount of measurement error, but the good news is that it is possible to correct for these sources of psychometric error. Jensen (1998, p. 383) describes how these corrections turn the observed correlation of r ≈ .6 into a true correlation of rho ≈ .9. The value of .9 represents the situation where all the studies going into the meta-analyses were carried out perfectly.

This extremely strong true correlation is in line with Jensen's default hypothesis of the causes of group differences in intelligence, stating that g is the most important variable but not the only variable. This extremely strong Jensen effect for racial/ethnic differences means environmental variables are less important than biological-genetic variables in explaining group differences in mean IQ scores. We emphasize that g loadings do not have a perfect correlation with racial/ethnic differences in IQ, so there is still a substantial amount of room for the influence of environmental, cultural and environmental, biological-non-genetic variables.

4. Do Drastically Changed Environments Make Jensen Effects for Races Disappear?

Flynn (2008, pp. 88-97) was interested in a fundamental theoretical question: do Jensen effects disappear when environments change drastically? Whether the force of genes can be prevailed over by the forces of a very strong environment is an empirical question; we supply two examples also discussed by Flynn (2008).

4.1 Mixed-race Children in Germany

Eyferth (1959) describes an interesting natural experiment on the IQ scores of mixed-race children in Germany, born to White German women and Black US soldiers after the end of the Second World War. The mean IQ scores of the mixed-race children were compared to the mean IQ scores of the children of White German women and White US soldiers, and the IQ scores of the mixed-race children were lower. Te Nijenhuis et al. (2019) estimate that the biracial German children had approximately 35% Black genes and 65% White genes because Jensen (1998, p. 432) states that US Blacks have about 75% sub-Saharan African genes and 25% European genes. The environment of the biracial children was 100% White because the German mothers were not married to the Black fathers and raised their children on their own. Te Nijenhuis et al. argue that it could be hypothesized that the completely White, German environment was so much stronger than the 35% Black genes that the Jensen effect ceased to exist. However, the value of Pearson's r = .42 (Flynn, 2008, pp. 313-314) means there is a quite strong Jensen effect. In all fairness, the mean value for racial/ethnic comparisons is .6, so the outcome of the Eyferth study is a third lower, which is substantial. One can clearly not conclude that the Jensen effect disappears, but the conclusion that the Jensen effect has lessened in the Eyferth study is undoubtedly warranted.

Flynn (2008) states that one should be cautious and not draw strong conclusions based on the outcomes of this single, limited dataset. It would be best to search for comparable natural experiments, apply MCV to the data, and then meta-analyze all the data points. Finally, Flynn should be applauded for bringing this dataset under attention and adding it to the nomological net of outcomes of MCV studies.

4.2 1940s US Whites versus 2000s US Blacks

Flynn (2008) came up with a theoretically fascinating comparison, namely of the IQ scores of US Whites in 1947-1947 with the IQ scores of US Blacks in 2002. The 54.5 years in between coincide with a dramatic increase in the quality of the environment. The brilliance of Flynn's comparison is that the 2002 Blacks are the only group benefiting from the effect of the improved environment on their mean IQ scores — the Whites are still stuck in the late 1940s environment. Flynn took the White mean of 1947-1948 of 100 as the standard, and in comparison, to that, the 2002 Blacks scored 104, a massive increase of 19 IQ points over 54.5 years; this means that the 2002 Blacks outscored the 1940s Whites with 4 IQ points. This outcome is without a doubt very strong proof that a dramatically improved environment leads to dramatically increased mean IQ scores.

However, the question of interest here is whether the Jensen effects vanished. Flynn (2008, p. 311) reported a value of r = .54, which should be compared to Jensen (1998) reporting an average correlation of r = .63 for a collection of early studies, mainly on Black children, and te Nijenhuis and van den Hoek's (2016) meta-analytical value of mean r = .57 for Black adults. It means that the tremendous improvement of the environment was not strong enough to make the Jensen effect vanish and that it only got slightly dented. It stands to reason that when an enormous change in the environment over 54.5 years that coincides with an IQ gain of more than a standard deviation cannot wipe out the Jensen effect, less impressive environmental changes will also not succeed. So, one would not expect the Jensen effects to disappear due to Headstart programs, cross-racial adoption, and schooling. However, these two examples show clearly that big environmental changes can lead to a less strong Jensen effect (te Nijenhuis et al., 2019). Finally, it would be good to conduct additional studies to understand this phenomenon more clearly.

5. Future Research

A large amount of research has been carried out using the MCV on group differences in mean intelligence scores, including meta-analyses of the largest US minority groups. However, there are still a lot of unanswered questions, so many additional studies could be carried out (see: te Nijenhuis et al., 2019).

5.1 How Far Do the Findings Generalize?

Cavalli-Sforza, Menozzi, and Piazza (1994) analyzed genetic data of 43 populations which yielded ten major "clusters", but traditionally the term "race" is used. Lynn (2015, p. 21) distinguishes between the same ten races: (1) Bushmen and Pygmies, (2) sub-Saharan Africans, (3) South Asians and North Africans, (4) Europeans, (5) East Asians, (6) Arctic Peoples, (7) Native American Indians, (8) Southeast Asians, (9) Pacific Islanders, and (10) Australian Aborigines and Aboriginal New

Guineans. Within the clusters or races, sub-clusters or sub-races can be distinguished, for instance, the sub-Saharan cluster comprises sub-races of Bantus, West Africans, Ethiopians, and Nilotics (Lynn, 2015, p. 57). So, there is still a lot of unexplored territory here. A couple of minority groups still need studying in the US, including Hawaiians, Puerto Ricans, Filipinos, and Cubans. Jensen (1998) states that 'the g pattern' is a law-like phenomenon, so it would be interesting to find racial or sub-racial differences that do not show clear-cut Jensen effects, like those of Northeast Asians.

5.2 Explaining Group Differences: Synthetic Correlation Matrix

Many studies have been carried out using MCV, and Rushton (1999) pioneered the use of independent MCV datasets to build a synthetic correlation matrix of all the correlations between the vectors and then apply factor analysis to this matrix to see how many meaningful factors appear and how the various variables load onto the factors. Rushton's synthetic correlation matrix yielded two factors: an environmental factor made up of only Flynn effect gains from various independent studies and a factor with loadings of heritability, inbreeding depression, g loadings, and Black/White differences, which he named the genetic factor. Interestingly, the B/W differences strongly loaded on the genetic factor and much less on the environmental factor.

Using different statistical techniques and analyzing much more datasets than Rushton, te Nijenhuis et al. (2019) came up with three clusters, where Rushton came up with two clusters. A new, enlarged synthetic correlation matrix should be created to test whether it yields three factors that resemble te Nijenhuis et al.'s three clusters. If three factors, biological-genetic; environmental, cultural; and environmental, biological-non-genetic indeed appear, it would be interesting to see how strongly racial/ethnic differences load on each factor. Jensen's default hypothesis (Jensen, 1998) would predict the strongest loading on the biological-genetic factor and substantial loadings on one or maybe even both environmental factors.

5.3 Carry Out More Meta-analyses

Schmidt (1992) convincingly argues that the amount of information in a single study is limited, and only the amount of information in a meta-analysis is sufficient to draw strong conclusions. Therefore, Schmidt states that the primary function of a single study is to be added to an upcoming meta-analysis. In the present book chapter, we discussed a lot of individual studies, and where possible, they should be combined into a meta-analysis. However, it is also clear that many studies using MCV have already been incorporated into a meta-analysis. Therefore, where possible, the individual studies should be meta-analyzed, and preferably additional searches should be carried out for independent datasets that allow using MCV, thereby allowing more powerful meta-analyses.

Frequently, the studies in a meta-analysis use various instruments. These instruments differ in their test-retest reliability, which influences the outcomes of these studies: instruments with low reliabilities tend to yield weaker correlations, and instruments with good reliabilities tend to produce stronger correlations. This additional variability between data points in a meta-analysis caused by differences in reliability usually results in a futile search for moderators. A better approach is to correct for the differences in reliability, yielding corrected correlations that describe a situation where every data point in the meta-analysis has the same, perfect reliability. Schmidt and Hunter (2015) developed psychometric meta-analysis, where study outcomes can be corrected for various statistical errors, also called artifacts. Jensen (1998, Ch. 10) describes how these techniques can be applied to a meta-analysis of the method of correlated vectors, albeit in embryonic form. Later, te Nijenhuis and co-authors more fully developed what came to be known as the psychometric meta-analytical-MCV hybrid model with corrections for five artefacts: sampling error, reliability of the *g* vector, reliability of the *d* vector, range restriction in *g* loadings, and imperfectly measuring the construct of *g* (see: te Nijenhuis, Jongeneel-Grimen, & Armstrong, 2015; te Nijenhuis, Jongeneel-Grimen, & Kirkegaard, 2014; te Nijenhuis, van den Hoek, & Dragt, 2019; te Nijenhuis & van der Flier, 2013; te Nijenhuis, van Vianen, & van der Flier, 2007; te Nijenhuis, Willigers, Dragt, & van der Flier, 2016). Correcting for these statistical artifacts tends to lead to a dramatic reduction in the variance between the data points in the meta-analysis, meaning there is no or almost no room for moderators. So, the outcomes of these meta-analyses are solid and help advance the cumulativeness of scientific knowledge.

6. Conclusion

Dr. Helmuth Nyborg was clearly on the right track when he studied the causes of racial differences in intelligence using the method of correlated vectors. Nyborg and Jensen (2000) focused on Black adults, and their value of $r = .81$ is the highest value for any of the data points in the meta-analysis of MCV used with Black adults by te Nijenhuis and van den Hoek (2016), which yielded a mean value of $r = .57$. Moreover, Hartmann, Kruuse, and Nyborg (2007) focused on Hispanics, and theirs was the first study in the field focusing on that ethnic group, using two datasets which yielded correlations of $r = .71$ and .74, respectively. Many replications, summarized in a meta-analysis and combined with Nyborg's two data points, show a mean $r = .63$, which shows that the two outcomes of the very first study are relatively strongly comparable to the meta-analytical outcome.

If Nyborg could be accused of anything, it is underestimating the effects' strength. MCV yields correlations between vectors that contain a considerable amount of measurement error, and correcting for various statistical artifacts yields the true correlation between the construct of *g* and the construct of group differences in intelligence. In the case of White-Hispanic group differences the meta-analytical mean $r = .63$ and the corrected meta-analytical *rho* = .91, so even

Hartmann, Kruuse, and Nyborg's Hispanics data point's $r = .74$ is 19% off from the true, meta-analytical value — a substantial underestimate.

The outcomes of Nyborg's two studies are clearly in line with Jensen's default hypothesis that the most important cause of within-group differences is the same as the most important cause of between-group differences, namely g. With this, Nyborg contributed two important studies to one of the hottest fundamental discussions in social science, namely the causes of the often-large differences in mean IQ scores between racial/ethnic groups. It seems clear his work as a young man as a stoker on a ship was not his intellectual zenith, and his primary-school classmates had foresight when calling him 'Fessor'.

Footnote

Several of the ideas in this chapter were taken from te Nijenhuis, J., Choi, Y.Y., van den Hoek, M., Valueva, E., & Lee, K.H. (2019). Spearman's hypothesis tested comparing Korean young adults with various other groups of young adults on the items of the Advanced Progressive Matrices. *Journal of Biosocial Science, 51,* 875-912.1.

References

Arend, I., Colom, R., Botella, J., Contreras, M. J., Rubio, V., & Santacreu, J. (2003). Quantifying cognitive complexity: Evidence from a reasoning task. *Personality and Individual Differences, 35,* 659-669.

Arendasy, M. E., & Sommer, M. (2013). Quantitative differences in retest effects across different methods used to construct alternate test forms. *Intelligence, 41,* 181-192.

Armstrong, E. L., te Nijenhuis, J., Woodley of Menie, M. A., Fernandes, H. B. F., Must, O., & Must, A. (2016). A NIT-picking analysis: Abstractness dependence of subtests correlated to their Flynn effect magnitudes. *Intelligence, 57,* 1-6.

Armstrong, E. L., Woodley, M. A., & Lynn, R. (2014). Cognitive abilities amongst the Sámi people. *Intelligence, 46,* 35-39.

Badaruddoza, & Afzal, M. (1993). Inbreeding depression and intelligence quotient among north Indian children. *Behavioral Genetics, 23,* 343–347.

Block, J.B. (1968). Hereditary components in the performance of twins on the WAIS. In S.G. Vandenberg (Ed.), *Progress in Human Behavior Genetics* (pp. 221-228). Baltimore, MD: The Johns Hopkins University Press.

Braden, J. P. (1989). Fact or artifact? An empirical test of Spearman's hypothesis. *Intelligence, 13*, 149-155.

Cavalli-Sforza, L. L., Menozzi, P., & Piazza, A. (1994). *The History and Geography of Human Genes.* Princeton, NJ: Princeton University Press.

Choi, Y. Y., Cho, S. H., & Lee, K. H. (2015). No clear links between g loadings and heritability: A twin study from Korea. *Psychological Reports: Sociocultural Issues in Psychology, 117*, 291-297.

Colom, R., Jung, R. E., & Haier, R. J. (2006). Distributed brain sites for the g-factor of intelligence. *Neuroimage, 31*, 1359-1365.

Crinella, F. M., & Yu, J. (1995). Brain mechanisms in problem solving and intelligence. A replication and extension. *Intelligence, 21*, 225-246.

Dahlke, J. A., & Sackett, P. R. (2017). The relationship between cognitive-ability saturation and subgroup mean differences across predictors for job performance. *Journal of Applied Psychology, 102*, 1403-1420.

Dalliard, (2013, December 8). Spearman's hypothesis and racial differences on the DAS-II. *Humanvarieties.com.* Retrieved from http://humanvarieties.org/. 2013/12/08/spearmans-hypothesis-and-racial-differences-on-the-das-ii/.

David, H., & Lynn, R. (2007). Intelligence differences between European and Oriental Jews in Israel. *Journal of Biosocial Science, 29*, 465-473.

Debes, F., Ludvig, A., Budtz-Jørgensen, Weihe & Grandjean, P. (2015). The effects of methylmercury on general intelligence in children and young adults. Oral presentation given at the 16th Annual Meeting of the International Society for Intelligence Research. Albuquerque, New Mexico, USA, September.

Eyferth, K. (1959). Eine Untersuchung der Negermischlingskinder in Westdeutschland [A study of Black interracial children in West Germany]. *Humana, 2*, 102-114.

Eysenck, H.J. & Barrett, P. (1985). Psychophysiology and the measurement of intelligence. In C.R. Reynolds & P.C. Wilson (Eds.), *Methodological and Statistical Advances in the Study of Individual Differences* (pp. 1-49). New York: Plenum Press.

Flynn, J. R., te Nijenhuis, J., & Metzen, D. (2014). The g beyond Spearman's g: Flynn's paradoxes resolved using four exploratory meta-analyses. *Intelligence, 42*, 1-10.

Flynn, J. R. (2008). *Where Have All the Liberals Gone? Race, Class, and Ideals in America.* Cambridge University Press.

Flynn, J. R. (2013). *Intelligence and Human Progress: The Story of What Was Hidden in Our Genes*. Oxford, UK: Academic Press.

Flynn, J.R. (2018). Reflections about intelligence over 40 years. *Intelligence, 70*, 73-83.

Goldstein, H. W., Yusko, K. P., Braverman, E. P., Smith, D. B., & Chung, B. (1998). The role of cognitive ability in the subgroup differences and incremental validity of assessment center exercises. *Personnel Psychology, 51*, 357-374.

Goldstein, H. W., Yusko, K. P., & Nicolopoulos, V. (2001). Exploring Black-white subgroup differences of managerial competencies. *Personnel Psychology, 54*, 783-807.

Haier, R. J., Siegel, B., Tang, C., Abel, L., & Buchsbaum, M. S. (1992). Intelligence and changes in regional cerebral glucose metabolic rate following learning. *Intelligence, 16*, 415-426.

Hartmann, P., Kruuse, N. H. S., & Nyborg, H. (2007). Testing the cross-racial generality of Spearman's hypothesis in two samples. *Intelligence, 35*, 47-57.

Hunter, J. E., & Schmidt, F. L. (1990). *Methods of Meta-Analysis*. London: Sage.

Jensen, A. R. (1980). *Bias in Mental Testing*. London: Methuen.

Jensen, A. R. (1985). The nature of the black-white difference on various psychometric tests: Spearman's hypothesis. *The Behavioral and Brain Sciences, 8*, 193-263.

Jensen, A. R. (1993). Spearman's hypothesis tested with chronometric information-processing tasks. *Intelligence, 17*, 47-77.

Jensen, A. R. (1994). Psychometric g related to differences in head size. *Personality and Individual Differences, 17*, 597-606.

Jensen, A. R. (1998). *The g Factor: The Science of Mental Ability*. Westport, CT: Praeger.

Jensen, A. R., & Faulstich, M. E. (1988). Difference between prisoners and the general population in psychometric g. *Personality and individual differences, 9*, 925-928.

Kane, H. (2007). Group differences in nonverbal intelligence: Support for the influence of Spearman's g. *Mankind Quarterly, 48*, 65–82.

Kirkegaard, E. O. W., Woodley of Menie, M. A., Williams, R. L., Fuerst, J., & Meisenberg, G. (2019). Biogeographic ancestry, cognitive ability and socioeconomic outcomes. *Psych, 1*, 1-25.

Lasker, J., Pesta, B., Fuerst, J. G. R., & Kirkegaard, E. O. W. (2019). Global ancestry and cognitive ability. *Psych, 1*, 431-459.

Lee, K. H., Choi, Y. Y., Gray, J. R., Cho, S. H., Chae, J.-H., Lee, S., et al. (2006). Neural correlates of superior intelligence: Stronger recruitment of posterior parietal cortex. *NeuroImage, 29,* 578-586.

Lynn, R. (2011). *The chosen people: A study of Jewish intelligence and achievement.* Washington, D.C.: Washington Summit.

Lynn, R. (2015). *Race Differences in Intelligence: An Evolutionary Analysis (Second revised edition).* Whitefish, MT: Washington Summit.

Lynn, R., & Vanhanen, T. (2002). *IQ and the Wealth of Nations.* London: Praeger.

Nagoshi, C. T., & Johnson, R. C. (1986). The ubiquity of g. *Personality and Individual Differences, 7,* 201-207.

Nyborg, H., & Jensen, A. R. (2000). Black-white differences on various psychometric tests. Spearman's hypothesis tested on American armed services veterans. *Personality and Individual Differences, 28,* 593-599.

Pedersen, N. L., Plomin, R., Nesselroade, J. R., & McClearn, G. E. (1992). A quantitative genetic analysis of cognitive abilities during the second half of the life span. *Psychological Science, 3,* 346-353.

Rae, C., Scott, R. B., Thompson, C. H., Kemp, G. J., Dumughn, I., Styles, P., Tracey, I. & Radda, G. K. (1996). Is pH a biochemical marker of IQ? *Proceedings of the Royal Society* (London), *263,* 1061-1064.

Ree, M. J., & Earles, A. A. (1991). Predicting training success: Not much more than g. *Personnel Psychology, 44,* 321-332.

Ree, M. J., Earles, J. A., & Teachout, M. S. (1994). Predicting job performance: Not much more than g. *Journal of Applied Psychology, 79,* 518-524.

Reeve, C. L., & Lam, H. (2007). The relation between practice effects, test-taker characteristics and degree of g-saturation. *International Journal of Testing, 7,* 225-242.

Rijsdijk, F. V., Vernon, P. A., & Boomsma, D. I. (2002). Application of hierarchical genetic models to Raven and WAIS subtests: a Dutch twin study. *Behavior Genetics, 32,* 199-210.

Rindermann, H., Baumeister, A. E. E., & Groper, A. (2014). Cognitive abilities of Emirati and German engineering university students. *Journal of Biosocial Science, 46,* 199-213.

Rindermann, H., & Thompson, J. (2016). The cognitive competences of immigrant and native students across the world: An analysis of gaps, possible causes and impact. *Journal of Biosocial Science, 48,* 66-93.

Rushton, J. P. (1998). The "Jensen Effect" and the "Spearman-Jensen hypothesis" of black-white IQ differences. *Intelligence, 26*(3), 217-225.

Rushton, J. F. (1999). Secular gains in IQ not related to the g-factor and inbreeding depression - unlike black-white differences. A reply to Flynn. *Personality and Individual Differences, 26*, 381-389.

Schafer, E.W.P. (1985). Neural adaptability: A biological determinant of g factor intelligence. *Behavioral and Brain Sciences, 8*, 240-241.

Schmidt, F. L. (1992). What do data really mean? Research findings, meta-analysis, and cumulative knowledge in psychology. *American Psychologist, 47*, 1173-1181.

Schmidt, F. L., & Hunter, J. E. (2015). *Methods of Meta-Analysis: Correcting Error and Bias in Research Findings (Third edition)*. Thousand Oaks, CA: Sage.

Schull, W. J. & J. V. Neel. (1965). *The Effects of Inbreeding on Japanese Children*. New York: Harper and Row.

Schoenemann, P. T. (1997). An MRI study of the relationship between human neuroanatomy and behavioral ability. *PhD dissertation*. Berkeley, California: University of California.

Tambs, K., & Sundet, J. M. (1984). Heritability analysis of the WAIS subtests. A study of twins. *Intelligence, 8*, 283-293.

te Nijenhuis, J. (2007). Een macho over sekseverschillen in intelligentie: Een interview met Helmuth Nyborg [A macho on sex differences in intelligence: An interview with Helmuth Nyborg]. *Talent: Tijdschrift over Hoogbegaafdheid, 9* (4), 28-31.

te Nijenhuis, J., Choi, Y.Y., van den Hoek, M., Valueva, E., & Lee, K.H. (2019). Spearman's hypothesis tested comparing Korean young adults with various other groups of young adults on the items of the Advanced Progressive Matrices. *Journal of Biosocial Science, 51*, 875-912.

te Nijenhuis, J., David, H., Metzen, D., & Armstrong, E. L. (2014). Spearman's hypothesis tested on European Jews vs non-Jewish Whites and vs Oriental Jews: Two meta-analyses. *Intelligence, 44*, 15-18.

te Nijenhuis, J., de Jong, M. J., Evers, A., & van der Flier, H. (2004). Are cognitive differences between immigrant and majority groups diminishing? *European Journal of Personality, 18*, 405-434.

te Nijenhuis, J., Jongeneel-Grimen, B., & Armstrong, E. (2015). Are adoption gains on the g factor?: A meta-analyis. *Personality and Individual Differences, 73*, 56-60.

te Nijenhuis, J., Jongeneel-Grimen, B., & Kirkegaard, E. O. W. (2014). Are Headstart gains on the g factor? A meta-analysis. *Intelligence, 46*, 209-215.

te Nijenhuis, J., Kura, K., & Hur, Y. M. (2014). The correlation between g loadings and heritability in Japan: A meta-analysis. *Intelligence, 46*, 275-282.

te Nijenhuis, J. & van den Hoek, M. (2016). Spearman's hypothesis tested on Black adults: A meta-analysis. *Journal of Intelligence, 4,* 6. doi:10.3390/jintelligence4020006

te Nijenhuis, J., van den Hoek, M., & Armstrong, E. L. (2015). Spearman's hypothesis and Amerindians: A meta-analysis. *Intelligence, 50,* 87-92.

te Nijenhuis, J., van den Hoek, M., & Dragt, J. (2019). A meta-analysis of Spearman's hypothesis tested on Latin-American Hispanics, including a new way to correct for imperfectly measuring the construct of *g. Psych,* 1, 101-122.

te Nijenhuis, J., van den Hoek, M., Metzen, D., & David, H. (2017). Spearman's hypothesis not supported? Three meta-analyses of Black and White prisoners, Northeast Asians, and Arabs and Jews. *Personality and Individual Differences, 117,* 52-59.

te Nijenhuis, J., van den Hoek, M., & Willigers, D. (2017). Testing Spearman's hypothesis with alternative intelligence tests: A meta-analysis. *Mankind Quarterly, 57,* 687-705.

te Nijenhuis, J, van der Boor, E., Choi, Y.Y., & Lee, K.H. (2019). Do schooling gains yield anomalous Jensen effects?: A reply to Flynn (2019) including a meta-analysis. *Journal of Biosocial Science, 51,* 917-919.

te Nijenhuis, J. & van der Flier, H. (2013). Is the Flynn effect on *g*?: A meta-analysis. *Intelligence, 41,* 802-807.

te Nijenhuis, J., van Vianen, A., & van der Flier, H. (2007). Score gains on *g*-loaded tests: No *g. Intelligence, 35,* 283-300.

te Nijenhuis, J., Willigers, D., Dragt, J., & van der Flier, H. (2016). The effects of language bias and cultural bias estimated using the method of correlated vectors on a large database of IQ comparisons between native Dutch and ethnic minority immigrants from non-Western countries. *Intelligence, 54,* 117-135.

van der Linden, D., Dunkel, C. S., & Madison, G. (2017). Sex differences in brain size and general intelligence (g). *Intelligence, 63,* 78-88.

Vernon, P. A. (1989). The heritability of measures of speed of information-processing. *Personality and Individual Differences, 10,* 573-576.

Vernon, P. A. (1993a). Intelligence and neural efficiency. In D. K. Detterman (Ed.), *Current topics in human intelligence,* Vol. 3 (pp. 171-187). Norwood, NJ: Ablex.

Vernon, P. A., & Mori, M. (1992). Intelligence, reaction times, and peripheral nerve conduction velocity. *Intelligence, 16,* 273-288.

Voronin, I., te Nijenhuis, J., & Malykh, S. (2016). The correlation between *g* loadings and heritability in Russia. *Journal of Biosocial Science, 48,* 833-843. Available on CJO 2015 doi:10.1017/S0021932015000395.

Whetzel, D. L., McDaniel, M. A., & Nguyen, N. T. (2008). Subgroup differences in Situational Judgment Test performance: A meta-analysis. *Human Performance, 21*, 291-309.

Wickett, J. C., Vernon, P. A., & Lee, D. H. (1994). In vivo brain size, head perimeter, and intelligence in a sample of healthy adult females. *Personality and Individual Differences, 16*, 831-838.

Woodley of Menie, M. A., & Dunkel, C. S. (2015). In France, are secular IQ losses biologically caused? A comment on Dutton and Lynn (2015). *Intelligence, 53*, 81-85.

Woodley of Menie, M. A., Fernandes, H. B. F., & Hopkins, W. D. (2015). The more g-loaded, the more heritable, evolvable, and phenotypically variable: Homology with humans in chimpanzee cognitive abilities *Intelligence, 50*, 159-163.

Woodley, M.A., te Nijenhuis, J., & Murphy, R. (2014). Is there a secular trend towards slowing simple reaction time?: Responding to a quartet of critical commentaries. *Intelligence, 46*, 131-147.

Woodley of Menie, M. A., Sarraf, M. A., Penaherra-Aguirre, M., & Fernandes, H. B. F. (2018). What caused over a century of decline in general intelligence: Testing predictions from the genetic selection and neurotoxin hypotheses. *Evolutionary Psychological Science,4*(3), 272-284.

Woodley of Menie, M., te Nijenhuis, J., Shibaev, V., Li, M., & Smit, J. (2018). Are the effects of lead exposure linked to the *g* factor? A meta-analysis. *Personality and Individual Differences, 137*, 184-191.

OTHER BOOKS PUBLISHED BY ARKTOS

OTHER BOOKS PUBLISHED BY ARKTOS

OTHER BOOKS PUBLISHED BY ARKTOS

OTHER BOOKS PUBLISHED BY ARKTOS

www.ingramcontent.com/pod-product-compliance
Lightning Source LLC
Chambersburg PA
CBHW020525270326
41927CB00006B/455